CHRONICLES

On the Political Economy of Plunder in Ethiopia (1991-2018)

AYELE GELAN

DEDICATION

As I was writing the articles in this book, popular uprising was raging all over Ethiopia, particularly in Oromia. Lives of thousands perished in the hands savage security forces. This book is dedicated to those selfless and brave young men and women who sacrificed their precious lives, steadfastly fighting injustice and eventually succeeding in freeing the people of Ethiopia from the shackles of tyranny.

CONTENTS

Preface

May 1991 was a watershed moment in recent Ethiopian history. A regime change took place and it was felt that was a regime change like no other. A military junta, known as the Derg, led by Colonel Mengistu Hailemariam, was ousted by the Ethiopian People's Revolutionary Democratic Front (EPRDF), a coalition of ethnically based liberation fronts.

EPRDF was not a coalition as such but the Tigrian People's Liberation Front (TPLF) camouflaging itself by creating proxy groups to gain legitimacy. TPLF's original goal was to liberate and breakaway Tigray from the rest of Ethiopia. However, as time went by, the Derg government got progressively weakened, literally imploding due to a backlog of political and economic policy blunders. Besides, the Derg was a communist regime whom the Western powers, as well as the people Ethiopia, loved to hate. Consequently, the TPLF got huge moral and material support from the governments and non-governmental organizations in the Western world.

Eventually TPLF abandoned their initial goal and decided to control the central government. However, the TPLF represented the Tigrean people that constituted only 6% of the population of Ethiopia. That was why even before they began to march towards Addis Ababa from their rebel base in Tigray, the TPLF had to cobble up a coalition by assembling proxy "liberation fronts" from such groups as militia and soldiers they captured in battlefields. This maneuvering enabled TPLF to seize power, EPRDF serving as a garb.

It was abundantly clear from the very outset that Ethiopia's democratic governance was at stake when regime change happened in 1991. Democracy essentially means majority rule with minority rights. Throughout Ethiopian history, on the contrary, minority has always ruled, bizarrely the majority has not only been deprived of their role to rule but actually even their right was never respected. In other words, democracy has always been standing on its head in Ethiopian history. In that sense, the situation simply gotten from bad to worse when the TPLF minority began to rule with the EPRDF as a cover.

Two additional factors further complicated the chance for genuine democratic governance to emerge during the post 1991 period in Ethiopia. First, yet another tactical maneuver by the TPLF who formed a government not just hiding behind the EPRDF but also by creating another layer of cover, a transitional government. This meant involving liberation fronts that refused to join the EPRDF coalition, notably the Oromo Liberation Front (OLF). This was essentially designed to gain credibility in the eye of the Ethiopian people by creating something that looked like a broad-based government. Second, the people of Ethiopia have clearly expressed their disgust regarding the ominous prospect of a tiny minority group monopolizing political power. In order to reassure the public, the US government, who effectively sponsored the TPLF or EPRDF takeover, warned the TPLF – "no democracy, no cooperation", a promise which was never kept [1]. The divergence in expectation between the US government and the people of Ethiopia persisted and shaped opposing viewpoints regarding the performance of the EPRDF regime.

Two strands of mutually exclusive and opposing narratives about Ethiopia have coexisted for nearly three decades. The first narrative painted a rosy picture of Ethiopia's social and economic progress. Ethiopia's economy was claimed to be among the fastest growing in the world so much that some reporters have gone so far as to calling the country as the lioness of Africa, analogous to Asian tigers. The story that "miraculous economic growth", double digit annual economic growth rate continuously being registered for more than a decade, has been repeatedly told that it became common knowledge among Ethiopia analysts. Proponents of this view claimed that Ethiopia has been making slow but steady progress in promoting democracy, citing that elections have taken place uninterrupted for over two decades with the EPRDF registering landslide victories. This narrative was produced primarily by the Ethiopian government propaganda, promoted by multilateral agencies, the World Bank and the IMF, and the diplomatic community and the Western powers, and finally sold by the global media houses to the international community.

The second narrative logically emerged from the fear manifested from the very outset among the people of Ethiopian that the TPLF ethnic minority rule would endanger the prospect of democracy taking root in the country. It did not take time for the EPRDF to emerge as a dictatorial regime. Representing the interest of the majority Ethnic group, Oromos who constitute at least 35% of Ethiopia's population, the OLF was the only real opposition to EPRDF in the transitional government formed in 1991. In a matter of a year, the TPLF kicked out the OLF from the transitional government, thereby consolidating its total control of political power. The cover up by using proxy groups in the EPRDF still remained intact. Some opposition groups, including the OLF were branded as terrorist groups, and their supporters were hunted down, killed in considerably large numbers, arrested en mass and incarcerated in concentration camps that dotted all over the country, particularly in Oromia. Human rights organizations have documented gross human rights violations continuously throughout the EPRDF reign. In order to prove elections were evidently fake, one did not need to go any further than referring to the embarrassing landslide victories the EPRDF has been announcing over the years, including the shocking 100% victory in 2015 [2].

In 2005 the EPRDF experimented with what looked like a genuinely free and fair election. However, they soon realized that power was about to escape from their grip. They snatched victory from the opposition by resorting to bullets. In a single bloody day, over 200 people, who went out to demonstrate opposing EPRDF's refusal to relinquish power, were massacred in Addis Ababa. That election proved to be a landmark event in the EPRDF governance. It signified a major shift in the EPRDF's ideology away from flirting with democracy to an openly dictatorial regime.

This was advanced by dovetailing two ideological pillars. First, 'democratic centralism' was made to resurface as matter of urgency and it became an overriding political principle for nearly a decade and half afterwards. Given the huge material and moral support the EPRDF government garnered from the western powers, particularly the USA government, it was prudent for them to hide it for much of the 1991 to 2005 period, otherwise democratic centralism was always there lurking hidden in the background, given the TPLF has always espoused the Marxist-Leninist political ideology.

Second, "developmental state" model emerged as a governing ideology of economic governance. In a way, the EPRDF was giving up with seeking legitimacy through democratic governance. EPRDF launched an intensive propaganda campaign that it would take long time for democracy to take roots in extremely poor country like Ethiopia. In effect, democracy was portrayed as a luxury Ethiopia could not afford. Priority shifted to economic development through a huge dose of government intervention, i.e., developmental state. There was a tacit understanding that firm political control through democratic centralism would inevitably cause pain to society but developmental state was meant to serve as a pain relief. In short, the political and economic ideological pillars were juxtaposed as stick and carrot respectively.

The popular uprising in Ethiopian between 2015 and 2018 signified a confluence of the different strands of narratives on Ethiopia. The people of Ethiopia could not tolerate the unfounded and fictitious narrative of miraculous economic growth and progressive EPRDF. A process of great unraveling was started by Oromo Protests, which was ignited on November 12, 2015 in Ginchi, a small town located at about 67 km west of Addis Ababa. At first glance the protest sounded a as if it was a localized dispute over corrupt ways a forested area was allocated to some investors. But corruption over land administration, illegal transfers to scrupulous investors, and mass eviction of farming households from their ancestral lands was commonplace everywhere in Ethiopia, but more intensely in Oromia.

For this reason, the Oromo Protest rapidly spread like a forest fire to all corners of Oromia. The EPRDF government unleashed its security forces to quell Oromo protestors. Thousands of protestors were killed, several thousands more were tortured, and still tens of thousands more were imprisoned and incarcerated in concentration camps. Rather than stopping the Oromo protesters, the killings, tortures and mass imprisonments further intensified the scale of upheavals in Oromia. Additionally, the popular uprising spread to the rest of regions in Ethiopia. Amhara resistance followed in the footsteps of Oromo Protests and eventually the whole of Ethiopia was engulfed in upheavals. The widespread popular protest forced the EPRDF to crack open. Progressive elements within the coalition effectively switched side and joined the protestors. This unleashed a process of political and economic reform. At the time of writing this introductory remark, the TPLF have already retreated to their base, Tigray. A number of their top level army and security chiefs were put in jail and many more were being hunted down for capturing and holding them accountable for corruptions and gross human rights violations they have perpetrated over the years.

This book brings together several articles I have published with newspapers, magazines and multi-media pages during the popular uprisings. Publication dates and platforms are indicated next to each title (*OP* for *Opride.com* and *AS* for *AddisStandard.com*). The articles were compiled with no further updating except for moving references presented as hyperlinked texts in the online versions to end notes. In the online versions, I used my real name for some articles and my pen name, Jabessa Bonsa, for others. The structure of the book reflects the chronological order in which the pieces were written, starting from August 2013 and ending with November 2018. Although the timing of the chronicles was concentrated around the years of the popular unrest, the contents of the pieces reflect circumstances that have prevailed during the entire period the EPRDF government was on power.

Economic policy was the focus of almost all of the articles included in this book, twenty two of the twenty five articles. The other three are devoted to explaining conceptual muddles with which varieties of Ethiopian nationalisms have often been discussed. Domestic and international human rights organizations, political activists and opposition parties have done a relatively good job in scrutinizing and exposing the lack of democratic governance and gross human right abuses during the EPRDF period. On the contrary, of all Ethiopia's current affairs, economic policies have always been analyzed in the most unsatisfactory manner throughout the post 1991 period. This became more apparent during the protest years.

The protest baffled the international communities who have been repeatedly told about Ethiopia's miraculous economic growth. If Ethiopia was really growing at double digit rate per annum for over a decade, then why have Ethiopians in all walks of life protested so vigorously? The existences of draconian press laws meant domestic print and broadcast press were decimated long before the protest years. Safety or geopolitical concerns meant foreign correspondents were simply unwilling or unable to even begin to scratch the surface, never mind digging deeper and providing answers to the burning questions. Some even resorted to using simplistic indicators, such proliferating high rise buildings in Addis Ababa, to pass judgment on Ethiopia's overall economic performance.

Journalists can be excused if they failed to capture every nuance of the Ethiopian society, theirs can mostly be down to inexperience in the field or unfamiliarity with the country context. The multilateral institutions, the World Bank and the IMF, should never be forgiven for their futile attempts to cover up for the regime that was obviously doomed to crumble, prolonging the agonizing pains to the people of Ethiopia. For instance, over four months into the Oromo Protests, in February 2016, the World Bank published an economic report entitled *Ethiopia's Great Run: The Growth Acceleration and How to Pace It*. A key message in that report was that between 2004 and 2014, Ethiopia had achieved an exceptionally high growth rate: 10.9% average annual growth rate and 8.0% in per capita terms.

I was intrigued by two things about this particular report. I was curious why that time interval was chosen. The authors of that report confessed why they excluded the pre-2004 period: "… our period choice is deliberately determined as the one which maximizes recent growth as the inclusion of earlier years would reduce average growth." Why was it necessary to report a "maximum" growth rate? Crucially, economic conditions during the post 2014 period were deliberately excluded in that report. The authors of that report knew that things were in disarray. Ironically, there was no mention of even a single word about the on-going protest in that report. Regardless World Bank continues to churn out high annual growth rates for Ethiopia, again the magic annual economic growth rate of 10.9% continued to prevail even in 2017[3].

It defied belief that 10.9% annual growth rate stayed on regardless of dramatic changes in the economic fundamentals – thousands of youth in active working age were killed, tens of thousands were on the streets, roads were blocked in many areas, and economic boycotts have happened a few rounds with the people staying at home as shows of defiance, and quite a number of factories were burned down by the protestors. A similar cover up by the IMF was explained in an article in this book, IMF *Chief Christine Lagarde's Venture to Wonderland Ethiopia: Why Now?* These cover ups were consistent with the Ethiopia rising narrative promoted by the two multi-lateral agencies who were staunch supporters of the EPRDF government.

Dismayed and somewhat frustrated by the misinformation about the Ethiopian economy, I started to write the articles and contribute to print and online media primarily to bring some rigor to the debate. I was particularly interested in scrutinizing the Ethiopia rising storyline. I am an economist and I spent most of my professional life studying the Ethiopian economy, writing and publishing articles in international peer reviewed journals. The flaws in the Ethiopia rising storyline were clear to me all along but I still remained in the academic domain that was until the popular protest was started.

However, I felt it would be irresponsible of me to sit by the side and read obviously inaccurate assessments of the reality on the ground. Specifically, I felt a sense of duty to offer some explanation as to why Ethiopians chose to rise up, risking their lives and dying in large numbers. What pushed me over the edge was the IMF and the World Banks' dogged determination to report double digit annual economic growth rates. That they chose to do so even two years after Ethiopia have come under a raging fire was nothing short of insulting the intelligence of Ethiopians, specifically those of us who have spent decades studying the Ethiopian economy.

Paucity of economic data used to be the main hurdle to undertake economic analysis on the Ethiopia. In post 1991 Ethiopia, a policy analyst would have the exact opposite trouble. In order to boast of great achievements, the EPRDF regime have churned out a huge dearth of economic data and made it available but its quality was highly questionable. I set out to do a serious economic analysis but I was confronted with economic data that I strongly believed was not trustworthy. Regardless, I believe I was able to unravel many complex issues on Ethiopia's political economy by using triangulation techniques, by bringing data together from disparate sources or digging out and revealing inconsistencies between data on different components in the economy.

The articles incorporated in this book were scattered in different magazines and multi-media pages published in different months. I have received suggestions and encouragements from many readers that there would be a value in collecting the pieces together and publish them in a single volume. As this book was being sent to the publisher, Ethiopia has already emerged from the troubled years and the reform process led by Prime Minister Abiy Ahmed has already been underway. This brought up an additional impetus for me to publish this book primarily to draw some useful lessons for establishing new rules of engagement between the new government of Ethiopia, donor agencies, multilateral institutions, and the international community.

Finally, I would like to thank Mohammed Ademo, editor of Opride, and Tsedi Lemma, editor of Addis Standard, for their time to edit and publish the online versions of the articles included in this book.

December 2018

References

[1] Craig R. Whitney. Ethiopian Seeks to Form Temporary Government. The New York Times, May 29, 1991.

[2] BBC News. Ethiopia Election: EPRDF Wins Every Seat in Parliament. 22 June 2015. https://www.bbc.com/news/world-africa-33228207

[3] The World Bank, Ethiopia at a glance, 2018. http://www.worldbank.org/en/country/ethiopia/overview

1. Typologies of Nationalisms in Ethiopia

August 1, 2013 (OP)

Over the last several weeks, a lot has been said on both sides of the "I am Oromo first" and "I am Ethiopian first" divide. But very little about why people choose those positions.

This piece is inspired by Abebe Gelaw's commentary on Jawar Mohammed's statement_[1]. In "I am Ethiopian First" I thought, Abebe presented a sensible and sober contrast to a catalogue of pieces with vulgar and repulsive sentiments from many Ethiopian writers"[2]. His call for calm among Amhara activists regarding their sudden Jawar mania as well as his plea for consensus and compromise between the two communities were commendable.

However, Abebe's characterizations of the typologies of national-isms in Ethiopia were rather troublesome. He writes,

> My understanding is that Jawar is an ethno-nationalist. As an ethno-nationalist, he says he is an Oromo first. Unlike him, I am a nationalist. But that is not the major problem. The problem is the way he has chosen to articulate and present his views in question that have been widely perceived as inflammatory and divisive. I firmly and fervently believe that I am an Ethiopian first. I do not wish to allow the ethnic origin of my predecessors and parents to

define me as a human being and overshadow my Ethiopian identity. Jawar said Ethiopian identity was imposed on him. On the contrary, I argue that such a position is fundamentally flawed. Nowhere in the world is anyone given choices of national identity.

While Abebe sees no problem in this statement, the notion that "I am a nationalist" and "you are an ethno-nationalist" is central to the simmering tensions between Amharas and Oromos. For starters, there is no such a thing as "I am a nationalist." One can only be a nationalist in some defined group. As such when Abebe says I am "an Ethiopian nationalist", it begs the question, but which Ethiopia?

The Euphemism

Oromos and most non-Amhara Ethiopians have a clear understanding of the existence of an Ethiopia with dual identity. The first is mythical Ethiopia, which is sufficiently described in Ethiopian history books. In this ancient Ethiopia with 3,000 years of history, everyone speaks Amharic and is an Orthodox Christian. In its heyday, mythical Ethiopia's geography stretched to the oceans before it was reduced to the current existence in recent centuries.

The second one is what I call the real Ethiopia where two minority groups dominated the majority of people within its borders in literally all spheres of life – politics, economy, culture, language, etc. for more than a century. This Ethiopia, created only during a time span of less than a century and a half, is made up of diverse nations with unique historical and cultural backgrounds.

If you are still reading, which Ethiopian nationalism do you embrace: the mythical or the real Ethiopia one? I relate to the real Ethiopia. Despite overwhelming evidence to the contrary, activists like Abebe often go to great heights to camouflage the facts. I have not heard them advocate for Oromo's or other groups rights. They do not write about the immense sufferings of nations and nationalities in Ethiopia's south, never mind admitting or even mentioning past atrocities and historical injustices. We often hear "free Eskinder Nega!" but rarely "free Bekele Gerba!" although Bekele is being treated harshly at the malaria infested Ziway prison.

Over the years, I saw numerous rallies organized by "Ethiopian nationalists", where they make little or no mention of human rights abuses perpetrated against Oromo and other nations in Ethiopia. Demonstrations are organized only when TPLF forces attack Amharas or Amhara interests. In other words, the likes of Abebe react only to Amhara related incidents. This inconsistency however is not true for Oromo groups. For instance, earlier this year the Oromo Studies Association organized a human rights rally [3] in front of the White House where members carried placards bearing mainly names of Oromo political prisoners. This is because OSA and the Oromo activists made no secret of their objective to raise the neglected Oromo voice. Even then, they called on U.S. government to put pressure on the Ethiopian regime for the release of "all political prisoners", not just the Oromo.

I find it baffling to hear "Ethiopian nationalists" shouting from the rooftops only about injustices perpetuated against Amharas. Even media groups like Abebe Gelaw's ESAT mention Oromo issues as an afterthought or much like a foreign news item. As such, Abebe's claim to represent the real Ethiopia is untenable.

In that sense, the Ethiopian nationalism Abebe represents is an Amhara nationalism wrapped in an Ethiopian garb. The Ethiopian nationalist discourse still remains a deliberate effort to hide Amhara nationalism under Ethiopia-ism. The history of mythical Ethiopia, which enhanced the political and cultural dominance of Amharas over other groups, serves as a "historical" background for the cover-up. As such, when Abebe says, "I'm Ethiopian First" he essentially means, "I'm an Amhara first." Ethiopian is only used as a euphemism for Amhara.

Abebe did not even differ to the Ethiopian euphemism when he said, "I am a nationalist but Jawar is an ethno-nationalist." This is a deliberate label meant to characterize his version of nationalism as superior, and Jawar's as inferior ethnic-nationalism. The truth is both Abebe and Jawar are ethnic nationalists. The only difference is Abebe wants to hide the fact that he's an Amhara nationalist whereas Jawar never hid his Oromummaa.

Ironically, over the last few years, Jawar made more tangible contributions to maintain Ethiopian unity, and has advocated for the emergence of real Ethiopian nationalism. For instance, Jawar has been at the forefront of debates to support Oromo political groups in Ethiopia who are engaged in peaceful movements to democratize Ethiopia. In this regard, Jawar fits what I characterized as a (real) Ethiopian nationalist than Abebe. As ethno-nationalist, Jawar advocates for equality and emancipation of Oromo while also engaging with others to bring about unity among various Ethiopian groups. However, as an Amhara nationalist, hidden behind Ethiopian euphemism, Abebe works to maintain the status quo; and hence he accuses Jawar of being divisive because he is engaged in a political activism that challenges the existing power structure, setup to keep mythical Ethiopia intact.

On Identity

I agree with Abebe that no one makes a conscious decision and chooses his/her identity. It is common for people with diverse cultural and historical backgrounds to be brought into a multination state. However, the extent to which the different groups achieve a harmonious identity, acceptable to each member of the group, would critically depend on the speed with which the multi-nation state becomes a melting pot for the diverse groups. For instance, Switzerland came into existence due to a certain historical accident that brought together Germans, French, and Italians.

The fact that they came from diverse backgrounds did not prevent the country from becoming one of the most peaceful and prosperous in the world. The reason is clear – no one member of the group wanted to impose its will on others. It has four national languages. Its French-speaking group constitutes about 20 percent of the population, roughly the same as Amhara in Ethiopia. But they never attempted to make French the only national language in Switzerland. The Italians make up about six percent of the Swiss population, the same ratio as Tigreans in Ethiopia, but never sought to control and monopolize the state machinery. These democratic attributes are at the core of the harmony and stability in Switzerland, and the problems in Ethiopia.

On Imposed Identity

During the now infamous AJStream segment [1], Jawar said, 'Ethiopia was imposed on me.' This statement has since been quoted repeatedly in Amhara media as being divisive. However, it should have been put in the proper context of everything else Jawar has said over the years. Jawar has appeared on numerous media outlets, including Amhara ones. That is why many are baffled to see the ensuing defamation campaign against him. It could be part of a wider effort to contain a rising Oromo politician that has great potential to become a threat to Amhara nationalist interests, primarily concerned with the maintenance of mythical Ethiopia

Like Jawar, many Oromo individuals and groups, at different times, tried to work with the Ethiopianist camp to only realize the futility of their efforts. They then retreated to the ethno-nationalist positions to bring about real change in that country. Today's young Oromo generation came of age at an era when the Oromo movement has gained momentum. Hence, they were initiated as Oromo nationalists. There is also a third category, like myself, who acquired Oromo nationalist status through evolutionary sequence triggered by real life anecdotes.

I would like to share one anecdote that relates to when, where and how I was "initiated" into becoming an Oromo nationalist. It was in early 1980s when I was a freshman at Addis Ababa University. Ethiopian history was one of the compulsory courses given to all incoming classes. The reading materials for the course were patched together from different sources, sorted into chapters, and then bounded up as a voluminous book. We had to read the material from cover to cover in order avoid dismissal come Christmas. The life of a freshman student was tough.

Toward the end of the book, there was a tiny section devoted to "Oromo history." After reading through the chapter, somewhat dismayed, I was left with numerous questions about my identity and history. Does this mean Oromos have nothing to do with the rest of the sections I already read? Is this all about Oromos? Is that all the Oromo people deserved, a tiny chapter at the end – like a footnote? I concluded the history of Ethiopia has little to do with me. That I am only an Oromo and no more Ethiopian or to use a familiar expression, I figured, *I am Oromo first*.

My mind rushed back to a small village in Western Oromia, no more than fifty households, where I was born and raised. I grew up hearing our neighbors swearing in the name of their fathers who lost their lives in Mekele (lafee abba kootii isa Mekeleti hafee) – reference to a battalion from that village perished in one of the battles around Mekele during the Italian invasion. As a young Oromo who just lost his faith in his Ethiopian-ness, I kept wondering whether those heroes lost their lives fighting the enemy to protect their fatherland or serving an army of their masters much the same way Indian and Nepalese fighters served in the British army during colonialism. I believe that they fought to protect their land but the real Ethiopia they died to protect is yet to emerge.

It should be noted that nobody influenced me in arriving at this conclusion. Logic and facts led me to take an Oromo first nationalist position. Suffice to say, mine was rather unique and a soft landing, but I know many other Oromos who have gone through a difficult journey on bumpy roads to discover their true identity. I lived happily ever after with my Oromo nationalism while also keeping an open eye on how to reach consensus with my fellow Ethiopians on establishing a genuinely united country, whose history and culture reflects the multitude of identities of all its constituencies.

In all, Oromo nationalism emerged not just as a rejection of Ethiopian identity. It is not only because Ethiopia was put together through violent force and Ethiopian identity was imposed on Oromos. This explains only part of the story. In my view, ethno-nationalism gained momentum largely because Amhara nationalists took center stage, confusing Ethiopian nationalism with their ethnic version.

This happened over extended period of time, for about a century, under Amhara's reign. By using state power, the Amhara elite made relentless, persistent, and irresponsible attempts to equate Amhara nationalism with Ethiopian nationalism, and then imposed it on other nations in the country's south. In effect, what Oromos vehemently resisted is not so much of Ethiopian identity but the deceptive way in which the Amhara identity was forced down their throats. Amharas stifled any opportunity for identities of other nations to exist and hence intimidated Oromos and others to retreat into a position of ethnic-nationalism, through which they are now seeking to establish a true Ethiopian identity.

Dialogue

I join Abebe in his plea for dialogue and consensus between the two communities. In "Ethiopian" nationalists' discourses though, even dialogue is practiced as a one-way lecture on unsuitability of ethnic nationalism for Ethiopia and the merits of "Ethiopian nationalism.". Such a discourse amounts to confusing dialogue with monologue. The former implies a two-way talk between two groups, a process in which various viewpoints are expressed to reach compromise and subsequently arrive at a consensus. As Abebe indicated, regardless of several decades of "debates" between Ethiopian nationalists and ethno-nationalists, we are yet to find the middle ground. But why has it taken Ethiopia so long to reach any meaningful consensus? I believe this is because there was no time in Ethiopian history when a meaningful dialogue took place among various stakeholders. It has become increasingly clear that Amharas are not interested in real dialogue while Oromos are not interested in monologues. The result is two separate community groups with different narratives and nationalisms.

Al Jazeera's broadcast revealed the extent to which Oromos and Amhara communities have drifted apart. If there were no such separations, then there would be no ground for Jawar's statement to trigger such uproar. On the other hand, Oromos couldn't understand what all the fuss was about, because this is an identification that most Oromos maintain on daily basis. The lack of dialogue and political space only exacerbates the fear and suspicion between the two communities. For instance, journalist Abdi Fite, in an audio commentary [4], explained how the lack of dialogue has led widening gaps. Abdi stated that we do not only have two communities but also separate soccer tournaments. He then underlined that it's time the two communities begin to deliberate on how they can resolve their differences and the future fate of that country. It looks to me that some Amhara nationalists have zero tolerance for such dialogue; that is why they physically attacked Abdi, whose only crime was calling for a dialogue.

In my view, Abdi's call was not only right but also timely. For instance, the two communities advocate for regime change in Ethiopia, however, it is not clear how they would deal with each other if change does come to Ethiopia. Perhaps the Abebe's of the world should re-watch Abdi's thoughtful commentary and start using their media to jumpstart such constructive dialogue.

References

[1] Do the Oromo have a voice in Ethiopia? The Stream - Al Jazeera
https://www.youtube.com/watch?v=idvJozrs284

[2] Abebe Gellaw , I am Ethiopian first, July 22, 2013.
http://www.zehabesha.com/i-am-ethiopian-first

[3] Mohammed A, Oromo activists rally for justice in homeland,
https://www.youtube.com/watch?v=idvJozrs284. January 30, 2013

[4]   Abdi Fixee, Are You Oromo First or Ethiopia? as Jawar and
millions of Oromos said PART 1. I'M OROMO FIRST!
https://www.youtube.com/watch?v=FoyqiC1s4_4

2. On Unraveling Ethiopia's Political Conundrums

October 8, 2013 (OP)

In a recent Op-Ed piece that appeared on OPride.com [1] , I discussed the types and nature of nationalism in Ethiopia. In response, I received a number of constructive comments and questions both on the site and via email.

In this piece, I will attempt to address some of these questions and comments raised by readers. I will start by responding to a specific question that I received by email regarding my brief reference to ongoing efforts by Amhara elites to "maintain the status quo."

I will then highlight some broader issues that I previously left aside and analyze the behavior of Ethiopian nationalists – how and why they have been resisting change for so long.

The Puzzle

The process of unraveling Ethiopia's political conundrums is analogous to peeling the onion – removing the unpalatable outer cover, cleaning away some rotten stuff between the layers or in the core, and then keeping the edible fresh leaves. The Abyssinian Empire has been around for a while but the Ethiopian empire began taking its current shape at about the same time when most countries in Africa and elsewhere in the world fell under the yoke of European colonization.

While most colonized countries have evolved through strings of changes, Ethiopia's internal colonization remained intact in so far as there were no genuine attempts to rewrite the social contract or democratize its governance. The empire might have undergone a few rounds of changes in governance but saw no substantial alterations in its structure or form.

There has been a cumulative build-up of fallacies at different social stratum as well as in Ethiopia's core establishment. A sober and genuine attempt to gain deeper understanding of Ethiopia's political puzzle requires peeling back those layers and clarifying misconceptions, and revealing deceptions. No doubt this process is bound to uncover inconvenient truths, which at times may raise emotions and even cause some to shed tears – much the same way chopping onions make some cry.

I believe it is a positive step in the right direction to go through such painful but essential exercise in the process of critical self-assessment to gain insights into the real problems befalling the country today. If various social groups continue to live in denial about the existence or nature of their deep-rooted problems, then the end result is bound to be catastrophic.

On the Cover

In the previous piece, I focused on two outer layers of misconceptions in Ethiopia's political discourse. It is useful to put these in the context of what has been said previously on these delusions.

The first one was the conceptual muddle regarding the mythical and real Ethiopia. I have attempted to establish that Ethiopians are yet to agree on what kind of nation they want to build or what exactly they mean by "Ethiopia", and who is really an "Ethiopian". In 1991 article[2], Professor Hamdesa Tuso aptly explained the incompatibilities between the mythical and real Ethiopia perspectives. He suggested that if Ethiopia is to be democratized and its "unity" is to survive, the Ethiopian nationalists should get over their obsession with their mythical Ethiopia paradigm and engage in honest debates on how to build real Ethiopia. However, over the last two decades, the so-called Ethiopian nationalists have only intensified their political activism to restore mythical Ethiopia with heightened zeal, ferocity, and fanaticism.

The second layer of deception is the exclusive manner in which the

Amhara elites shaped Ethiopian nationalism to serve their own narrow interests. In a short-lived attempt in 1990s, the Amhara elites briefly threw away their Ethiopian mask by forming the All-Amhara People's Organization (AAEO) as an ethnic based political organization. This caused a huge uproar within members of the group because they found themselves in a rather embarrassing position. Even in this context, a certain Getinet Belay, writing in the May 1993 issue of *The Ethiopian Review* magazine,committed yet another logical fallacy in Amhara nationalist discourse.

He claimed that the only legitimate ethnic political group in Ethiopia was the AAPO because the interest of that ethnic group coincided with that of Ethiopia. As Dereje Alemayehu explained in his August 1993 response [3], Getinet's bizarre line of argument was actually consistent because what he had in mind was a mythical Ethiopia. The Amhara elites quickly and fully retreated back to their usual position by simply replacing "Ethiopia" for "Amhara" to transform AAEO to AEUP (All Ethiopian Unity Party). I would argue that other ethnic-based political parties are even more legitimate because their interests coincided more with the real Ethiopia.

The Core "Establishment"

A couple of readers asked "what status quo?!" They reasoned that Amharas are no longer in a position of power to maintain any status quo. However, the reader should remember that the foundation of mythical Ethiopia was firmly built with three analogous structures: Amharanization, the Orthodox Church, and State Power. A marriage between these three served as the basis for "the establishment" of an Ethiopian empire. The roles of the first two pillars have barely been interrupted ever since. The third pillar is taken away partly but the bureaucracy of the "establishment" largely survived with a proven capacity to regroup and re-establish itself using the military and even the weaknesses of the current regime.

The underlying cause of this dichotomy between the types of nationalism and Ethiopia's identity lie in the phenomenon of Amharanization. The architects of the Ethiopian empire rather naively envisaged converting Ethiopia into a melting pot of diverse nations and nationalities by simply Amharanizing everybody living within its borders. This is the first and most fatal error that remains unresolved and is at the core of Ethiopia's political troubles. As any mathematician would tell you, if one starts solving a problem using the wrong formula, then the person can spend the rest of his/her life trying but would never arrive at the correct solution.

I am not talking about Amharanization and its origin in some distant past but the aggressive manner in which Amhara elites and the Orthodox clergy are currently advocating the value of Amharanization to "maintain" the unity and survival of Ethiopia.

Following Dergue's downfall, the "establishment" launched a stiff resistance to limit the use of Afaan Oromo as the official language in Oromia. By openly supporting the "establishment," Amhara activists living in Oromia fiercely opposed the use of Oromo language and utilized all kinds of tricks to evade rules and regulations [4] of the Oromia regional state. Similarly, Amhara students often clash with their Oromo counterparts – sometimes through tacit approval of senior elites – simply because Oromo students spoke in their language to each other or organized Oromo cultural events.

Official Language

Amharic is still the only official working language at the federal level in Ethiopia. There have been vigorous campaigns by the "establishment" to pre-empt any possibility of the Oromo language becoming a second working language. In a recent interview with SBS radio Amharic program, Birhanemeskel Abebe Segni [5] compared the present day Ethiopia to a sick person in bed and receiving glucose. Segni reasoned that a nation, which relies only on less than a third of its potential capacity, couldn't be seriously considered as healthy and fully alive. The status of the remaining two-third is reduced to second-class citizenship with their identity hidden and their sense of belonging grossly diminished.

One unique behavioral characteristic of those who preach Amharanization is their zero-sum game mentality. First, Amharanization was more of a religious movement than a social phenomenon. For proponents of this movement, if one deviates from mythical Ethiopia's Amharic "scriptures" and uses his own native tongue, the gods would be seriously disappointed. Like devotees to a religious sect, followers of

Amharanization consider it an unforgiveable sin or treason to speak a language other than Amharic or maintain an identity different from Ethiopian. This remains a source of continuous friction and irritation between the minority "followers" and majority "non-converts" in that country.

Advocates of Amharanization, particularly the Orthodox clergy, once propagated that modern communication devices such as radio and telephone would immediately shatter into pieces if the Oromo language was used. The fact that the Qubee generation is building vibrant Oromo TV and radio stations may not necessarily mean the end of such mythology. The advocates of Amharanization may still be worrying that the roof of Ethiopian parliament would suddenly collapse if Oromo parliamentarians speak to the microphone in their own native language.

There is a great deal that the establishment could learn from the progress attained over the last four decades. In spite of the relentless defense by advocates of Amharanization, today most nations in Ethiopia are developing and promoting their respective cultures. Ethiopia has experienced perhaps the fastest social change and cultural revival during this period since the formation of the empire.

Denials and Falsifications

Lately, Ethio-nationalists have moved beyond attempts to block ongoing changes and pre-empting possible future changes. They are now engaged in futile attempts to prove that the changes that took place over the last forty years were unnecessary and counter-productive. For instance, Professor Messay Kebede, a pioneer in this school of thought, has been vigorously cursing the student movement [6] that triggered the Ethiopian revolution and the abolition of the feudal system.

Messay asserts:

> The very fact that we are dealing with students and intellectuals easily suggests that we direct our attention to the mental process triggered by the exposure to modern, Western education. Because modern ideas and methods did not grow from the native culture, modern education took the form of displacement of native values and beliefs. It became a process of acculturation, of Westernization resulting in the depreciation of the traditional legacy.

A casual reader may think the above text is taken from a political satire, but it is a reasoning advanced by presumably the best brain the elites of establishment could offer. According to Kebede, if Ethiopia's education policy was fully indigenized in line with the mythical Ethiopian doctrine, then millions of *Debrtera Liqawunts* would have been produced and Ethiopia would have achieved a middle-income status years ago.

There is now an ongoing movement established along Kebede's line of thinking to deny, revise, and falsify Ethiopia's pre-1974 history of land holding system. As James McCann noted in *An Agricultural History of* Ethiopia [7], one claim is that "Menelik had never taken land away from Oromo farmers." And that the elites had the right to a share of income from the land but the actual entitlement to the land remained in the hand of Oromo farmers. These kinds of ill-informed conclusions arise from a deliberate effort to falsify history through biased rural development research particularly in Oromia. An Oromo farmer would typically be asked where or how he acquired the plot he is currently farming. Naturally, he would say, "I inherited it from my father." Then the "enlightened" researcher would ask, "Where did your father get it from?" and the farmer would respond, "He inherited from my grandfather."

The "researcher" then tabulates the data and concludes that most Oromos had entitlement to their land throughout the feudal regimes and, therefore, land was never taken away from them. What is lost in this story is, what Oromo sons inherited from their fathers was actually serfdom rather than land ownership. This is a rather obvious historical fact but Ethiopian nationalists would not relent on re-writing history to suit their ulterior motives.

This begs another question: What is their ulterior motive? For some formerly CUD (Kinijit) and now G7 politicos, their primary political agenda is to privatize land. In order to fit this narrative into their "democratic Ethiopia" agenda, they needed to revise and re-write history with a claim that "life was much better when land was in the hand of the landlords." Toward that end, these nationalists used their clouts with multilateral agencies such as the World Bank Group to put pressure the EPRDF regime into privatizing land. The EPRDFites, known to be masters of political opportunism, used these pressures as a pretext and went on a land-selling spree on a gigantic scale. However, all the Ethio-nationalists really wanted was "effectively surrendering land back to the sons and daughters of ex-landlords in whose custody they believe Ethiopia's land would be safer."

The Paradox

As we keep peeling back the layers of Ethiopian polity, we encounter many more misconceptions and deceptions. The sum total yields a grand paradox whereby the very people who occupied the core of the establishment and claim to protect its unity have become the worst enemy of Ethiopia – the ultimate source of its disunity and misery. In a bizarre twist in Ethiopia's history, we have now reached a stage where Ethno-nationalists are having hard time to save Ethiopia from the dangers posed to it by the so-called Ethiopian nationalists.

In the past, Ethiopian nationalists presented themselves as the only group who cared about Ethiopia's existence and excluded the rest of Ethiopia's political groups from playing a part in the nation building drills. The Amhara saying *man baqenaw hager* – meaning *this is my country, none of your business* – which reduces the entire country to a private property for the benefit of a small group, succinctly sums this truth up. One way or another, this mentality still lurks in the background of Ethiopian nationalist rhetoric.

Ethiopian nationalists' all-time favorite motto has been *Ethiopia First*. It still beams from their affiliate FM radio stations, which obey the Amharanization doctrine by playing music in no other language except Amharic. "Ethiopia Tikdem!" punctuates each song and program throughout the broadcasts. Ironically, the very people who have formulated and preached the *Ethiopia First* mantra are the ones who practice it the least. Ethiopia First requires a serious commitment to putting aside *group* interests for the sake of *national* interest. Other ingredients include tolerance, respect, consensus, and compromise. But these are buzzwords completely absent from the Ethiopian nationalist's political narratives.

Based on several years of experience working in and researching in the country, former U.S. Ambassador to Ethiopia, David Shinn [8]_once concluded: "I believe that at least in highland Ethiopian society, the concept of compromise as I understand it in the United States is sorely lacking."

I concur with his observation. If genuine democratization was to be envisioned, Ethiopia is going to need a lot of it.

References

[1] Ayele Gelan, Typologies of National-isms in Ethiopia, August 1, 2013. http://opride.com/2013/08/01/typologies-of-national-isms-in-ethiopia

[2] the Demise of Mythical Ethiopia [2]

[3] Dereje Alemayehu. A Diktat or a Perspective For A Democratic Discourse? (A Reply Of A "National-Nihilist To A Mature Neopatriot).
http://www.gadaa.com/DAlemayehuWalelignsEthiopia2012.pdf

[4] Gigsa Tesso, Commentary on the current status of Afan Oromo in Gimbi town, West Oromia . http://ayyaantuu.com/horn-of-africa-news/oromia/commentary-on-the-current-status-of-afan-oromo-in-gimbi-town-west-oromia/

[5] An interview with SBS Radio Part 1.
https://www.youtube.com/watch?v=FVKQEbsfiEA

[6] Messay Kebede. Ethiopia: Guilt And Atonement: the Genesis of Revolutionary Spirit in Ethiopia.
https://allafrica.com/stories/200408060599.html

[7] James McCan 1995. People of the Plow: An Agricultural History of Ethiopia, 1800-1990. University of Wisconsin Press

[8] David Shinn 2010. Ways to Contribute to the Future of EthiopiaRemarks to the Ethiopian American Youth InitiativeEthiopian EmbassyWashington, D.C.2 January 2010.
https://www.scribd.com/document/24710474/Future-of-Ethiopia

3. Scottish Lessons for Oromo Nationalists

September 17, 2014 (OP)

In a landmark referendum on Sept. 18, the people of Scotland will vote Yes or No to determine the future of their 300-year-old union with England.

The simplicity of the question and the answers are by no means indicative of the intensity of the debates and emotions in this campaign. There have been passionate debates over the years between the unionists and Scottish nationalists. The publicity of the campaigns has generated a lot of interest around the world. As a result, this week's vote is being closely watched by Oromo activists [1] and nationalists the world over who are still trapped in old empires. What lessons can be gleaned from the Scottish case for the decolonization of the Ethiopian empire and the Oromo people's aspiration for an independent statehood?

Involuntary Unions

There are several remarkable similarities between Scotland and Oromia. First, both are endowed with abundant natural resources. Second, both Scotland and Oromia were involuntarily incorporated into empires by their next door neighbors. The Scots have a humorous saying which goes something like this: During creation, God gave Scotland many good things — fascinating lakes, beautiful beaches, majestic mountains and etc. One of his companions commented: Lord, this is not fair; you are being too generous to Scotland, you do not seem to mix it with anything bad. To which God replied, "just wait and see what kind of neighbor I will give Scotland!"

The Scottish people spent several hundreds of years fending off the English. This culminated in the Acts of Union[2] in 1707 when the English and Scottish parliaments voted to create the United Kingdom. Scotland was in economic bankruptcy[3] and it had no more energy left to resist another invasion and continued meddling by the English. Like the Scottish wars of independence[4], Oromos in Central, Southern and Eastern Oromia put up years of stiff resistance against Abyssinian occupation. In some ways, the act of union also resembles the incorporation of Western Oromia into the Abyssinian empire. The beheading of William Wallace, a prominent Scottish hero, resonates well with cases of Oromo heroes who perished, amputated or mutilated at the battles of Gulale, Aanolee [5], Chalanqo [6] and many others.

Like the Scots, the Oromo were treated inhumanely by the invading Abyssinian feudal lords. For instance, the industrial revolution in England was fueled by wool supplied by absentee landlords who evicted Scottish highlanders[7] from their lands to give way for large scale sheep rearing. Similarly, the Oromo experienced a grand scale dispossession under the Gabbar system [8], which appropriated virgin farmlands to feudal landowners. For the Scots, the greatest victim was their language, Gaelic [9], which suffered hugely in part due to the highland clearance [10] and relocation of Scottish farming communities to faraway territories such as Nova Scotia in Canada. In contrast, Oromo farmers endured the brunt of exploitation toiling their own land for absentee landlords as serfs and slaves. This together with the demographic balance helped the survival of the Oromo language against all odds.

Empire Building

To borrow an Orwellian expression, all empires are wicked but some are less wicked than others. With regard to the relative successes of the empires that absorbed them, the fate of Scotland and Oromia could not be more different. In Oromia's case, it goes without saying that the Ethiopian empire failed to establish any degree of cohesion among its constituencies. The fact that a situation similar to the Scottish highland clearances is still happening in Oromia — nearly a century and a half later — is a testament to the farcical nature of the Ethiopian empire.

By contrast, despite all the setbacks that came with losing independence, Scotland thrived in the UK, where the whole became greater than sum of the individual parts. For one, under the terms of the Acts of the Union, Scotland retained most of its institutions, e.g., legal system, education, church and etc. This helped energize the union. Success in domestic economy through a series of revolutions (e.g. agricultural and industrial) propelled the UK to emerge as one of the most powerful nations on earth, so much so that it came to be known as *"the empire on which the sun never sets."* In effect, Scotland and England built solid institutions and sustained enviable democratic governance. The same can't be said about Oromia. The Amharanization doctrine was essentially designed to wipe out all aspects Oromo socio-political, religious and cultural institutions and aggressively replace it by official state functions.

What Can Oromos Learn from the Scottish Nationalists?

There is no doubt that both Scotland and Oromia were victims of internal colonization. Both nations experienced brutal wars of conquest in the centuries leading up to and during their involuntary incorporation into burgeoning empires.

Both Scotland and Oromia maintain distinct culture and history from their neighbors. Thus, it is ironic that the Scottish nationalists did not anchor their case for independence on history. They have not campaigned on the principle of decolonization.

Past history or injustices during wars of resistance did not play any part in the Scottish independence rhetoric during the referendum debate. In fact, most cases for Scottish independence dramatically contrast with Oromia's circumstances.

Demography

The Scots, who constitute about 8.4 percent of the UK's population, are a minority group. This led to a phenomenon commonly referred to as democratic deficit, meaning political parties could form a government in the Westminster regardless of which way the Scottish people voted. For instance, for far too long, the Conservative Party has been governing the UK with no electoral mandate in Scotland.

This is why the Scottish National Party (SNP) firmly anchored their argument on the principle that no matter how hard they try to perfect the union, democracy is unlikely to work in favor of the Scottish people so long as Scotland remained in the UK. Needless to say, in contrast to Scotland's clear disadvantage, Oromia enjoys a massive demographic advantage. This means democracy will work exceptionally well for Oromos.

Economy

Several attempts have been made to address Scotland's democratic deficits through referendums for Scottish devolution [11]. This culminated in the formation of the Scottish Parliament in Edinburgh in 1999. However, the devolution of the political power has not led to any meaningful economic power. For instance, the parliament had power to spend funds allocated to it from the Westminster but it had no power to raise its own revenues [12] through taxes. This fuelled the rationale for independence advocated by the SNP who rested their economic case on the fact that the oil-rich Scotland is actually a net contributor to the UK treasury, by about 400 pounds per person [13].

In Oromia's case, it would be unfair to talk about the state's share in government revenue in terms of some marginal net contribution; it suffices to say the bulk of Ethiopian government revenue from domestic sources is generated in Oromia.

However, it should be noted that Scotland's economic case for independence is rooted in the incurable democratic deficit, which in turn is explained by its demographic disadvantage. On the contrary, Oromia is not expected to encounter the Scottish economic dilemma provided that Oromos assert their power to establish a democratic and genuinely federal system of government.

Geography

Scotland is located in the periphery of the UK. Peripheral locations often find themselves in disadvantageous positions because resources (human and financial) tend to move and concentrate in the center through forces of agglomeration. More and more jobs are created in London and its surroundings in England. The youth and the skilled among the Scottish people migrate to England in search of jobs.

Similarly, investment resources follow suit through the banking system. It requires a good deal of government intervention to slow down this self-reinforcing cumulative process of resource outflow from the periphery to the center. The Scottish independence is essentially meant to reduce or stop the resource outflows by creating jobs in Scotland.

By contrast, Oromia occupies a vast landmass in Ethiopia, comparable more to England in the UK than Scotland. In fact, Oromia is already a magnet, a preferred destination for investors from domestic and international sources. Under normal circumstances, such resource inflows are considered a blessing.

However, circumstances are not normal in Oromia so we see resources as a curse to our people. The main reason for this is that Oromos do not participate in critical aspects decision-making (e.g., investor selection, business location, or employment contracts).

Contested viewpoints

The similarities and differences between Oromia and Scotland may enable us to shed some light on established contrasting viewpoints in Oromo nationalist rhetoric. From the foregoing discussion, it is clear that the SNP has mainly campaigned on democratic principles. In that sense, SNP's strategy is consistent with the pro-democracy viewpoint in the Oromo movement. The former to justify departure from the UK empire and the latter to justify feasible and possible achievements of democracy within Ethiopia.

While similar to the pro-independence camp in Oromia, the SNP chose not to invoke decolonization as a rallying cry. To be fair, colonial trappings are a thing of distant past within the boundaries of the UK. In contrast, archaic colonial behaviors and sentiments are still rife in the Ethiopian empire. This has made the road to freedom a lot more complicated for Oromos than the Scots, with clashes between contesting viewpoints.

At this juncture, it is useful to draw attention to a few conceptual muddles that might have exacerbated the differences. One is related to the issue of "democratic principle" as discussed in the context of the Ethiopian empire. It should be clear that "democratic deficit" does not mean "lack of democracy." Oromo nationalists often say, "the Ethiopian empire has been ruled by dictators who do not give democracy to the people." This expression comes from a misconception that democracy is in fact "given."

The reality is democracy is never given, it is "earned" by establishing power balance through a resolute struggle. As such, it is not tenable to rest the case for Oromia's independence on the supposition that democracy will not work in the Ethiopian empire. This amounts to resigning from endeavoring to establish power equilibrium through which democracy can come to existence.

Similarly, we often hear assertions such as "an empire cannot be democratized." The UK is the mother of all empires and yet it is one of the most democratic countries on earth. The English, who are the majority group in the UK, do not seem to have any trouble with UK's democratic governance.

But the minority Scots have expressed a legitimate grievance that UK's democracy did not work for them. It is true that the English were colonizers in the context of the UK but then again we should note how they "achieved" democracy through Magna Carta [14] long before they became colonizers.

In a nutshell, Scotland's potential independence offers little in a way of practical lessons for Oromia. Oromo nationalists should instead look at multi-ethnic states such as Malaysia and South Africa on how the majority can and should assert themselves to build democracy. If anything, Oromo leaders should emulate the SNP's vision and style of effective leadership to mobilize and energize their base in order to realize the aspiration of Oromo people for freedom.

References

[1] Boruu Barraaqaa 2014. Essence of the Scottish Referendum in the Eyes of an Oromo Nationalist.
http://gadaa.net/FinfinneTribune/2014/09/boruu-barraaqaa-essence-of-the-scottish-referendum-in-the-eyes-of-an-oromo-nationalist/

[2] Act of Union 1707, https://www.parliament.uk/about/living-heritage/evolutionofparliament/legislativescrutiny/act-of-union-1707/

[3] Darien scheme. https://en.wikipedia.org/wiki/Darien_scheme

[4] The Wars of Independence.
http://www.bbc.co.uk/scotland/history/articles/the_wars_of_independ
ence/

[5] Mohammed Ademo. Aanolee: 'a tragedy on which Ethiopian
sources are silent'. April 2014.
http://www.opride.com/2014/04/08/aanolee-mutilation-a-tragedy-on-
which-ethiopian-sources-are-silent/

[6] Jaffar Ali, Fictional Account of Calanqoo Massacre (audio in
Afaan Oromoo).
https://www.youtube.com/watch?v=3x4lVZXXknk&feature=youtu.b
e

[7] The Patterns of the Highland Clearances.
http://www.scottishhistory.com/articles/highlands/clearances/clearan
ce_page1.html

[8] Bichaka Fayisa 1992. Rent-seeking behavior or Ethiopian rulers
as a constraint to the economic development of the Oromo People.
The Oromo Commentary. II(1): 17-20.
https://oromocommentary.files.wordpress.com/2010/07/rent-seeking-
behaviour-of-the-ethiopian-rulers.pdf

[9] Scottish Gaelic.
https://en.wikipedia.org/wiki/Scottish_Gaelic#From_the_Middle_Ag
es_to_the_end_of_Classical_Gaelic_education

[10] The Highland Clearances, and their causes, effects, and results
Chapter One. http://www.scottish-history.com/clearances.shtml

[11] History of Scottish devolution.
https://en.wikipedia.org/wiki/History_of_Scottish_devolution

[12] SNP growth commission to set out fresh economic case for
Scottish independence. https://www.holyrood.com/articles/news/snp-
growth-commission-set-out-fresh-economic-case-scottish-
independence

[13] Reporting the Referendum.
http://reportingthereferendum.blogspot.com/2014/01/economic-case-

for-scottish-independence.html

[14] The Magna Carta. https://www.archives.gov/exhibits/featured-documents/magna-carta

4. Crony Capitalism and the Myth Behind Ethiopia's Economic Miracle

July 15, 2014 (OP)

Over the last decade, Ethiopia has been hailed as the fastest growing non-oil economies in Africa, maintaining a double-digit annual economic growth rate. The Ethiopian government says the country will join the middle-income bracket by 2025 [1].

Despite this, however, as indicated by a recent Oxford University report [2], some 90 percent of Ethiopians still live in poverty, second only after Niger from 104 countries measured by the Oxford Multidimensional Poverty Index. The most recent data shows an estimated 71.1 percent of Ethiopia's population lives in severe poverty.

This is baffling: how can such conflicting claims be made about the same country? The main source of this inconsistent story is the existence of crony businesses and the government's inflated growth figures. While several multinational corporations are now eyeing Ethiopia's cheap labor market, two main crony conglomerates dominate the country's economy.

Meet EFFORT, TPLF's Business Empire

The seeds of Ethiopia's economic mismanagement were sown at the very outset. We are familiar with rich people organizing themselves, entering politics and protecting their group interests. But something that defies our knowledge of interactions between politics and business happened in 1991 when the current regime took power.

Ethiopia's ruling party, the EPRDF, came to power by ousting the communist regime in a dramatic coup. A handful of extremely poor people organized themselves exceptionally well that they quickly took control of the country's entire political and military machinery.

In a way, this is analogous to a gang of thieves becoming brutally efficient at organizing themselves to the extent of forming a government. Once in power, the ruling Tigrean elites expropriated properties from other businesses, looted national assets and began creating wealth exclusively for themselves.

This plan first manifested itself in the form of party affiliated business conglomerate known as the Endowment Fund for Rehabilitation of Tigray (EFFORT). EFFORT has its origin in the relief and rehabilitation arm of the Tigrean People Liberation Front (TPLF) and the country's infamous 1984 famine.

As reported by BBC's Martin Plaut and others, the TPLF financed its guerilla warfare against the Dergue in part by converting aid money into weapons and cash [3]. That was not all. On their way to Addis Ababa from their bases in Tigray, the TPLF confiscated any liquid or easily moveable assets [4] they could lay their hands on. For instance, a substantial amount of cash was amassed by breaking into safe deposits of banks all over Ethiopia. Those funds were kept in EFFORT's bank accounts. TPLF leaders vowed to use the loot to rehabilitate and reconstruct Tigray, which they insisted was disproportionately affected by the struggle to "free Ethiopia."

Intoxicated by its military victory, the TPLF then turned to building a business empire. EFFORT epitomizes that unholy marriage between business and politics in a way not seen before in Ethiopian history. According to a research by Sarah Vaughan and Mesfin Gebremichael [4], EFFORT, which is led by senior TPLF officials, currently owns 16 companies across various sectors of the economy.

This figure grossly understates the number of EPRDF affiliated companies. For example, the above list does not include the real money-spinners that EFFORT owns: Wegagen Bank, Africa Insurance, Mega Publishing, Walta Information Center and the Fana Broadcasting Corporate. The number of companies under EFFORT is estimated to be more than 66 business entities [5]. Suffice to say, EFFORT controls the commanding heights of the Ethiopian economy.

While it is no secret that EFFORT is owned by and run exclusively to benefit ethnic Tigrean elites, it is a misnomer to still retain the phrase "rehabilitation of Tigray." Perhaps it should instead be renamed as the Endowment Fund for Rendering Tigrean Supremacy (EFFO*RTS*).

MIDROC Ethiopia, EPRDF's Joker Card

In Ethiopia's weak domestic private environment, EFFORT is an *exception to the rule*. Similarly, while Ethiopia suffers from lack of foreign direct investment, MIDROC [6] Ethiopia enjoys unparalleled access to Ethiopia's key economic sectors. Owned by Ethiopian-born Saudi business tycoon, Sheik Mohammed Al Amoudi, MIDROC has been used by the EPRDF as a joker card in a mutually advantageous ways. The Sheik was given a privilege no less than the status of a domestic private investor but the EPRDF can also count it as a foreign investor. For instance, the United Nations Conference on Trade and Development [7] reported that about 60 per cent of the overall FDI approved in Ethiopia was related to MIDROC.

MIDROC stands for Mohammed International Development Research and Organization Companies. Despite reference to development and research in its name, however, there is no real relationship between what the crony business says and what it actually does. Ironically, as with EFFORT, MIDROC Ethiopia also owns 16 companies. But this too is a gross underestimation given the vast sphere of influence and wealth MIDROC commands in that country.

Like EFFORT, Al-Amoudi's future was also sealed long before the TPLF took power. He literally entered Addis Ababa [9] with the EPRDF army, fixing his eyes firmly on Oromia's natural resources. Shortly after the TPLF took the capital, Al-Amoudi allegedly donated a huge sum of money to the Oromo People's Democratic Organization.

Why the rush? The calculative Sheik sensed an eminent threat to his business interests from the Oromo Liberation Front (OLF), a groups that was also a partner in the transitional government at the time. In return for its "donation," MIDROC acquired massive lands in Oromia – gold mines, extensive state farms and other agricultural lands. In a recent article entitled, "The man who stole the Nile," journalist Frederick Kaufman [8] aptly described Al Amoudi's role in the ongoing land grab in Ethiopia as follows:

In this precarious world-historic moment, food has become the most valuable asset of them all — and a billionaire from Ethiopia named Mohammed Hussein Al Amoudi is getting his hands on as much of it as possible, flying it over the heads of his starving countrymen, and selling the treasure to Saudi Arabia. Last year, Al Amoudi, whom most Ethiopians call the Sheikh, exported a million tons of rice, about seventy pounds for every Saudi citizen. The scene of the great grain robbery was Gambella, a bog the size of Belgium in Ethiopia's southwest whose rivers feed the Nile.

It is little wonder then that Al-Amoudi said, "I lost my right hand" [9], when Ethiopia's strongman of two decades Meles Zenawi died in 2012. If EFFORT is a curse to the Ethiopian economy, MIRDOC is EPRDF's poisoned drink given to the Ethiopian people.

Mutual Distrust

The marriage between politics and business has had damaging effects on the country's economy. One of its most far-reaching consequences is the total breakdown of trust between the EPRDF and the Ethiopian people. In economic policy, trust between private investors and the government is paramount. The deficit of trust is one of the hallmarks of Ethiopia's much-touted development.

After all youth unemployment [10] hovers around 50 percent. Every year, hundreds of young Ethiopians risk their lives trying to reach Europe or the Middle East, often walking across the Sahara desert or paying smugglers to cross the Red Sea or Indian Ocean aboard crowded boats. The desperation is a result of the lack of confidence in the government's ability to provide them with the kind of future they were promised.

Ironically, aside from their crony businesses, the EPRDF does not have any confidence in Ethiopian entrepreneurs either. It is this mutual distrust that culminated in the prevalence of an extremely hostile environment for domestic private investment.

This is not a speculative claim but a well-documented fact. The World Bank's annual survey, which measures the ease with which private investors can do business, ranks Ethiopia near the bottom. In the 2014 survey, Ethiopia [11] came in 166th out of 189 countries in terms of difficulties in starting new business or trading across borders. Moreover, year on year comparison shows that the investment climate in Ethiopia is actually getting worse, sliding down the ranking both in the ease of doing business and trading across borders.

Farms but No Firms

The TPLF cronies do not engage in competitive business according to market rules but act as predators bent on killing existing and emerging businesses owned by non-Tigrean nationals. However, the ruling party, which largely maintains its grip on power using bilateral and multilateral aid, is required to report its economic progress to donors (the regime does not care about accountability to the people). In this regard, the lack of foreign direct investment (FDI) has been a thorn in the throat of the EPRDF. Donors have repeatedly questioned [12] and pressured the EPRDF to attract more FDI. The inflow of FDI is often seen as a good indicator of the confidence in countries stability and sound governance. Despite widespread belief in the West, the EPRDF regime cannot deliver on these two fronts.

To cover up these blind spots, the regime has persuaded a handful of foreigners to invest in Ethiopia, but until recently few investors considered any serious manufacturing venture in the country. Besides, considered "cash cows" for the government, banks, the Ethiopian Airlines, telecommunication and energy sectors remain under exclusive monopoly of the state. They provide almost free service to the crony businesses. Any firm looking to invest in manufacturing and financial sectors have to overcome insurmountable bureaucratic red tape and other barriers.

One sector that stands as exception to this rule is agriculture. Since the 2008 financial crisis and the rise in the global price of food, the regime opened the door widely for foreigners who wanted to acquire large-scale farms. These farms do not hurt their crony businesses but they do harm poor subsistence farmers. Vast tracts of lands have been sold to foreigners at ridiculously cheap prices, often displacing locals and their way of life.

Contrary to the government rhetoric, the motivation for opening up the agricultural sector has nothing to do with economic growth but everything to do with politics – to silence critics, particularly in the donor community who persistently question EPRDF's credibility in attracting FDI. In essence, hundreds of thousands of poor farmers were evicted to make way for flower growers and shore up the government's image abroad. This tactic seems to be working so far. Earlier this year, Ethiopia received its first credit rating from Moody's Investors Service [13]. In the last few years, in part due to rising labor costs in China and East Asia, several manufacturers have relocated to Ethiopia.

Addis' Construction Boom as a Smokescreen

Crony businesses and flower growers may have created some heat but certainly no light in Ethiopian economy. EFFORT and MIDROC were in action for much of the 1990s and early 2000s but GDP growth was not satisfactory during that time. In fact, since other private businesses were in dismal conditions (and hence domestic market size is very limited), even the crony businesses encountered challenges in getting new business deals.

The setbacks in political front during the 2005 election shifted EPRDF's strategies to economic front to urgently register some noticeable growth. This partly explains the motives behind the ongoing construction rush in and around Addis Ababa. In several rounds of interviews on ESAT TV [14], former Minister d'etat of Communications Affairs, Ermias Legesse, provided interesting accounts of cronyism surrounding Addis' explosive growth and its tragic consequences for Oromo farmers.

It is important to understand the types of construction that is taking place around or near Addis. First, private property developments by crony estate agents mushroomed overnight. A lion's share of land expropriated from Oromo farmers were allocated to these regime affiliates through dishonest bids. Luxury houses are built on such sites and sold at prices no average Ethiopian could afford, except maybe those in the diaspora. The latter group is being targeted lately due to shortages of hard currencies.

Second, EPRDF politicians and high ranking military officers own multi-storey office buildings, particularly aimed at renting to NGOs and residential villas for foreign diplomats who can afford to pay a few thousand dollars per month. It is a known fact that the monthly salary cap for Ethiopian civil servants is around 6000 birr (about $300). As such, that these individuals could invest in such expensive properties underscores the extent of the daylight robbery that is taking place in Ethiopia.

Third, the government was engaged in massive public housing construction but under extremely chaotic circumstances. The condominium rush in Addis is akin to the Dergue regime's villagization schemes in rural Ethiopia. Families are uprooted from their homes without any due consideration for their social and economic well-being.

Most households that once occupied the demolished homes in Addis Ababa's shantytowns made a living through informal home businesses such as brewing local drinks and preparing and selling food at prices affordable to the poor. It was clear that the condominiums were not suitable for them to continue doing such businesses. The construction of the public houses was financed by soft loans from various donor agencies to be sold to target households at affordable prices. However, the government often priced them at the going market rates for condos.

As a result, the poor households simply rented out the properties to those who could afford, while struggling to find affordable houses for themselves. Solving the public housing crisis was never the government's intention in the first place, as they were only interested in creating business opportunities for their crony construction companies.

Fourth, roads and railway networks are by far the most important large-scale public sector construction projects taking place in Addis. There is no doubt that Addis Ababa's crowded roads, equally shared by humans, animals and cars, need revamping. But, what is happening in the name of building roads and railways simply defies belief. First, the sheer scale and magnitude as well as the obsession with construction makes the whole undertaking look suspicious. Every time I travelled to Addis, I witness the same roads being constructed and then dug up to be reconstructed over and over again.

The ulterior motive behind these projects is nothing more than expanding TPLF's business empire and benefit crony allies. Having exhausted opportunities within the existing perimeter of Addis, the so-called master plan had to be crafted to enlarge the size of "the construction site" by a factor of 20 to ensure that the cronies will stay in business in the foreseeable future. In effect, the large-scale construction projects are being used to siphon off public funds. And there seems to be no priority or accountability in the whole process from the project inception, planning to implementation.

Lies and Damn Lies

The construction boom in Addis serves as a two edged sward. On the one hand, the funds generated from selling Oromo lands to private property developers adds to the ever-expanding business empire of Tigrean political and military elites. On the other hand, the appearances of several high-rise buildings and complex road networks give the impression that Ethiopia is witnessing an economic boom. The target audience for the latter scenario is foreign journalists and the diplomatic community in Addis Ababa, some of whom are so gullible that they fall in love with ERDF's economic "miracle" from the first aerial view even before landing at the Bole airport.

The fact remains however: no such economic miracle is actually happening in Ethiopia. A pile of concrete slabs cannot transform the economy in any meaningful way. After all, buildings and roads are only intermediaries for doing other businesses. For instance, it is not enough to build highways and rural roads – a proportionate effort is required to enhance production of goods and services to move them on the newly built roads in such a way that the roads will get utilized and investments made on them get recovered. Otherwise, the roads and buildings can deteriorate without giving any service, and hence more public money would soon be required to maintain them. This is exactly what is happening in Ethiopia.

Meanwhile, the EPRDF has been engaged in a frantic effort to generate lies and damn lies to fill the gap between the rhetoric and the reality of Ethiopia's economy. The government-controlled media has been used for extensive propaganda campaign to create a "positive image" in the eyes of ordinary citizens. They literally compel viewers or listeners to see or feel things that do not exist on the ground. The Ethiopian television zooms onto any spot of land with a colony of green grass or lush crop fields to "prove" the kinds of wonders the government is engineering.

Barring rain failures, much of Ethiopia's lush-green countryside has a decent climate for agriculture. But the EPRDF regime tries to convince the public that anything positive that occurs in the Ethiopia is because of its economic policies. But, as evidenced in ongoing multifaceted grievances around the country, the government is fooling no one else but itself (and perhaps a few gullible individuals in the diplomatic community).

Its lies also come in the form of dubious economic statistics, which are generated in such a way that EPRDF could report double-digit economic growth year after year. The story of the double digit economic growth rate in Ethiopia has been such that a lie told hundreds of times, no matter how shambolic the numbers are, is becoming part of the western vernacular. Donors often point to the abundance of high-rise buildings and impressive road networks in Addis Ababa in regime's defense.

In a brief conversation, it is not possible to take such casual observers through details of the kind I have attempted to narrate in the preceding paragraphs. And, unfortunately for millions of Ethiopia's poor, in the short run the government's lies and crony capitalism may continue to ravage the country's economy until it begins to combust from within.

References

[1] World Bank. Can Ethiopia Become a Middle Income Country by 2025? (A video archive)
http://www.worldbank.org/en/news/video/2013/07/01/can-ethiopia-become-a-middle-income-country-by-2025.

[2] Oxford Poverty and Human Development Initiative (OP

HI). Country Briefing: Ethiopia OPHI Country Briefing 2013.
http://www.ophi.org.uk/wp-content/uploads/Ethiopia-2013.pdf?79d835

[3], Ethiopia: Live Aid-Arms Aid? Was food aid pilfered? The Economist http://www.economist.com/node/15641802. March 8, 2010.

[4] Sarah Vaughan and Mesfin Gebremichael

Rethinking business and politics in Ethiopia The role of EFFORT, the Endowment Fund for the

Rehabilitation of Tigray. Research Report No. 02. August 2011.

http://www.institutions-africa.org/filestream/20110822-appp-rr02-
rethinking-business-politics-in-ethiopia-by-sarah-vaughan-mesfin-
gebremichael-august-2011

[5] Ethiopia is looted by EFFORT and The TPLF Business Empire.
Ethiopiantimes. July 30, 2012
http://ethiopiantimes.wordpress.com/2012/07/30/ethiopia-is-looted-
by-effort-and-the-tplf-business-empire/

[6] Mohammed International Development Research and
Organization Companies. https://en.wikipedia.org/wiki/MIDROC

[7] UNCTAD. Investment and Innovation Policy Review Ethiopia/.
UNCTAD/ITE/IPC/Misc. 4
http://unctad.org/en/docs/poiteipcm4.en.pdf. New York. 2012

[8] Frederick Kaufman The Man Who Stole the Nile: An Ethiopian
billionaire's outrageous land grab. Harper's Magazine (July 2014
issue). http://harpers.org/archive/2014/07/the-man-who-stole-the-
nile/.

[9] "It's like I lost my right-hand" - Al Amoudi on Meles Zenawi
death. http://nazret.com/blog/index.php/2012/08/29/ethiopia-it-s-
like-i-lost-my-right-hand-al-amoudi-on-meles-zenawi-death

[10] Andualem Sisay. Youth unemployment: lessons from Ethiopia.
Africa Renewal May 2013.
http://www.un.org/africarenewal/magazine/may-2013/youth-
unemployment-lessons-ethiopia

[11] World Bank. Ease of Doing Business in Ethiopia
http://www.doingbusiness.org/data/exploreeconomies/ethiopia

[12] US Trade Representative. Ethiopia: Trade Summary 2013.
http://www.ustr.gov/sites/default/files/2014%20NTE%20Report%20
on%20FTB%20Ethiopia.pdf

[13] Moody's
https://www.moodys.com/Pages/rr003_0.aspx?bd=4294966708&ed=

4294966848&rd=4294966708&tb=0&po=0&sb=&sd=&lang=en&cy
=global&searchfrom=SearchWithin&kw=ethiopia

[14] ESAT Yesamintu Engeda Ermias Legese The former Miniseter
d'etat May 2014 http://ethsat.com/video/esat-yesamintu-engeda-
ermias-legese-the-former-miniseter-detat-may-2014/

5. Is Devaluation of Birr the Answer to Ethiopia's Economic Troubles?

August 19, 2014 (OP)

In a new report released last month [2], the World Bank recommended a 10 percent devaluation of the Ethiopian birr, saying depreciating birr can "increase export growth by more than 5 percentage points per year and increase economic growth by more than 2 percentage points."

This piece will be presented in two parts. Part I focuses on devaluation and exports, specifically regional and sectoral policy biases that explain Ethiopia's poor export performance. Part II will scrutinize Ethiopia's trade data and highlight implications of devaluation for import prices. The later will be published in a separate piece (the next one in this book).

Ethiopia's external trade position [2] has rapidly deteriorated in recent years. In 2012, payments for imports exceeded receipts from exports by about $8.1 billion. In 2005 the deficit in commodities trade was $1.6 billion but this gap widened by two-fold by 2012, and reached about 7 percent of Ethiopia's Gross Domestic Product.

As such, the devaluation of birr alone may not improve Ethiopia's troubles in external trade. If any improvement is to be made, authorities should first rein in the entrenched policy biases and power structures in Ethiopia that underlie poor export performance that is grossly overlooked in the World Bank report.

Devaluation and Exports

The World Bank researchers acknowledge that they arrived at this recommendation after running an extremely simple theoretical analysis, which they then juxtaposed with Ethiopia's trade data. Under this textbook approach, and leaving the economics jargon aside, devaluing birr means reducing its price in foreign exchange markets, where currencies are bought and sold like any other commodity.

Reducing price of any commodity is bound to increase demand for it. So, after devaluation, demand for birr by foreigners is expected to increase. For instance, currently the official exchange rate for 1 USD is 19.745 birr. The recommended 10 percent devaluation would increase the quantity of birr offered per 1 USD to about 22.

Since the ultimate need for the birr by foreigners is to purchase Ethiopian goods and services, the depreciation of the birr will immediately translate to making Ethiopian exports cheaper in USD (or any other foreign currency for that matter). For instance, in June 2014 Ethiopia was selling a ton of coffee at $4,360 but after devaluation the price will fall to $3,924. The faith in the effectiveness of devaluation as a means of promoting coffee exports follows from a belief that Ethiopia will become more competitive by lowering the price of its exports. The hope is that, if all goes well, coffee buyers may turn to Ethiopian coffee.

Policy Context

When exports become cheaper, exporters may incur losses from a given quantity. But if larger quantity is sold then gains will more than compensate for losses incurred. So, devaluation is justified if lack of demand for Ethiopian exports is the only obstacle and there are no troubles on the supply side.

However, Ethiopia does not have a stockpile of exportable commodity waiting to be sold. Still worse, there are entrenched policy biases against exportable products such as coffee and its producers raising concerns that export supplies may not increase in the near future.

Thus, the most likely immediate effects of devaluation will be deterioration in revenues from a given quantity of available exports. The power imbalance between coffee exporters and coffee growers is such that most of the reduction in revenue will be directly passed to coffee farmers, who will be the ultimate victims.

The World Bank seems to have grossly overlooked these most fundamental policy contexts. It is essential to examine in some detail the policy bias against export producing regions and sectors.

Regional Policy Bias

Public investment decisions need to be based on potential returns. A dollar invested in resource rich region generates much larger returns and more quickly than if it is invested in resource poor regions. It pays to initially invest in resource rich regions, recover the returns and then worry about ways to subsidize poorer regions on equity considerations. After all, wealth has to be created before it can be distributed.

Ethiopia's ruling party has turned this logic upside down by adopting a lopsided development pattern whereby the government leads the private sector by example. There are strong complementarities between public and private investments.

Ethiopia's public investment is hugely concentrated in and around the capital Addis Ababa and a few selected regional centers such as Mekelle, Hawassa and Bahir Dar. The private sector have followed suit and most economic activities have gravitated to these centers. However, these rapidly growing urban centers make little, if any, contribution to Ethiopia's commodity exports. On the other hand, resource rich areas, e.g., Oromia's coffee growing regions, have received little attention in terms of public investments — giving private investors no incentives to move into such resource regions.

To illustrate this point, let's briefly contrast the economic fortunes of Jimma and Mekele cities. Jimma is located in the Oromia state, 335 kms southwest of Addis Ababa. Situated in coffee heartland, Jimma is Ethiopia's economic nerve center. The bulk of Ethiopia's coffee exports come from this region. However, the EPRDF regime has long abandoned the city and other nearby towns such as Agaro, relegating them to a status of decay.

By government's own statistics, between the last two censuses (1994 and 2007) [3], the population of Jimma city grew by 2.8 percent per annum, far lower than the national average annual growth rate. Resource rich region such as Jimma were supposed to attract workers seeking employment opportunities. But since no effort has been made to create jobs and attract more talent, Jimma's population saw only natural increments — the number of births exceeding deaths.

A few months ago I travelled to Jimma. While I was fully aware of the fact that the region was long neglected, nothing could have prepared me for what I witnessed upon arrival. Dismayed by Jimma's total stagnation, I went to Agaro hoping to get a better perspective. If I was dismayed by my observations in Jimma, I was shocked and disturbed with my encounters in Agaro. I confided to a friend about my observations in Agaro. He referred to a local saying (in Amharic): "Agaaroo diro moote, ahun gin Jimma betam tamowal," roughly meaning "Agaro died long ago, while Jimma is now seriously ill."

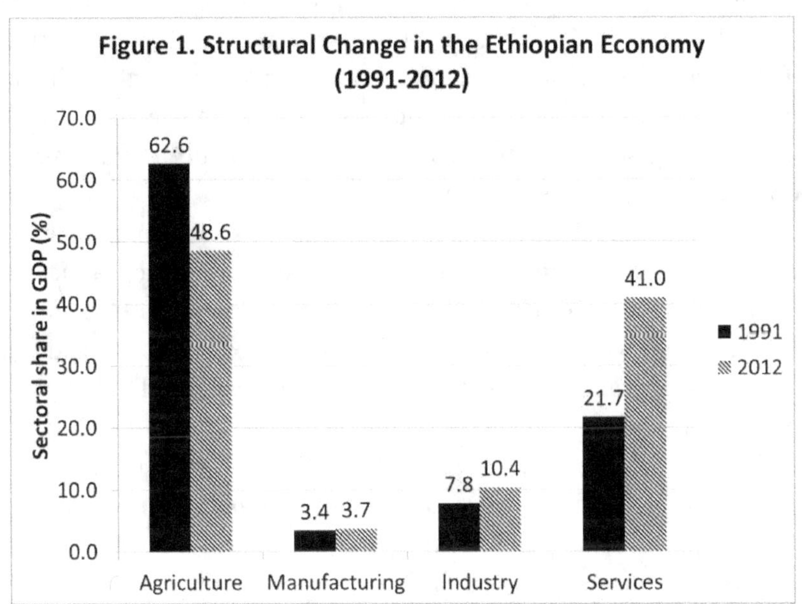

By contrast, in 1994, Mekelle [4], the capital of Tigray state, had about the same level of population as Jimma. However, between 1994 and 2007, with an average annual growth rate three times Jimma's (9.4 percent), Mekelle's population more than doubled. The growth was largely a result of huge investments and job creations in Mekelle — people followed jobs and jobs followed people in a circular causation.

A handful of early public investments were more than enough to trigger the town's explosive growth. Mekele received colossal amounts by Ethiopian standard — an international airport, became a hub for a network of government-affiliated conglomerate called EFFORT, an expanded Mekelle University, and etc.

Today, the economic boom in Tigray is so crucial that the Ethiopian Airlines maintains [5] four daily flights between Mekelle and Addis Ababa. Ironically, unlike Jimma, Mekelle or Tigray do not make any contribution to Ethiopia's exports. In other words, the return to Ethiopia from investing in Tigray is next to nothing.

Sound economic development is accompanied by structural transformation, with a rising relative share of manufacturing. **Figure 1** display [5] structural transformation in the Ethiopian economy under the EPRDF regime. Between 1991 and 2012, the share of agriculture declined from 63 to 49 percent. However, share of manufacturing in GDP remained stuck at around 3.5 percent. In other words, Ethiopia's much hyped economic miracle did not increase the relative share of manufacturing sector by even half a percentage point in more than two decades.

The EPRDF achieved an extremely shallow structural change. This led to the relative shrinkage of the commodity producing agricultural sector. In contrast, the share of the service sector expanded from 30 to 41 percent. The non-manufacturing industrial sector, which includes the state-run energy and telecommunication sectors, expanded only by about 2 percent.

The bloating service sectors are almost entirely dominated by government owned businesses such as the Ethiopian Airlines and other service sectors such as the military where salary payments for civil servants are counted as part of GDP.

These figures reveal the extent of inherent policy biases against production of tradable or exportable commodities in Ethiopian economy. EPRDF's shoddy policies simply bypassed a transition from agriculture to manufacturing and directly entered a service-based economy. This means ignoring the role of agro-processing, e.g., value addition to coffee production rather than exporting raw beans. The EPRDF have move the economy consistently in undesirable direction — even the shallow structural transformation was accompanied by a relative shift from private to public ownership.

The diminishing role of coffee in Ethiopia's exports explains the situation. Given the policy bias against coffee producing regions in public investment allocation and the absence of incentives for private investors to grow or process coffee inside the country, the share of coffee in Ethiopia's commodity exports [7] plummeted from 65 percent in 1995 to 32 percent in 2012. Meanwhile, the share of cut flowers increased from zero to 6 percent during the same time. Ethiopian Airlines began to fill the gap in the foreign exchange revenues.

The recent dramatic structural changes in Ethiopia must be understood in its proper politico-economic context. The regional and sector biases are deeply rooted in Ethiopia's simmering political tensions. Coffee is mostly grown in the Oromia region, a hotbed of political opposition to the EPRDF government. Therefore, both the regional and sectoral policy biases are part of the regime's overall strategy to progressively weaken Oromia's continued economic significance.

The deliberate creation of a nexus of export enclave built on interdependencies between flower farming and Ethiopian Airlines is meant to destroy the livelihoods coffee farmers in Oromia and other resource rich regions.

It is disturbing that the World Bank is now consciously or unknowingly caught up in this quagmire. It is hard to imagine their experts were unaware of the political machinations that underlie Ethiopia's recent export sector developments. The cover of the Bank's report bears wrapped up cut flowers. That's not all. The authors shower praise on the regime for dramatically increasing the number of flower farms in less than a decade.

However, it is unclear to what extent they understood that those red roses were grown by destroying livelihoods of hundreds of thousands of Oromo farms that were forcibly evicted from their ancestral lands[8]. The report contains a nod to jobs created by the flower farms but makes no mention of the jobs that were destroyed to create the farms.

The process of job destruction and then creation was a negative-sum-game. The workers moved from sustainable organic family farms to unsustainable and chemical infested flower farms, exposing them to extremely damaging health hazards. The long term risks [9] on the flower farms is not limited to human health but also the soil and wider environmental pollution, which will take hundreds of years to remove. Sustainable development [10], which World Bank advocates, stands on three legs: economic, social and environmental. And yet, the Bank's mission to Ethiopia seems to recognize sustainability that stands on only one footing: economic gains to a few elites.

References

[1] World Bank. Unleashing the Potential of Ethiopia's Export Industry
http://www.worldbank.org/en/country/ethiopia/publication/ethiopia-economic-update-strengthening-export-performance-through-improved-competitiveness, July 2014

[2] World Bank, Ethiopia. http://data.worldbank.org/country/ethiopia

[3] http://en.wikipedia.org/wiki/Jimma

[4] Mekelle's profile. https://en.wikipedia.org/wiki/Mekelle

[5] All airlines flying from Mekele (MQX) to Addis Ababa (ADD).

http://info.flightmapper.net/route/YY_MQX_ADD

[6] World Bank, Ethiopia. http://data.worldbank.org/country/ethiopia

[7] UN Comtrade Database. http://comtrade.un.org/

[8] ESAT Yesamintu Engeda Ermias Legese The former Miniseter d'etat May 2014.

http://ethsat.com/video/esat-yesamintu-engeda-ermias-legese-the-former-miniseter-detat-may-2014/

[9] Gudeta, D. T., 2012. Socio-economic and Environmental Impact of Floriculture Industry in Ethiopia

6. Ethiopia's Trade Data and the Effect of Devaluation on Import Prices

September 2, 2014(OP)

This is part II of *"Does devaluation of birr as a way to fix Ethiopia's economic troubles"* [in this series]. This part focuses on Ethiopia's trade data and highlights the implications of devaluation of the birr for import prices.

Trade Data

As noted in part I, the World Bank's recommendation for devaluation of the birr was based on statistical analysis using Ethiopia's trade data. But Ethiopia's trade data is simply not reliable to undertake such statistical estimations to make sound policy recommendations.

To illustrate the fallacy of the Bank's analysis, let's look at Ethiopia's trade value in recent years. First, there is no easy way to tell the size of Ethiopia's exports or imports. The discrepancies between export and import trade data is displayed in figure 2 (*click on the image to enlarge*). In the graph, "comtrade" refers the figure reported by Ethiopia to the United Nations Statistical Division (UNSD)[1] while the "total trade" represent figures compiled by the UNSD using mainly the International Monetary Fund (IMF) financial statistics.

For most countries, the two data series fall within close ranges, some discrepancies are inevitable but differences often fall in single digit percentage points in either direction. This was the case even for Ethiopia until around 2005, but then the trade data series starts to show significant degree of abnormality.

If we start with exports, the value of goods and services registered by Ethiopia as exported have consistently exceeded the actual total export earnings registered by the IMF. For instance, in 2011, Ethiopia exported goods worth about $2.6 billion but IMF's records show only $1.9 billion.

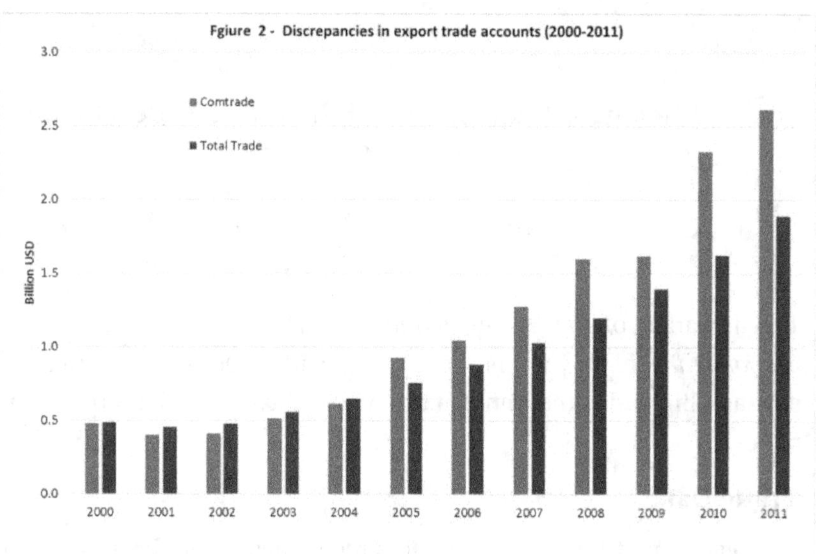

Fgiure 2 - Discrepancies in export trade accounts (2000-2011)

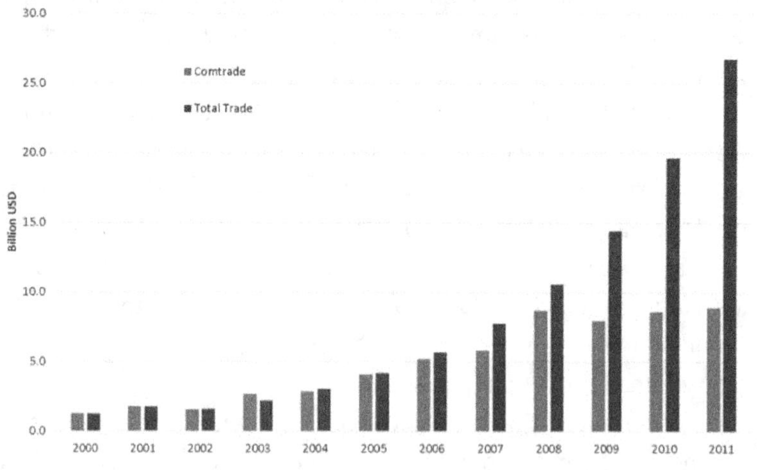

Fgiure 3 - Discrepancies in import trade accounts (2000-2011)

The discrepancies between import data series are even worse. The ways the discrepancies occur are systemic. For exports what government have reported have consistently exceeded IMF records but the reverse is true for imports. For example, in 2011 IMF records show three times larger imports than the Ethiopian government records.

The systemic and suspicious discrepancies in trade data points to the existence of illicit trade for which Ethiopia is already known. Foreign trade has been used as a vehicle to transfer finance abroad. This is commonly done through trade mis-invoicing.

In other words, the export revenue reported by the government have consistently exceeded IMF records, implying that less than the full amount of export revenue was actually been channeled back into Ethiopia. Besides, payments abroad in the name of imports seem to considerably exceed the true value of goods and services actually shipped to Ethiopia.

In its 2014 report, the Global Financial Integrity estimated[2] that the cumulative illicit financial flow out of Ethiopia between 2002 and 2011 was over $20 billion. That is an average of about $2 billion per annum, nearly twice the average annual export revenue earnings from commodity exports during the period.

Devaluation and Imports

In contrast to exports, devaluation will increase prices of imported goods in the domestic market. In theory, higher price can discourage imports as consumers shift from foreign goods to domestic products.

In practice, however, the situation is a lot more complicated. Most items Ethiopia imports are not domestically produced, e.g., capital goods and industrial inputs. Besides, a good proportion of Ethiopia's payments abroad go to imports of military hardware although this is safely hidden in the midst of statistical data through aggregations or is reported as statistical omissions. It is unrealistic to expect that the government would reduce spending on such strategic items simply because their prices have increased.

Under such circumstances, there will be no change in the quantity and types of imports but just that they will be sold at price much higher than warranted by the rate of devaluation. This happens because of the power imbalances between importers and consumers. A handful of import companies enjoy an oligopolistic status, they conspire and fix prices to exploit the general public. In fact, all previous devaluations of the birr were followed by higher inflations because importers increased prices of all goods and services, not just imported ones, in part justifiably so since imports constitute a bulk of inputs (e.g., petrol). This makes Ethiopia a seller's market, where buyers are too powerless because they do not have alternative suppliers for imported products.

Ultimately, the essential prerequisites for devaluation to become effective are lacking. As a result, Ethiopia's envisaged devaluation is unlikely to lead to improvements in the country's foreign trade position. Far from producing intended benefits, devaluation is likely to exacerbate Addis Ababa's economic troubles.

Finally, while the media singled out devaluation, the Bank also made a number of other interrelated recommendations [3]. These include increasing value-addition in the agricultural sector through agro-processing and easing constraints on regulatory frameworks and distributive channels.

Ironically, the Bank's researchers merely listed the recommendations without any sense of prioritization or sequencing of policy reforms. For instance, it is pointless to devalue birr without putting in place incentives for businesses that do value-addition (e.g. coffee processing), removing numerous hurdles for starting new businesses and opening up opportunities for foreign trade in import and export businesses to reduce the dominance of oligopolistic market.

A focus on value-addition to exportable commodities would have addressed the aforementioned regional and sector biases. For instance, coffee-processing plants should be located near production areas (e.g. Jimma), not least because coffee is normally collected wet and loses weight as it dries and gets processed.

Ethiopia's State Minister of Finance Ahmed Shide recently stated [4], "A decision to adjust the exchange rate would be made on the basis of what its wider impact on the economy would be." However, there's an ominous prospect that the EPRDF will jump onto devaluation, leaving aside other more important and far-reaching recommendations.

I expect this will happen for the following reasons. First, past experiences suggest that the Ethiopian government does not hesitate to devalue the currency even when the conditions were not right. In fact, it is very likely that the regime was behind the idea, taking the initiative and indirectly engineering the recommendations.

Second, EPRDF politicians control a network of party affiliated business conglomerates that dominate the bulk of import and export businesses. These importers and exporters will be the net beneficiaries of devaluation but its adverse consequences will be borne by the general public both consumers and producers.

Reference

[1] Monthly Bulletin of Statistics Analytical Trade Tables.
Unstats/Comtrade.
http://unstats.un.org/unsd/trade/imts/annual%20totals.htm

[2] Dev Kar, Brian LeBlanc. Illicit Financial Flows from Developing Countries: 2002-2011 http://www.gfintegrity.org/report/2013-global-report-illicit-financial-flows-from-developing-countries-2002-2011/. December 11, 2013

[3] World Bank. Third Ethiopia Economic Update : Strengthening Export Performance through Improved Competitivenesshttp://www-wds.worldbank.org/external/default/WDSContentServer/WDSP/IB/2 014/07/18/000470435_20140718101850/Rendered/PDF/895480WP0 Wb03d00Box385285B00PUBLIC0.pdf. June 2014

[4] William Davison. World Bank Urges Ethiopia to Devalue Birr to Boost Exports. Bloomberg. http://www.bloomberg.com/news/2014-07-22/world-bank-urges-ethiopia-to-devalue-birr-to-lift-export-revenue.html. July 22, 2014.

7. Does Ethiopia Really Need Another Mega Airport?

April 13, 2015 (OP)

In his recent piece, *"How Ethiopia Is Shaking Off Its Famine-Stricken Image,"*[1] AP's Ethiopia correspondent Elias Meseret portrayed the country's current rulers as visionary leaders who pulled millions of Ethiopians out of misery.

Meseret uses plans for yet another mega construction project as a jumping off point: Ethiopia is planning to build a new multibillion airport in order to increase the Bole International Airport's capacity by four fold.

Meseret quotes the authorities at length:

> The airport we are planning to build is going to be huge. Very huge…. It will be one of the biggest airports in the world. I don't know what other countries are planning in this regard for the future but no country has created this much capacity so far in Africa.

The excitable reporter adds:

> Ethiopia, once known for epic famines that sparked global appeals for help, has a booming economy and big plans these days. The planned airport is one of several muscular, forward-looking infrastructure projects undertaken by the government that have fueled talk of this East African country as a rising African giant…. Addis Ababa increasingly looks like an enormous construction site,

with cranes and building blocks springing up in many corners of the city.

Meseret's assertions clearly overlap with the authorities' audacious claims. In fact, he expounded on the official statements as part of his expressed mission to promote the feel-good, "Ethiopia rising" story [2]. It's also one of those simplistic, Africa rising stories that the western media like to run from time to time as if to makeup for their otherwise sloppy coverage of the continent. Needless to say, Meseret's report was extremely biased and lacked any sense of balance.

By abolishing free press and criminalizing freedom of expression, Ethiopian authorities have avoided closer scrutiny of their policies. The void is filled by opportunist local reporters who align themselves with the officials to either serve their own specific self-interests or to avoid risks of persecution.

Similarly, foreign correspondents in Addis Ababa have shunned issues deemed sensitive and often regurgitate official statements for fear of harassment by the authorities or at times to align their coverage with geopolitical interests of their home countries.

Consequently, reporters have time and again failed to hold corrupt officials accountable by conducting thorough investigation in their reports. For example, a balanced report on the plan to build another huge international airport would require some investigation into whether or not there is any justification for such extravagant projects and how they'll be financed. Meseret's justification for the new airport is rather laughable: "The old airport has been engulfed by residential areas — a major reason behind the decision to build a new airport on the capital's outskirts." "Addis Ababa's Bole International Airport, whose passenger terminal is undergoing a $250 million expansion amid growth in passenger numbers from 900,000 in 2000 to more than 7 million in 2014."

It is silly to juxtapose and present these two statements, directly quoting the authorities, without saying a word on the shocking extents of inconsistences. If the justification for the new airport is that the old airport has been engulfed by housing developments, then surely this raises another question: why keep expanding the existing airport by such a large magnitude?

Why was residential development allowed to engulf Bole, given that land is the exclusive property of the government, which also owns and operates the airport? The housing developments themselves are mega construction projects, implemented by the government in the form of large-scale social housing developments or private developers who buy land from the government and also get permission to build around the airport. Clearly, this indicates the haphazard ways various construction projects are implemented without proper planning.

Importantly, the reporter completely misses or deliberately overlooks the context for the circus about Bole airport. The latter is part and parcel the infamous Addis Ababa Master plan, which has been the source of simmering tensions for more than a year now. Mega construction projects have led to evictions of hundreds of thousands of farming households from their ancestral lands and destroyed their livelihoods. This has led to protests and clashes that ended up in bloodshed [3].

Benchmarking Bole

Let's take the Bole airport and examine some basic facts. Bole has two terminals. The second terminal is relatively new, its construction began in 1997 and it was completed in 2003 at a total cost of $130 million [4]. At the terminal's inauguration, it was announced that the new terminal was one of the largest in Africa, with a runway length of 4,725 metres and a capability to handle some 3,000 passengers an hour [5].

Per Meserat's report, the official justification given for building a new airport hinges on a claim that Bole is not meeting the rapidly growing demand, estimated at 6.5 million passengers a year. This implies that Bole has reached its full capacity.

But how can one reconcile this with the 3,000 passengers per day figure announced earlier? Most international airports operate 24 hours a day and 365 days a year. The chart below displays possible scenarios of total numbers of hours Bole International Airport remains open and serves customers. For instance, if Bole operates 24 hours per day, then it can serve just more than 26 million passengers per year. This would mean that it is currently utilizing only 25 percent of its total capacity, and hence there is no justification for expansion.

Even if Bole operates only 12 hours per day, it could still serve more than 13 million passengers a year, which is still less than 50 percent of its full capacity. This is the kind of nuance that's missing from Meserat's rehashing of official talking points.

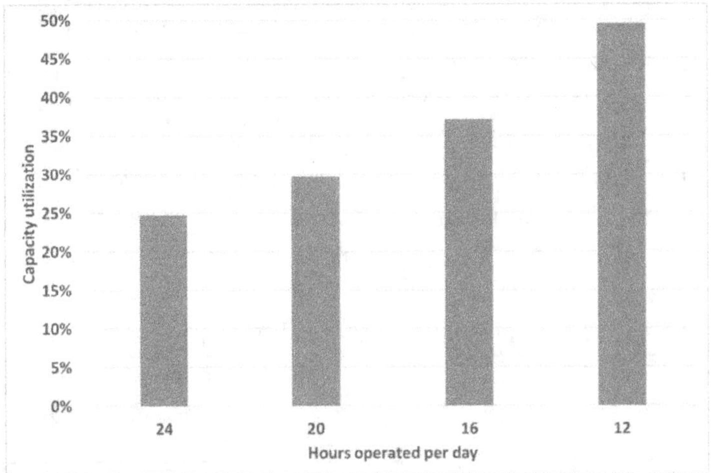

Figure 1. Bole International Airport Capacity Utilization Rate.

Another way of looking at the rationale for Bole's expansion is to compare its performance with similar airports in the region and around the world. This is done by collating data from disparate sources (as I have in the table below). Let's begin by comparing Bole with Kenya's Jomo Kenyatta International Airport (JKIA). But for a more accurate comparison of Bole and JKIA's performances, I will compare the two with Standstead, a small airport outside of London.

Runways are one of the most important limiting factors in facility at airports. Bole has two long runways. JKIA and Stanstead each have only one runway. In terms of runway length, Stanstead's is the shortest of the three. In 2012, Bole and JKIA reportedly serve nearly equal number of passengers per year, i.e., 6.5 million.

By contrast, even with its one, smaller sized runway, Stanstead served 17.5 million passengers in 2013, three times the number of passengers served by the two East African airports. In other words, as Stanstead's case demonstrates, Bole could serve more than 17 million passengers with just one runway.

This confirms my prior conclusion about Bole's capacity utilization, i.e., Bole is probably utilizing only 25 percent to 50 percent of its full capacity. Given these facts, how would one explain the rush to build yet another mega airport at the cost several billion dollars?

So far I used the 6.5 million passengers a year figure reported by the Ethiopian authorities. However, as illustrated in the table above, this figure does not stand up to scrutiny.

While the total number of passengers served at Bole and JKIA are reportedly equal, the JKIA figure appears more credible. Tourists constitute the bulk of passengers served at major international airports. As such, the statistics on the number of passengers served by a given airport should be roughly compatible with tourist data.

Table 1. Bench-marking Bole International Airport

	Bole	Jommo Kenyatta	Stanstead [9]
Numbers of runways [6]	2	1	1
Sizes of runways	3,700m x 45m 3,800m x 45m	4,117m x 45m	3,048m x 46m
Number of passenger [7] passing through the airport per year (millions)	6.50	6.46	17.5*
Number of tourist arrivals per year (millions)*[8]	0.47	1.47	NA
Number of airlines currently operating to this airport with scheduled services[9]	13	31	12
Number of Airlines currently operating to this airport via codeshare [6]	25	27	NA

* 2010 data, 2013 data

In 2010, about half a million tourists arrived in Addis Ababa, while some 1.5 million arrived in Kenya via JKIA during same year, according to the World Bank [8]. This shows that JKIA serves at least three times the number of tourists passing through the Bole airport. Information on airline movements is not available but we know how many airlines regularly fly [10] to Bole and JKIA.

Bole serves 38 airlines, out of which only 13 actually fly to Bole through scheduled flights. The remaining 25 airlines work with Ethiopian airlines through codeshare agreements, whereby other airlines purchase or sale seats with the Ethiopian Airlines without any provisions of landing or taking-off services. By contrast, JKIA serves 58 major airlines, with 31 scheduled flights to JKIA and 27 through codeshare.

This means the number of airlines with scheduled flights to JKIA is more than twice the number of scheduled flights to Bole airport. More important, there are several major international airlines that have scheduled flights to JKIA, including Air France, British Airways, Emirates, KLM Royal Dutch Airlines and Lufthansa. Out of these airlines, only Emirates and Lufthansa maintain scheduled flights to Addis Ababa. If we combine the tourist data and the number of airlines serving the two airports, it then becomes difficult to accept the premise that Bole and JKIA serve equal number of passengers.

Besides, it is a known fact that there are more headquarters of international organisations and UN agencies in Nairobi than in Addis Ababa. Similarly, it is untenable to argue that there are millions of Ethiopian tourists travelling abroad. In 2008 Bole and JKIA served 3.33 and 4.75 million passengers respectively. Since then Bole and JKIA experienced 95 percent and 36 percent growth in passenger numbers in that order. But how can Bole's explosive growth in passenger numbers be explained? There has been no change in Ethiopia's tourism sector during this period. The authorities' narrative of "explosive" GDP growth cannot be taken seriously.

Construction Mania

In normal circumstances, the construction sector is subservient to the needs of the overall economy. In other words, public construction projects are launched mostly when the requirements of other economic sectors necessitates it, or to expand gaps in capacity to stimulate economic activities. All of that is primarily geared toward creating material wealth and improving the living standards of the country's citizens in equitable manner.

In Ethiopia, this logic has been turned upside down – expansive construction projects are being launched without taking into account the need or affordability of the country's economy. The foregoing discussion on the Bole airport is one such example. As discussed, the available evidence on the whole indicates that there is little for building another mega airport. In fact, as I have illustrated here, the existing airport is operating considerable below its full capacity.

Even without the numbers and figures I provided, it's easy to see that Bole operates below its full capacity. I have travelled reasonably well to different parts of the world, but Bole is perhaps the quietest major airport I recall passing through. As I wait in departure terminals, I do not see many aircrafts landing and taking off. When I arrive, I rarely see any other airliner parked on the tarmac, except for a few Ethiopians dotted here and there, with lots of empty parking spaces between them. The comparative analysis above only validated my subjective assessments.

Smoke Screen

The regime uses large construction projects as a double edge sword in *the myth of Ethiopia's crony capitalism and economic miracle* (in this series). It suffices to say that the motivation for mega projects lie in crony business interests among politicians and business elites, who happen to be the same ethnic background.

Small group of elites control the commanding heights of the Ethiopian economy. They have created large and complex civilian and military engineering companies, which need large construction contracts to thrive. Long before they have completed one mega construction project, opportunities to start yet another mega project has to be created, mainly by manipulating facts on the ground to justify upcoming projects and continuity of business opportunities.

In this case, the Bole airport passenger numbers had to be manipulated and inflated a few years back to justify its envisaged expansion. In addition to serving narrow business and political interests, large construction projects are also used as a means of siphoning off public funds.

Large construction projects in and around Addis Ababa have created a *façade of economic boom* taking place in Ethiopia. This is by far the most important explanation for Ethiopia's construction-driven economic policy during the last decade.

This is not to suggest all construction is bad. However, the emphasis on public works projects had starved the rest of Ethiopian economy. Agriculture remains among the most neglected sectors. To understand this point, one needs to look beyond official statistics on agricultural output and examine consumer prices of agricultural products in both rural and urban areas.

Authorities in Addis Ababa shamelessly cite "high income among consumers and improvements in their standard of living" as a reason for the crisis in the agricultural sector, particularly the skyrocketing prices of foodstuff that consumers have to bear. This could not be further from the truth. The high consumer prices are fuelled by agricultural supply shortage relative to considerable expansions in the non-productive service sector, particularly public administration and defense.

To add insult to injury, reporters like Meseret work hard to link the construction boom with famine and poverty reduction. But what has construction got to do with famine? How would Ethiopia ever shake off famine without actually tackling poverty at its roots?

It does not produce food after all, it has the weakest link to agriculture – it does not use raw materials or supply inputs to agriculture. We are not talking about agro-processing or fertilizer manufacturing industry.

In reality, the construction boom has been used to gloss over and hide the dire state of agriculture, rampant famine and poverty among millions of destitute households in rural and urban Ethiopia. I disagree with Meseret's assertion that Ethiopia is *shaking off its famine-stricken image.* What the authorities are doing is actually to use mega construction projects to camouflage *Ethiopia's famine-stricken image.*

References

[1] Elias Meseret. How Ethiopia Is Shaking Off Its Famine-Stricken Image. March 29, 2015

[2] Elias Meseret. Facebook post
https://www.facebook.com/elias.meseret/posts/10206541467275411

[3] BBC, Ethiopia protest: Ambo students killed in Oromia state. 2

May 2014

[4] The New Bole International Airport Terminal Due to Open in May 2001. http://www.ethiopians.com/bole_airport.htm. (March 2001 - EOW).

[5] Ethiopia: State of the Art Airport Terminal Opens http://allafrica.com/stories/200301220109.html. 22 January 2003

[6] Center for Aviation. Airport profiles. https://centreforaviation.com/profiles/airports

[7] List of the busiest airports in Africa http://en.wikipedia.org/wiki/List_of_the_busiest_airports_in_Africa

[8] World Bank, International tourism, number of arrivals http://data.worldbank.org/indicator/ST.INT.ARVL

[9] Facts and figures about London Stansted Airport. https://www.stanstedairport.com/about-us/london-stansted-airport-and-mag/facts-and-figures/

[10] Airports in Africa http://en.wikipedia.org/wiki/List_of_the_busiest_airports_in_Africa

8. Ethiopia's Fake Economic Growth Borrows from ENRON's Accounting

December 19, 2015 (OP)

More than 70 people have been killed and dozens wounded in an ongoing crackdown on peaceful protesters in Oromia. One of the underlying causes of the prevailing tense political situation is Ethiopia's bogus claim about "miraculous" economic growth in the last decade.

The youth is not benefitting from the country's supposed growth and doesn't anticipate the fulfillment of those promises given the pervasive nepotism and crony capitalism that underpins Ethiopia's developmentalism.

The ruling Ethiopian People's Revolutionary Democratic Front (EPRDF) came to power in 1991 and briefly experimented with democratic transition. However, a little over a decade into its rule, the party's former strongman, the late Meles Zenawi, realized that their pretentious experiment with liberal democracy was not working. Zenawi then crafted a dubious concept called, "developmental state."

Stripped of the accompanying jargons and undue sophistications, Zenawi was simply saying that he had abandoned the democratic route but will seek legitimacy through economic development guided by a strong hand of the state. This was a ploy, the last ditch attempt to extend EPRDF's rule indefinitely.

Using fabricated economic data to seek legitimacy and attract foreign direct investments, the regime then advanced narratives about its double-digit economic growth, described with such catch phrases as Ethiopia rising, the fastest growing economy in the world and African lioness. The claims that EPRDF has delivered economic growth at miraculous scales has always been reported with a reminder that it takes several decades to build democratic governance. The underlining assumption was that, as long as they deliver economic growth, Ethiopia's leaders could be excused on the lack of democracy and human rights abuses associated with the need for government intervention in the economy.

EPRDF spent millions to retain the services of expensive and well-connected Western lobbying firms [1] to promote this narrative and create a positive image of the country. These investments were also accompanied with a tight grip on the local media, including depriving foreign reporters' [2] access if they cross the government line. Ethiopia's communication apparatus was so successful that even serious reporters and analysts started to accept and promote EPRDF's narrative on rapid economic growth.

However, a few recent events have tested the truthfulness of Ethiopia's economic rise. Drought and the resulting famine remain the Achilles heels of the EPRDF government. The government can manipulate data on any other sector, including the aggregate Gross Domestic Product, and get away with it, but agriculture is a tricky sector whose output is not so easy to lie about. The proof lies in the availability of food in the market, providing the absolute minimum subsistence for the rural and urban population.

The sudden translation of drought into famine raises serious questions. For example, it is proving difficult to reconcile the country's double-digit economic growth with the fact that about 15 million Ethiopians [3] are currently in need of emergency food aid.

Rampant Famine

Except for some gullible foreign reporters or parachute consultants, who visit Addis Ababa and depart within days, serious analysts [4] and students of Ethiopian economy know that authorities have often fabricated economic statistics in order to generate fake GDP growth. For a trained eye, it does not take a lot to find inconsistencies in the data series. In fact, Ethiopia's economic growth calculus is so reminiscent of

Enron accounting. (See my recent pieces questioning EPRDF's economic policies, including anomalies in the alleged achievements of *millennium development goals*, *crony businesses*, *devaluation*, *external trade* and *finance* (all included in this series).

The tacit understanding in using GDP as a measure of economic growth is that responsible governments generate such data by applying viable international standards and subjecting the data to scrutiny and consistency checks.

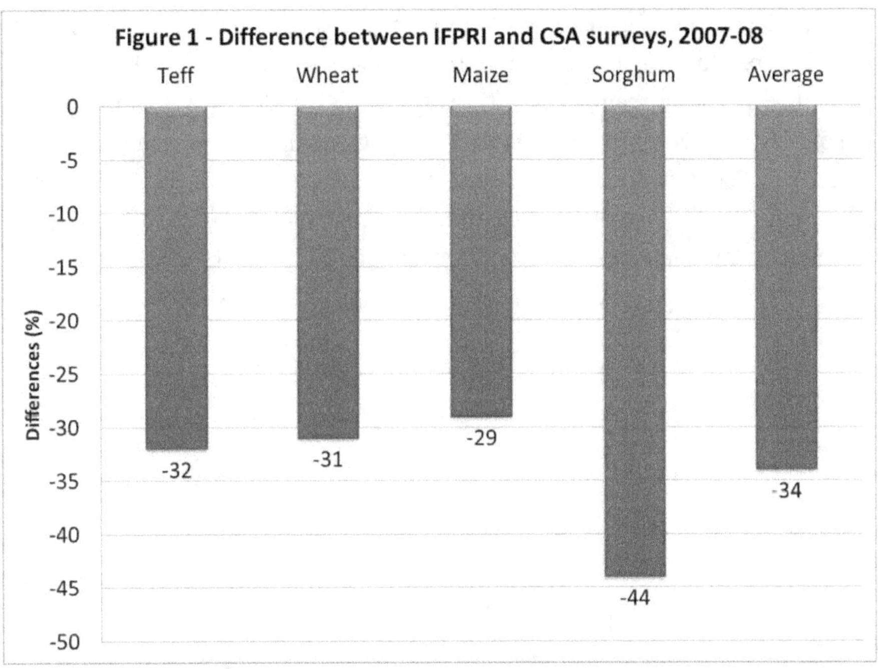

Unfortunately, these standards are not foolproof; irresponsible governments with mischievous motives can abuse them. There is credible evidence that show Ethiopian authorities deliberately inflated economic statistics to promote feel-good, success stories.

Let's take the agricultural data, which is timely and topical given the ongoing famine. This came to light recently as the European Union tried to understand anomalies in Ethiopia's grain market, particularly persistent food inflation which the EU found incompatible with the agricultural output reported by the Central Statistical Authority (CSA) of Ethiopia.

The EU's Joint Research Centre (JRC) then developed the technical specification for studying the scope of the Cereal Availability Study in order to account for the developments in the Ethiopian cereal markets. The International Food Policy Research Institute (IFPRI) was selected to carry out the study [5].

Figure 1 (above) compares the EU-sponsored survey and the Ethiopian government's survey produced by the CSA. I am using the data for 2007/08 for comparison. The negative numbers indicate that the IFPRI estimates were consistently lower than the CSA data. For instance, CSA overstated cereal production by 34 percent on average. This ranged from 29 percent for maize to 44 percent for sorghum. The actual amount of *Teff* produced is lower by a third of what's reported by the CSA.

The research team sought to explain this "puzzle" by examining the sources of the confusion, the methodological flaws that might have led CSA to generate such exaggerated economic data. Toward that end, they compared CSA's crop yield estimates with comparable data from three neighboring countries: Kenya, Tanzania, and Uganda (see Figure 2).

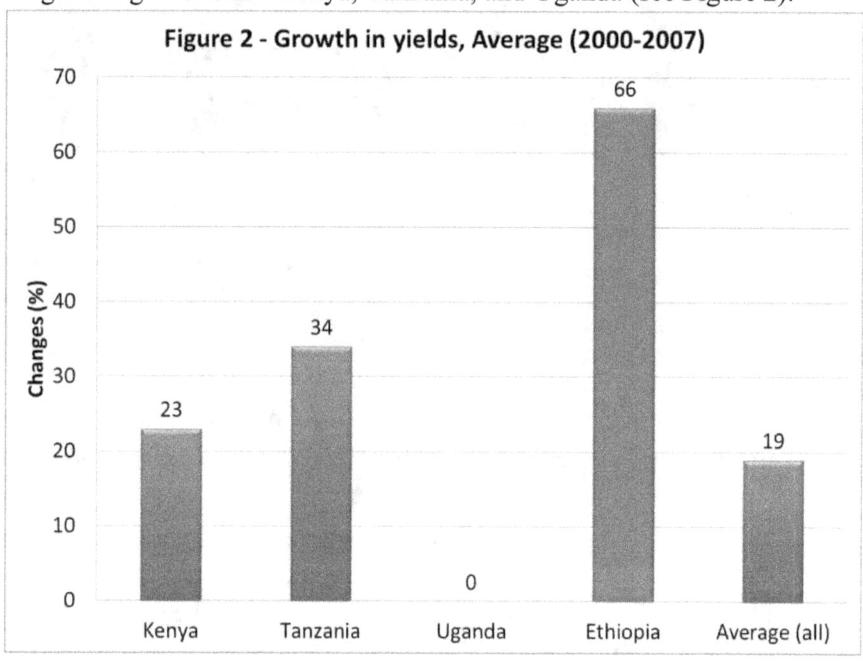

From 2000 to 2007, the average increase in cereal yield for these countries, including Ethiopia, was 19 percent. Yet the CSA reported a whopping 66 percent for Ethiopia's yield growth. The country was not experiencing an agricultural revolution to justify such phenomenal growth. It is unrealistic that Ethiopia's yield growth would be greater than the neighboring East African countries, particularly Kenya, where the agricultural sector is at a much more advanced stage. If anything, the reality in Ethiopia is closer to Uganda, which did not report any yield increase during that period.

This reveals the extents of data manipulation by Ethiopian authorities to create an inexistent economic success story and seeks political legitimacy using a bogus record. We now know the widespread distortions in official statistics on cereal production thanks, in no small part, to EU's intervention in sponsoring a study and explaining the disparities. Cereals represent only a sub-sector in the agricultural realm. It is likely that worse distortions would be revealed if similar studies were done on Ethiopia's growth statistics in other sectors, including manufacturing and service divisions.

'Poverty Reduction'

The IMF [6] has praised Ethiopia for achieving accelerated growth with a focus on equity and poverty reduction, a challenging dilemma for most countries. However, a closer look at three interconnected facts turns this claim on its head.

First, as noted above, Ethiopia's agricultural output has been inflated by 34 percent on average. Second, a 33 percent poverty reduction [7] since 2000 is widely reported. Third, there is a consensus that poverty reduction has happened mostly in rural Ethiopia. Now we put these three facts together and apply a simple logic to establish that the 33 percent poverty reduction is explained by the 34 percent exaggerated agricultural outputs. Notice that it is not by accident that the two percentage points are almost identical. Therefore, the ups and downs cancel each other out. In the best-case scenario, poverty rate must remain at the same level as in 2000.

The World Bank, IMF and other donors have often anchored their conclusions on poverty reduction on alleged changes in the agricultural sector, where the bulk of the poor live and work. Little do they know that the data they used to compute the poverty index comes from agricultural statistics with hugely inflated yield assumptions as shown above.

This raises the question: where has the billions of dollars in bilateral and multilateral aid pumped into Ethiopia in the name of poverty reduction and the millennium development goals gone?

'The Enclave Economy'

The 'Ethiopia rising' storyline is a standard set by foreign correspondents who often repurpose official government press releases, or report based on the construction projects in the capital, Addis Ababa.

For example, Bloomberg Africa's, William Davison, often uses the proliferating high-rise buildings in Addis Ababa as tangible evidence of Ethiopia's double-digit economic growth. In his latest whitewash [8], Davison writes, "such growth is already visible in parts of the capital, where shopping malls and luxury hotels are sprouting up." That a veteran reporter for a business website unashamedly passes judgment on economic success by referring to heights and width of buildings underscores his shallow understanding of the country's social and political fabric.

Here are some of the questions that reporters aren't asking and seeking answers for: Who owns those building? Where did the investment money come from? Are there any firm linkages between these physical infrastructures and the rest of the Ethiopian economy? I have partially answered some of these questions in *the myth of Ethiopia's crony capitalism and economic miracle* (in this series) and will soon provide additional insights.

For now, I would like to draw attention to the *existence of an "enclave economy" within the mainstream Ethiopian economy*. This enclave is made up of highly interconnected crony businesses, which are owned and operated by Tigrean elites, who also have a tight grip on the political and military command structures. Take, for example, the Endowment Fund for Rehabilitation of Tigray (EFFORT), a business conglomerate affiliated with the Tigrean People's Liberation Front (TPLF). EFFORT has a humble origin in the relief and rehabilitation arm of the TPLF. However, it has undergone amorphous growth and now controls the commanding heights of the Ethiopian economy. By some estimates, EFFORT now controls more than 66 business entities [9]. Since its "rehabilitation" function is obviously redundant, I have previously suggested, "it should instead be renamed as the Endowment Fund for Rendering Tigrean Supremacy (EFFORT*S*)."

The EFFO*RTS* controlled enclave and related military engineering complexes have created a semi-autonomous economy in Ethiopia. They made smart choices and specialized in engineering and construction businesses. This means they do not have to rely on the Ethiopian public for their products; instead, each specialize in separate industrial branches and buy from each other and also sell to the government, which is also in their hand. The huge government infrastructural projects necessitated by the "developmental state" model create business opportunities for these engineering companies.

The enclave economy is only loosely linked to the mainstream economy and it does not benefit the bulk of the Ethiopian people in any meaningful way. The luxury hotels and supermarkets that Davison refers to cater for the needs of the affluent business classes, their families, and the expatriate community.

In other words, Ethiopia's miraculous economic growth, if it in fact exists, must have happened only in the enclave economy. Statistically, it is possible to generate a double-digit economic growth at the national level through a combination of some real astronomical growth in the enclave component and stagnation or declines hidden, through some accounting tricks, in the rest of the economy.

Lock-in Style of Reporting

Unfortunately, the unquestioned reporting on Ethiopia's economic success has continued. Even the EU study appears to have been shelved, or deliberately ignored despite the significant findings. Even as a fifth of the population is in need of emergency aid, the World Bank is sticking with the outdated data and has recently released a sensationalized report entitled "Ethiopia's Great Run: the growth acceleration and how to pace it."[10]

The ensuing famine has shaken the foundation of Ethiopia's growth narrative, yet western NGOs and media outlets appear to suffer from the lock-in effect in adopting consistent storylines. They continue to link and refer to the World Bank, IMF and others reports and indexes by multilateral organizations.

That's why we continue to see comical headlines such as *Ethiopian Drought Threatens Growth as Cattle Die, Crops Fail [11],* which assumes that Ethiopia's growth is actually occurring. This acquiescence does not only display ignorance, but it also underscores an effort to evade accountability for previous mistakes and failure to report accurate information.

In a recent interview with The Ethiopian Reporter [12], Prime Minister Hailemariam Desalegn made a rare and fateful admission: "if we crave for too much praises for our achievements, we might run the risk of undermining the challenges we are facing. These challenges could grow bigger and become irreversible and that would be detrimental."

Over the past 25 years, the EPRDF worked tirelessly to create a distorted image of the country and began craving and lobbying foreigners for praises.

Enron's success involved an elaborate scam, but the firm was named *America's Most Innovative Company* [13] for six consecutive years. This fame did not stop Enron from crumbling. EPRDF's fate will not be any different. The Oromo uprising has already started the unraveling of its elaborate scams devised to attain legitimacy on the back of non-existent economic and democratic advancement.

References

[1] Joshua Kurlantzick. When Lobbyists Work for Authoritarian Nations. Newsweek. http://www.newsweek.com/when-lobbyists-work-authoritarian-nations-74781. July 26, 2010

[2] Human Rights Watch. World Report 2015: Ethiopia, Events of 2014 https://www.hrw.org/world-report/2015/country-chapters/ethiopia

[3] DFID Press Release. Crisis in Ethiopia needs global response. https://www.gov.uk/government/news/hurd-crisis-in-ethiopia-needs-global-response. 11 December 2015.

[4] Social Progress Index 2014. http://www.socialprogressimperative.org/data/spi?gclid=Cj0KEQiA7rmzBRDezri2r6bz1qYBEiQAg-YEtv3FmfJWJkfEJbKRFhP35nrnADCf3iVS_yMA9MpDM60aApBI8P8HAQ.

[5] ALEMU Dawit; et. al. 2011. Cereals Availability Study in

Ethiopia, 2008.
http://publications.jrc.ec.europa.eu/repository/handle/JRC64683.
Publications Office of the European Union

[6] IMF 2015. The Federal Democratic Republic of Ethiopia:
Selected Issues IMF Country Report No. 15/326.
http://www.imf.org/external/pubs/ft/scr/2015/cr15326.pdf

[7] World Bank. Poverty in Ethiopia Down 33 Percent Since 2000.
PRESS RELEASEhttp://www.worldbank.org/en/news/press-
release/2015/01/20/poverty-ethiopia-down-33-percent. January 20,
2015

[8] William Davison. Ethiopia Growth Clashes With Politics as
Oromo Protests Rise. Bloomberg.
http://www.bloomberg.com/news/articles/2015-12-16/ethiopian-
growth-clashes-with-politics-as-oromo-protests-surge. December 16,
2015

[9] Ethiopia is looted by EFFORT and The TPLF Business Empire.
Ethiopiantimes
http://ethiopiantimes.wordpress.com/2012/07/30/ethiopia-is-looted-
by-effort-and-the-tplf-business-empire/ July 30, 2012

[10] World Bank 2015. Ethiopia's great run : the growth acceleration
and how to pace it.
http://documents.worldbank.org/curated/en/2015/11/25475811/ethiop
ia%E2%80%99s-great-run-growth-acceleration-pace.

[11] William Davison. Ethiopian Drought Threatens Growth as
Cattle Die, Crops Fail. Boomberg.
http://www.bloomberg.com/news/articles/2015-10-15/ethiopian-
drought-threatens-growth-as-cattle-die-crops-fail. October 15, 2015

[12] Ethiopian Reporter TV | Exclusive Interview w/ PM
Hailemariam https://www.youtube.com/watch?v=wzMiXdJEZEk

[13] Enron. https://en.wikipedia.org/wiki/Enron.

9. The Great Unraveling: A Political Endgame is Underway in Ethiopia

December 15, 2015 (OP)

The finale of the Ethiopian regime's tragic political drama is being played out on the streets of Oromia, Ethiopia's largest state. Oromo students have been ratcheting up tensions in ongoing protests that began in early November. The protesters oppose the encroaching of Addis Ababa, a federally administered city, into Oromia's jurisdiction, which has already evicted hundreds of thousands of Oromo farmers from their ancestral lands.

The dust has not yet settled to clearly predict what happens next, but the endgame appears imminent. It is important to start taking stock of what has been happening over the last two and a half decades. This piece provides a broad overview of the Machiavellian political and economic policies of Ethiopia's ruling party. The first of two-part analysis discusses the ongoing dramatic showdown between Oromo students and Ethiopian security forces, as well as the circumstances that triggered the standoff, including Addis Ababa's deceitful experiment with federalism and democratization.

The Oromo Uprising

The dramatic events unfolding in numerous districts and townships across Oromia represent an unprecedented popular uprising in modern Ethiopian history. The uprising began on November 12, in Ginchi town, 81 kms southwest of the capital. This was set off by transfer in ownership of a school playground and stadium by local authorities and the clearing of pristine natural forest near the town to make way for investors.

Ginci is located 32 kms from Ambo, the site of Oromo resistance for many years and where security forces killed dozens of peaceful protesters in 2014.

The protests in Ginci were suppressed brutally, but the resistance spread to other parts of Oromia like a forest fire, galvanizing university, high school and even elementary school students. As usual, security forces responded heavy-handedly, killing at least 50 people. The death toll is growing by the hours and is estimated to be higher. Hundreds of protesters have been injured and taken to hospitals and hundreds more are jailed in a heightened crackdown.

The Oromo uprising has expanded to include the wider Oromo public who intervened to stop security forces from firing at young and unarmed students. In most cases, the public joined in because soldiers refused to heed their call for restraint and demands for proper burials of dead students.

Protesters are blocking roads in many localities to obstruct the movement of security forces, but the protests have remained largely peaceful.

A Grand Land Grab Scheme

The main trigger for the protesters the so-called "Addis Master Plan," which they refer to as the "Master Killer."

Addis Ababa is located in the Oromia state, but it was unjustly made an independent federal region, with a constitutional guarantee for Oromia's "special interest" over the city. The rationales for this were that: Addis Ababa is located in the heart of Oromia, Oromo resources are used in its development and surrounding Oromo communities are exposed to severe urban pollution.

The special privilege remained on paper, but Oromos continue to suffer from the city's expansions. For instance, most Oromia rivers passing through or near Addis Ababa have been poisoned to a catastrophic extent so much that fishing in them has become a thing of the past. The livelihoods of downstream Oromo farming communities are completely destroyed. Addis Ababa has aggressively encroached into Oromia almost unrestricted, forcibly evicting native Oromo farmers from their ancestral lands with paltry compensations far below the value at which the authorities resell the land to private developers.

The number of farming households evicted from and near Addis Ababa has not been properly documented, but it's estimated that about 150,000 farming households [1] were displaced in a single round of eviction campaign in the early 2000s. Since then, evictions has intensified as the city expanded horizontally in all directions, which means, at least, a million households have been dislocated over the last decade. This estimate does not include widespread evictions taking place elsewhere in Oromia, for instance, to make way for flower farms and other export-oriented investments in the vicinity of Addis Ababa.

The convenience to foreign businessmen in accessing the Ethiopian Airlines services for exports was given a priority over the lives and welfare of millions of Oromo farmers. As a result, once thriving farming communities have become destitute, thrown onto the streets and now make a living by working as daily laborers or beggars on the streets of Addis Ababa.

The ill-fated master plan was an effort to further entrench the city's expansion. Government technocrats without any public participation prepared it. If implemented, the plan will enlarge the city by 20 times its current size. Clearly, the master plan was a deliberate act to weaken Oromia's status within Ethiopia's federal structure. It will divide the state into two parts, rendering it a non-viable regional unit.

The government "spin doctors" are busy fabricating distorted stories to misrepresent the popular opposition as anti-development. However, as discussed in *Crony capitalism and the myth behind Ethiopia's economic miracle (in this series),* the ploy to expand the city is nothing more than a grand scam aimed at grabbing Oromo land by government cronies, private developers, and corporations that aspire to maximize their own profits at any costs.

'Illegitimate Parliament'

The dramatic events of last month underscore the fact that the regime in

Addis Ababa lacks legitimacy and popular mandate. In general elections last May, the EPRDF declared that it won 100 percent of parliamentary seats. By declaring a total victory, the regime shot itself in the foot – inadvertently exposing its abuses of the electoral system and process.

The gap between the rhetoric and the reality becomes apparent when we juxtapose this total victory against extraordinarily large turnouts at opposition rallies during the campaign period. EPRDF reluctantly "allowed" opposition parties to campaign for a few weeks, presumably to create a façade of a free and fair election in Ethiopia.

On the campaign trail, the Oromo Federalist Congress (OFC) galvanized the youth, attracting huge crowds in all corners of Oromia. It is a gross understatement to view EPRDF's victory as "stolen election" even by the standards of its previous polls. The bald-faced announcement was a humiliating insult to voters. EPRDF cadres displayed an utter contempt for the very people they claim to govern.

The gap between EPRDF's words and deeds has become ever wider. Steadfast Oromo resistance has frequently led to widespread killings and imprisonments. Human right groups have relentlessly documented some of the atrocities committed by EPRDF leaders. This includes the Amnesty International's landmark *Because I am Oromo* [2] report that provided compelling evidence that "being an Oromo is a good enough reason to be incriminated and put in jail under the EPRDF government."

In part II of this piece, *Ethiopia's fake economic growth borrows from ENRON's accounting (in this series),* I will examine the unraveling of the EPRDF rule, focusing on the bogus claim around Ethiopia's miraculous economic growth over the last decade.

References

[1] Ex-Minister Ermias Legesse Spills the Been. Tesfanews. http://www.tesfanews.net/ex-ethiopian-minister-ermias-legesse-spills-the-beans/. A Review of Ermias Legesse's book entitled: The Gifts of Meles - A City without an Owner (in Amharic)

[2] Amnesty International Report. Because I am Oromo, https://www.amnesty.org/en/documents/afr25/006/2014/en/

10. The Addis Milk Scare: A Precautionary Tale as False Alarm

(An revised version of this piece was published in Addis Fortune December 10,2015)

A recent research report produced by ILRI [1] has triggered panic among milk consumers in Addis Ababa, the capital city of Ethiopia. The milk market in and around Addis Ababa plunged into a serious crisis, at a level unheard before. As anyone with some familiarity with conditions of small holder dairy in Ethiopia would attest, it does not need a crisis of this magnitude to push Ethiopia's poor dairy farmers off the edge.

A crisis of this proportion can wreck the livelihood of poor dairy producers, given the conditions of feed market in Addis and its peri-urban districts. While thinking about potential victims, dairy producers come to mind immediately but one can trace more number of sufferers along the value chain – milk traders, processors, and, above all, milk consumers, particularly children and the elderly, whom the milk scare have deprived of the desperately needed nutrition from dairy products.

ILRI's mission statement has always been about supporting the livelihood of small holder farms. The latest version is stated as *better lives through livestock,* and previously it used to be expressed more explicitly as *poverty reduction through livestock.* Although ILRI's mission indicates commitment to producer support, ILRI is also dedicated to consumer protection from animal-born or zoonotic diseases. A number of research programs have been implemented utilizing substantial sum of public funds to support food safety.

Reconciling or balancing conflicts between producer and consumer interests requires rigorous scientific methods in coming up with sound public policy prescriptions on food safety. As long as policy recommendations are rooted in scientific consensus, then it may not matter much if ILRI's research outcomes end up in conflicts with meeting commitments to producers and consumers.

However, if ILRI research priority has tilted to one side or another would inevitably give rise to awkward situations, particularly when such bias is compounded with lack of scientific rigor. The research project which ended up with the Addis milk scare seems to be a good case in point. It is appropriate to investigate into this particular case which seems to have contradicted ILRI's mission in a fundamental way.

The main objective of this commentary is to explain why the research report had such a catastrophic outcome. This commentary is structured as follows. First, a brief overview of the ILRI research report is provided. This is followed by a discussion of conceptual and methodological problems with the research report. Finally, the ILRI research report is discussed in the context of the spectrum of food safety related public policy discourses in the literature.

Overview of the Survey

A cross sectional survey was conducted in the Greater Addis Ababa milk shed [2]. This location was selected for it is the most commercialized dairy production system in Ethiopia. Intensification has progressed ahead of the rest of Ethiopia. The study site largely falls in the central highlands in the Oromia regional state, urban and peri-urban locations surrounding Addis Ababa. The study adopted a value chain approach, covering input and output nodes in milk production.

A survey was conducted, 110 milk and 156 feed samples were

collected. Data was analyzed using what seems to be a standard procedure. I will refrain from commenting on the sampling method and procedures of laboratory analysis, although it is reasonable to ask some questions on these aspects of the research. I will focus on the manner in which research results on the milk samples were framed, presented and discussed in the research report. Also, I will confine discussion research results related to milk. The reason is that the presence of aflatoxin in feed would ultimately affect milk, and it would suffice to deal with the latter.

The most fundamental problem in ILRI's research was the fact that the research findings put undue emphasis on establishing the mere confirmation of *existence* of aflatoxin in milk rather than its quantity. This misguided emphasis was bound to adversely influence the research outcome. In the remaining sections of this commentary, I will discuss how this approach proved to be a fatal mistake.

Inappropriate Standard

It was stated "that dairy feeds and milk are highly contaminated with aflatoxin in the Greater Addis Ababa milk shed. All milk and feed samples had detectable levels of aflatoxin. The majority (93%) of milk samples exceeded the limit of 0.05 µg/L set by the EU." [2, p. 776].

Table 1: Contamination of milk samples in the Greater Addis Ababa milk shed.

Row	Aflatoxin	Number	(%)	Cumulative (%)
1	*< 0.05*	*9*	*8.2%*	*8.2%*
2	0.05 - 0.10	49	44.5%	52.7%
3	0.10 - 0.50	33	30.0%	82.7%
4	0.50 - 1.00	10	9.1%	91.8%
5	1.00 - 2.00	4	3.6%	95.5%
6	> 2.00	5	4.5%	100.0%
7		110	100.00%	

Source: [2, p. 777]

While interpreting research findings, the authors have strictly applied EU milk standard. However, there is no rationale to superimpose EU standard on Ethiopia; it is unclear why the researchers opted for EU standard. The role of researchers is to provide a range of options and assist policy-makers. It is misleading to present research results in just one scenario and imply that the authorities should adopt it. The motivation to choose the EU standard indicates that the researchers were set to create a highly sensationalized report from the very beginning.

In the research paper, the levels of aflatoxin in milk were presented in a bar graph. In order to bring out hidden information, I presented the data below in a tabular format (Table 1).The EU standard is shown in the first and *italicized* row of the table. The undue emphasis on this part of the data has led the researchers to end up with producing an excessively sensational report. Statements like "all samples contain aflatoxin" exaggerated the message and created a sense of fear in the mind of the reader. However, we know that mere presence of the substance does not mean anything – what matter is the amount of aflatoxin found in milk. Now in terms of the extent of aflatoxin in milk, the researchers confined their interpretation to row 1, which displays EU standards, < 0.05 microgram per liter.

The reporting style emphasized the very presence of aflatoxin as "dangerous". More sensational statements were presented as key findings: "The prevalence and concentration of AFM1 in milk in this milk shed was among the highest reported in the world."

Crucially, the research report, which was initially released for the wider public [1], does not even mention the existence of USA standard, row 3 in Table 1, the other shaded row in the table, which displays <0.5 microgram per liter. Curiously, there is a mention of USA standard in the version of the report published as a scientific paper [2]. However, this was hidden as far away from the general public, and by then the damage was already done. Even in the scientific journal article, the tone of the discussion remains as in the early report.

Ironically, the urge to exaggerate the figures was so much that even in the scientific paper [2, p.773], there was a factual error in stating that 29 of the milk samples (or 26.3%) were greater than 0.5 microgram per liter. Of course, this is obviously wrong, as shown in the table above, the correct figures were 19 samples (or 17.2%), which is the correct number or percentages of milk samples that exceeded the USA standard.

The bottom line is that as soon as we expose the data to the alternative standard available, then the problem begins to unravel. This states that

83% of the sample meets USA standard! With this, the policy implication of the research report changes dramatically. It becomes immediately clear that there is no ground for the chaos to occur in the Addis milk market. A consumer with this information would definitely feel a great deal more confident about consuming dairy products supplied from the Addis milk shed area. Now the first point to establish is this: the authors chose a reporting style that created fear and panic among public. Perhaps this was meant to raise awareness but this is precisely the wrong and the most risky way to go about raising public awareness on food safety. It is a certain way of increasing the chance of panic occurring among the general public and generate all the havocs that resulted from it.

Reinterpreting the Results

Now it is important to say a few words as to why the EU standard and the USA standards are so divergent [6]. In other words, why is the USA standard set at a level ten times higher than that of the EU standard? After all, there is no scarcity of scientists in the USA to raise public awareness in food safety and alert the authorities to come up with a stricter safety regime. Importantly, if the USA standard is somewhat more relaxed than that of EU, possibly due to some legitimate reasons, then perhaps it would be alright if standards of other countries including Ethiopia have diverged slightly from the USA standard? I raise these points for very important reasons.

First, it was reported (again unfortunately only in the scientific paper) that the median of aflatoxin contamination level in the milk samples was 0.09. In order to illustrate this, imagine the 110 milk samples were analyzed for their aflatoxin contents. The samples were sorted and then ranked according to their aflatoxin contents, the lowest, 1st and the highest, 110th. Now if we count the samples starting from the container with the lowest aflatoxin content upwards, we would still be around the EU standard until we reach the 55th container. This is astonishing since we know the EU standard is the strictest in the world. Therefore, in contrast to the claim in the report, amazingly Ethiopia is much closer to the EU than USA standard, since 0.09 is much closer to 0.05 than 0.5! A further breakdown of the distribution of the 49 samples (row number 2) in the 0.05 to 0.5 range would reveal interesting insights.

Second, if some of the Ethiopian dairy farms are allowed to have aflatoxin levels twice the USA limit, then actually in 92% of the cases, the aflatoxin level is less than 1.0 microgram per liter. In a nutshell, if the data was interpreted more cautiously, taking the Ethiopian context and possible ranges of global variations into account, then the research findings wouldn't have to cause any panic.

Lack of Scientific Consensus

Research reports that aim to influence public policy on critical matters such as food safety are expected to maintain some balance which in turn should be rooted in scientific consensus. Clearly, ILRI's research report does not fulfill this criterion.

The fact that the researchers chose a rather stricter regime, the EU standard, rather than presenting results in ranges of the alternative safety standards implies that they subscribe to a one-sided approach, commonly known for pushing the ideology of "precautionary principles" in advocating public policy regarding food safety. Further below I will return briefly to the consequences of food safety regulations that are guided by such extreme ideological viewpoint. Here it suffices to note that the deep-seated reason for the co-existence of EU and USA standards with such wide gap is rooted in lack of scientific consensus on the effect of aflatoxin on public health.

For the same reason, aflatoxin does not appear in the top priority list prepared by the World Health Organization (WHO). I stress here that I do not mean aflatoxin is not a health hazard, it is known that aflatoxin is harmful; after all it is a toxic substance. However, it is not well established in exactly what ways it does cause the harm except for known associations with liver cancer. The exposure-and-hence-fatality linkages are not so well known. For instance, it would have helped if ILRI's research report provided recorded and confirmed cases of aflatoxin related fatalities at different levels – global, regional or country scales. In a comprehensive report [7] that worldwide annual age-standardized incidence rate among men is 15.8 per 100,000 and 5.8 per 100,000 among women". This indicates 0.016% for male and 0.006% for female, extremely small rate of fatality rate.

Even this is further complicated by compounding factors, since aflatoxin's effects are often associated with other causes of liver cancer. In order to put matters in perspective, and build a sense of proportion to the debate, I would like to present relevant WHO estimates for Ethiopia. In global estimates on age-standardized alcohol related death, WHO reported that 133 person deaths per 100,000 alcohol consumers in Ethiopia [3].   On the other hand, comparison of observed and predicted incidence rate of aflatoxin-related liver cancer study on 33 countries puts Ethiopia's estimate below 5 per 100,000 [4].

The Danger of "False Positives"

It is important for authorities to guard against extreme viewpoints advocating regulations, including food safety [5, 9]. Earlier I mentioned that there are problems with regulations rooted in precautionary principles, also known as "false positives". In order for precautionary principles to be relevant to sound public policy, they should not involve some trade off in risks – minimizing some and maximizing others.

The trouble with false positives is that they often exaggerate the impacts of small risks and alter priorities in public policy targeting [8]. Assigning priority to obviously low risks means neglecting or undermining genuinely high risks, particularly given the scarcity of resources to satisfy all public policy objectives. The Addis milk scare provides a classic example. We know that malnutrition is the biggest killer and the highest risk to public health in developing countries including Ethiopia. It is for this reason that fighting malnutrition is on top in the list of priorities advocated by WHO. The Addis milk scare seems to have already adversely influenced the food intake decisions among households in Addis Ababa. Households are led to make wrong decisions – minimize a risk which is already low, perhaps health effect of afflatoxin does even exist to any significant extent. The net outcome is making an already bad situation worse, in terms of exacerbating malnutrition and hence increasing mortality, particularly among children.

Concluding Remarks

In this commentary, I have attempted to draw some lessons from ILRI's recent research that proved to be harmful to milk producers and consumers alike. Interpreting research results and drawing policy conclusions is a balancing act, requiring harmonization of various social and economic objectives. Policy conclusions with tunnel vision are bound to have damaging effects on the very group whose interest the research project was set out to serve.

It is likely that the Addis milk scare will have far reaching consequences. The milk scare can open up another front whereby Ethiopia's fledgling dairy sector would encounter an insurmountable barrier in the domestic dairy market. It is possible that the ongoing crisis would open up opportunities for importers of dairy products.

The increased intensity of imported dairy brands advertisement in Ethiopia after the Addis Milk scare indicates that there are already some interest groups jostling to exploit the opportunity created by the crisis unleashed by the infamous ILRI report. If such a group gets its way, then it would mean a certain death for Ethiopia's infant domestic dairy industry.

References

[1] ILRI 2015. New ILRI study finds high levels of aflatoxin in milk and dairy feeds in Greater Addis Ababa milk shed https://aghealth.wordpress.com/2015/07/20/new-ilri-study-finds-high-levels-of-aflatoxin-in-milk-and-dairy-feeds-in-greater-addis-ababa-milk-shed/

[2] Dawit Gizachew, Barbara Szonyi, Azage Tegegne, Jean Hanson, Delia Grace 2016. Aflatoxin contamination of milk and dairy feeds in the Greater Addis Ababa milk shed, Ethiopia. Food Control, 59: 773-779

[3] WHO 2008. Global Health Observatory data repository, Age-standardized DALYs, alcohol and drug use disorders Data by country. http://apps.who.int/gho/data/view.main.58140

[4] Scott A. McDonald, Brecht Devleesschauwer, Niko Speybroeck, Niel Hens, Nicolas Praet, Paul R Torgerson, Arie H Havelaar, Felicia Wu, Marlène Tremblay, Ermias W Amene & Dörte Döpfer. 2014.

Data-driven methods for imputing national-level incidence in global burden of disease studies. Bulletin of the World Health Organization, 93: 228-236

[5] Steffen Foss Hansen and Joel A. Tickner. The precautionary principle and false alarms — lessons learned. In Lessons from Health Hazards. http://www.eea.europa.eu/publications/late-lessons-2/late-lessons-chapters/late-lessons-ii-chapter-2

[6] Richard Lawley 2013. Aflatoxin. Food Safety Watch, the Science of Safe Food.
http://www.foodsafetywatch.org/factsheets/aflatoxin/

[7] Thomas W. Kensler, Bill D. Roebuck, Gerald N. Wogan, and John D. Groopman 2011. Aflatoxin: A 50-Year Odyssey of Mechanistic and Translational Toxicology. Toxicological Sciences 120(S1) -S28–S48. doi:10.1093/toxsci/kfq283
http://toxsci.oxfordjournals.org/content/120/suppl_1/S28.full.

[8] Calum G. Turvey, Eliza M. Mojduszka 2005. The Precautionary Principle and the law of unintended consequences. Food Policy 30 (2): 145-161 http://dx.doi.org/10.1016/j.foodpol.2005.04.001.

[9] Noel S. Weiss 2006. When Can the Result of Epidemiologic Research Not Eliminate the Need To Invoke the Precautionary Principle? Journal of Evidence Based Dental Practice, 6(1): 16-18.
http://dx.doi.org/10.1016/j.jebdp.2005.12.016.

11. Sovereign Bond May Prove to be a Nightmare for Ethiopia

December 15, 2014 (OP)

Ethiopian has recently joined the sovereign bond market, where governments sell debt to investors with a guarantee that they would pay periodic interest rates and the initial investment value at maturity.

The bulk of sovereign bonds are bought by institutions and governments, individual investors constitute a relatively small proportion of total bond buyers. Sovereign bonds are often denominated in local currencies.

Ethiopia's foray into the sovereign bond market has raised eyebrows in the world of financial market for at least three reasons. First, Ethiopia is the poorest country ever to venture into this market. Second, the real value of Ethiopia's currency has been deteriorating at alarming rates, devalued by close to 40 percent in the last three years alone. Third, the 108-page long prospectus [1] that the Ethiopian government prepared and submitted to formally enter the market contained astonishing revelations. In a bizarre twist, the government made unfamiliar and strange declarations about risks associated with purchasing the bond it is about to issue.

Among other things, authorities warned about: famine, Ethio-Eritrean war, social unrest and upheaval in the aftermath of the May 2015 election. These are extra-ordinary admissions of risks to a scale not heard in this market before. But what is the motive of the Ethiopian government in exhibiting such an extraordinary behavior? What are the triggers for the move to enter the sovereign bond market? In this piece, I will attempt to seek answers to these questions.

Carrot and Stick

The local English weekly Addis Fortune [2] reported rumors in Addis Ababa that the unusual admission of the risks was due to naivety of junior staff. However, central government in Ethiopia is known for ordering lower level units to do things a certain way only to deny involvement to avoid blame at a later stage. For example, federal government officials often deny and attribute human rights abuses to local authorities. The latest screw up seems to be an extension of that logic to international diplomacy. The fact that this rumor was leaked through a pro-government newspaper provides further clue about some sinister motives beyond a simple act of incompetence by those who prepared the prospectus.

It is likely that the government used the document as a carrot and stick tactic aimed at Western governments. An evidence of this comes from the revelations about Ethiopia's [3] "credit lines from China and Chinese entities accounted for 42 per cent of all external loan disbursements in 2013-14, and for 69 percent in 2012-13." This fact underscores Ethio-Chinese partnerships have been considerably strengthened. Western countries, particularly the U.S., recognize Ethiopia's support in the global fight against terrorism. But they also know that that support has often been offered to them so officiously with hidden motives, which at times jeopardized Western interests in the Horn of Africa[4].

The issuance of the sovereign bond and rare admission about the scale of Ethio-China relations appear like a warning to the U.S.: Buy the bond generously if you want to stop us from lurching toward China. The categories of hazards the government chose are even more telling. For instance, the possibility of another war with Eritrea is inserted to gain sympathy and also imply that terrorism is still rampant in Horn of Africa. The likelihood of social unrest after the next election is meant to warn the West that they should not seriously consider pressing the government on human rights and democratization.

Other motivations are rooted in domestic politics. The government knows that the risks are real and investors will find out sooner or later. In that case, by declaring the risks upfront, the regime tries to present itself as a brutally honest and transparent government. In doing so, they might be trying to pre-empt opposition claims about lack of transparency in areas of governance and economic management.

Liquidity Crisis

The Ethiopian government has a strange habit of biting more than it could chew. For example, it plans to invest [5] about $5.1 billion per year over the next decade on mega infrastructural projects: power, roads, and telecommunications. Another $6 billion is required to build a 2.4 thousands km railway network. The construction of the Grand Ethiopian Renaissance Dam (GERD) on the Nile River is expected to cost about $4.8 billion. The World Bank [6] has warned that this level of investment (more than 40 percent of GDP and three times the $1.3 billion in infrastructure spending that the country managed during the mid-2000s) is well beyond the country's modest means.

This created a self-inflicted wound in the form of a very messy liquidity crisis [7]: an acute shortage or drying up of funds in the economy. This *crisis is the main trigger for the foray to the sovereign bond market*. The shortage of funds is specially manifested in difficulty to borrow funds from the banking system. The crisis has been around in the Ethiopian economy for a good part of the last decade. The government left no stone unturned in the sphere of the domestic economy to overcome the severe liquidity crisis.

But the regime squandered huge sums of free grants and concessionary or low interest loans from donors, annual net-inflows [8] in the upwards of $2 billion, excluding other humanitarian aid. If wisely invested, the unprecedented and extremely generous foreign aid would have already pulled Ethiopians out of poverty. On the contrary, foreign aid created perverse government behavior — the abundance of foreign hard currency meant authorities did not see the need to economize. A good chunk [9] of the funds was embezzled and transferred abroad. The rest has been wasted on white elephants that have no prospect of yielding returns at least in the short to medium term.

The debacle from the 2005 election and the 2009 Charities Law [10], which restricted operations of foreign NGOs, saw a noticeable reduction in foreign aid. The government had to seek non-concessionary loans, particularly from China, to finance its mega projects. Meanwhile, the ill-designed project locations in less productive sectors or regions means sharp declines in export earnings [11].

For much of the last decade, the government simply printed more and more birr and engaged in a spending spree. However, a limit was reached when inflation hit the roof, approaching 60 percent in 2008 [12]. Fearing political backlash through social unrest and also due to pressures from international financial institutions, the government backed down from its inflationary financing strategy.

Involuntary Savings

Absent foreign funds, the government maintained a dogged determination and vowed to proceed with the mega projects by entirely relying on domestic savings. This began with sales of government savings bonds [13] to domestic institutions, to raise about $892.2 million in five years. Obviously, this was not realistic. About 70 percent of Ethiopians still live in extreme poverty, and one cannot expect households to voluntarily save even a small proportion of the target amount of saving. Consequently, the government resorted to force savings, using unorthodox methods.

The involuntary savings was accompanied by an intensive propaganda campaign to rally the public around the mega infrastructural projects by creating wartime like atmosphere. It is not only "unpatriotic" to question the suitability or merit of the large projects, it borders with criminality to express any reservations specifically about the GERD. Every civil servant has been forced to buy a saving bond paying her one-month salary in 12 installments. They have also made a relentless but unsuccessful campaign to entice the Ethiopian diaspora. The perverse method applied to sell bonds to households was followed by an even more crude procedures meant to force bonds on the business community. Private Banks have been compelled to purchase bonds equivalent to 27 percent [14] of their annual loans. However, this does not apply to government owned banks. Banking is effectively government monopoly [15], the three major state-owned banks hold 73 percent of the total bank assets in the country, 63 percent for the Commercial Bank of Ethiopia alone.

The extent of ignorance among Ethiopia's policy makers is baffling. The involuntary saving is meant to boost *public investment expenditure,* which is part of aggregate demand that fuels economic growth. But the authorities grossly overlooked the very act of involuntary saving is bound to reduce the other components of expenditure — *household consumption expenditure* on goods and services as well as *business investment expenditure.* Sure enough, the government has belatedly realized there was a limit to achieving their goals through involuntary savings, and with all options in the domestic economy already exhausted.

Sovereign Bond

The sovereign bond saga is a yet another maneuver to raise funds the government so desperately needed to finance the ill-conceived mega projects. This time the movement is on a less comfortable and unfamiliar terrain beyond Ethiopia's borders, in the international market arena where the regime cannot apply brute methods to enforce bond purchases. Perhaps for the first time in its rein, Ethiopia's ruling party will have to play by the rules.

Accordingly, it set out with a calculated move to secure a "sound" credit rating from known global agencies. In a quick succession during the first half of May 2013, credit rating agencies [16] offered the government exactly what it needed. Fitch Ratings [17] and Moody's assigned 'B' and 'B1' ratings to Ethiopia, respectively. These endorsements opened the door for a debut on international capital markets.

However, the government rhetoric notwithstanding, most economic analysts know that the fundamentals of the Ethiopian economy have not reached the level that warranty the kinds of credit ratings offered to Ethiopia. For instance, in May 2012, three months before Meles Zenawi died, the Economist observed[18]:

JUST how sustainable is Ethiopia's advance out of poverty? This is a vexed topic among bankers and others in Ethiopia who hold large wads of birr, the oft devalued currency. Despite hard work by the World Bank, oversight from the International Monetary Fund, and studies by economists from donor countries, it is not clear how factual Ethiopia's economic data are. Life is intolerably expensive for

Ethiopians in Addis Ababa, the capital, and its outlying towns. Some think Ethiopia's inflation figures are fiddled with even more than those in Argentina. Even if the data are deemed usable, the double-digit growth rates predicted by the government of Prime Minister Meles Zenawi look fanciful.

Similarly, soon after Ethiopia received the favorable credit ratings, the International Monetary Fund [19] "warned that the pace of accumulation of public sector debt to finance major investments in dams, factories and housing construction "deserves close attention."" Given these reservations about the credibility of Ethiopian authorities, it is perplexing as to why the ratings agencies endorsed Ethiopia to enter the global capital market.

This could have happened only if Ethiopian authorities have utilized their familiar strategy: buying the services of powerful and highly connected lobbying firms. This has become a familiar last resort for authoritarian regimes in Africa [20]. Ethiopia reportedly allocates a sizeable budget [21] to pay for prohibitively expensive lobbyist service fees.

Public sector debt has been growing at alarming rate. As Horn Affairs [22] reported recently, "Ethiopia's public sector debt grew threefold in the past five years. The total outstanding external debt surged from $5.6 Billion in 2009/10 to $14 Billion in 2013/14."These are increasingly becoming commercial or non-concessionary loans such as those from China. Ethiopia's premature entry into the sovereign bond market amounts to adding fuel to a flame.

IMF [23] predicts Ethiopia's "total debt to GDP increases from 24 percent to 48 percent of GDP in 5 years, posing risks to debt sustainability. External commercial borrowing entails risks even under the assumption of a highly efficient big-push public investment program." This means unlike in the past when funds have been flowing in through free grants or soft loans, debt servicing will soon become a huge burden on the Ethiopian economy, given the government's wasteful investment and a shift from soft to commercial loans. However, it is anybody's guess whether or not the regime will stay long enough to face the consequences of its decisions.

References

[1] FT. Ethiopia issues unfamiliar investor warning over war and famine. http://www.ft.com/intl/cms/s/0/c8691100-7a07-11e4-8958-00144feabdc0.html

[2] Addis Fortune. Many in the gossip corridors found it perplexing to see the administration shooting. http://addisfortune.net/columns/many-in-the-gossip-corridors-found-it-perplexing-to-see-the-administration-shooting/. Published on December 07, 2014 [Vol 15 ,No 762]

[3] FT. Ethiopia issues unfamiliar investor warning over war and famine. http://www.ft.com/intl/cms/s/0/c8691100-7a07-11e4-8958-00144feabdc0.html

[4] PBS News, Islamic Militia Takes Control of Somali Capital. http://www.pbs.org/newshour/bb/africa-jan-june06-somalia_06-06/. June 6, 2006

[5] Tigraonline. Ethiopia Compels Private Banks to Buy Bonds to Fund Development http://www.ethiopian-news.com/ethiopia-compels-private-banks-to-buy-bonds-to-fund-development/

[6] Vivien Foster and Elvira Morella. 2010. Ethiopia's Infrastructure: A Continental Perspective http://siteresources.worldbank.org/INTAFRICA/Resources/Ethiopia-Country_Report_03.2011.pdf. ACID (African Country Infrastructure Diagnosis), Country Report.

[7] Liquidity crisis. http://en.wikipedia.org/wiki/Liquidity crisis

[8] Getnet Alemu. A Case Study of Aid Effectiveness in Ethiopia: Analysis of the Health Sector Aid Architecture http://www.brookings.edu/research/papers/2009/04/ethiopia-aid-alemu. April 28, 2009

[9] Dev Kar, Brian LeBlanc. Illicit Financial Flows from Developing Countries: 2002-2011 http://www.gfintegrity.org/report/2013-global-report-illicit-financial-flows-from-developing-countries-2002-2011/.

December 11, 2013

[10] Human Rights Watch Report. Ethiopia: New Law Ratchets up Repression http://www.hrw.org/news/2009/01/08/ethiopia-new-law-ratchets-repression. January 8, 2009

[11] Jabessa Bonsa. Ethiopia's trade data and the effect of devaluation on import price. Opride. http://opride.com/2014/09/02/ethiopia-s-trade-data-and-the-effect-of-devaluation-on-import-prices/

[12] African Development Bank 2011. Inflation Dynamics in selected East African countries: Ethiopia, Kenya, Tanzania and Uganda http://www.afdb.org/fileadmin/uploads/afdb/Documents/Publications /07022012Inflation%20East%20Africa%20-%20ENG%20-%20Internal.pdf

[13 Ethiopia Compels Private Banks to Buy Bonds to Fund Development. Tigraonline. http://www.ethiopian-news.com/ethiopia-compels-private-banks-to-buy-bonds-to-fund-development/

[14] Ethiopia Compels Private Banks to Buy Bonds to Fund Development. Tigraonline. http://www.ethiopian-news.com/ethiopia-compels-private-banks-to-buy-bonds-to-fund-development/

[15] Moody's assigns B1 issuer ratings to the Government of Ethiopia. Financial Times. https://www.moodys.com/research/Moodys-assigns-B1-issuer-ratings-to-the-Government-of-Ethiopia--PR_298848. May 2014.

[16] Ethiopia receives first sovereign rating. http://www.ft.com/intl/cms/s/0/cb3a02ee-d9c7-11e3-b3e3-00144feabdc0.html?siteedition=intl#axzz3LUYFlxvm

[17] Fitch Rates Ethiopia 'B'; Outlook Stable. Reuters. Market News. http://www.reuters.com/article/2014/05/09/fitch-rates-ethiopia-b-outlook-stable-idUSFit69988020140509. Market News. May 9, 2014

[18] A peculiar case. How well is Ethiopia's economy really doing? The Economist.
http://www.economist.com/blogs/baobab/2012/03/ethiopian-economics. May 2012.

[19] Ethiopia receives first sovereign rating. Financial Times. http://www.ft.com/intl/cms/s/0/cb3a02ee-d9c7-11e3-b3e3-00144feabdc0.html?siteedition=intl#axzz3LUYFlxvm

[20] Joshua Kurlantzick. When Lobbyists Work for Authoritarian Nations. Newsweek. http://www.newsweek.com/when-lobbyists-work-authoritarian-nations-74781. July 26, 2010

[21] Jennifer LaFleur. Opening the Window on Foreign Lobbying, Propublica. http://www.propublica.org/article/opening-the-window-on-foreign-lobbying-718 . Aug. 18, 2009

[22] Daniel Birhane, Ethiopia's external debt surged to 14 Billion USD. Horn Affairs. http://hornaffairs.com/en/2014/10/26/ethiopias-external-debt-surged-to-14-billion-usd/

[23] IMF. The Federal Democratic Republic of Ethiopia: Selected Issues Paper. IMF Country Report No. 14/304. http://www.imf.org/external/pubs/ft/scr/2014/cr14304.pdf

12. Foreign Investment in Ethiopia: A Blessing or a Curse?

March 3, 2016 (AS)

In conflict prone contexts, foreign investors, especially whose actions while entering a given country were not subject to checks and balances, may undermine political stability and fuel social unrest.

Depending on the level of accountability in the recipient country, foreign direct investment (FDI) could be a blessing or a curse. In this piece, I will attempt to highlight Ethiopia's political economy and the setting for the operations of foreign investors.

Peculiar Political Context

Notwithstanding the announcement of a 100% electoral victory by the ruling EPRDF, the fact remains that Ethiopia has never had a fully representative government. This rather unique situation means it is naïve to discuss Ethiopia's current affairs by applying standard rhetoric. Doing so fails to capture the peculiarity of the situation on the ground. For instance, familiar phrases such as "dictatorial regime" or "totalitarian government" do not fully capture the essence of the current political system in Ethiopia.

The key to understand the strange nature of the ERPDF government, a coalition of four parties, is to recognize it as a system of "internal colonial rule" led by one powerful party, the Tigrean People's Liberation

Front (TPLF). It is a conspicuous knowledge held by many that EPRDF essentially means TPLF.

The loyalty towards TPLF of Ethiopia's military and security apparatus has remained the only source of EPRDF's strength and tight grip on power. Without further ado it suffices to mention that the country's army generals and high ranking officers hail from Tigray, the geographic location home to TPLF. In turn the army's brutal efficiency in military and security command system has earned the TPLF an extraordinary reputation and near complete political upper hand in the eyes of the other three parties within the coalition.

Technically that leaves Ethiopia with a reverse political system: the world is familiar with majority-rule and minority-rights, Ethiopia's, on the other hand, is a political system without even some majority-rights. Today's TPLF dominated EPRDF needed to be certain that the majority would not have the bare minimum of rights, because, if allowed, this might eventually lead to the emergence of democracy.

Business as Unusual

The political and military power disparity favoring a single party has also caused divergences in economic and domestic private investment opportunities. This resulted in the emergence of domestic crony capitalism of the ugliest type. Endowment Fund for Rehabilitation of Tigray (EFFORT), the acronym that has more than 50 companies under its control, owns its presence and dominance to the growing trend of domestic crony capitalism.

In the last 25 years EFFORT has emerged as the most powerful domestic business conglomerate controlling the commanding heights of the Ethiopian economy. Its monopoly on the Ethiopian economy ranges from heavy engineering, construction, import and exports (of key capital and raw materials including fertilizers on which all Ethiopian farmers rely) to freight and passenger transport, wholesale and retail distributions. And yet, there is little information about EFFORT that is available for the general public.

It is a misnomer to describe EFFORT as a business group "affiliated to the government". But Ethiopians know that the same groups of people who occupy government positions are also owners of the companies under EFFORT.

And as of late another unlikely business monopoly has emerged in the form of the military establishment, the same military whose top leadership is either loyal to or under the indirect control of TPLF. METEC, a company run by the national army, is having an elaborate business interest from production of computers and flat screen TVs to heavy metals, car assembly and hotels. Once again, there is no or little information available to the public on the exact nature of METEC's business empire.

The Dark Horse

It is within this political reality that one needs to look into the economic aspects, including the manner by which the EPRDF led government is regulating the flow of FDI. It is a public knowledge that cronyism has, by and large, emerged as the trade mark of EPRDF's economic governance over the past two decades, including its deals with foreign companies operating in the country.

As of this writing, news is coming those protesters in Gujji zone of southern Ethiopia and Dembi Delo of western Ethiopia are targeting the two gold mines in the area owned by the MIDROC Ethiopia Investment Group. To understand this boiling public frustration, it is important to acknowledge that the people of Ethiopia have no knowledge about how these two gold mines were sold to MEDROC in the first place, and to evaluate whether the people in the areas where the natural resources are being ferociously extracted have stood to benefit from it in any way.

It is also important to know that the name MIDROC stands for Mohammed International Development Research and Organization Companies, a name that implies nothing about the nature of the vast business functioning under its umbrella. For Many Ethiopians, therefore, MIDROC is the dark horse that appeared on the scene from nowhere but spread itself in all sectors of the Ethiopian economy at alarming pace.

For much of the first decade under EPRDF's rule, Ethiopia suffered a serious setback in attracting foreign investment. Foreign investors were cautious (rightly), observing the unhealthy governance system as a risk not worth taking. However, during those days, MIDROC Ethiopia was often presented as a cover up to entice other foreign investors, giving the impression that the EPRDF regime was trustworthy and foreign investment was safe to flow in. That, and its sworn allegiance to the ruling party in power, gave MIDROC the opportunity to enjoy unparalleled access to Ethiopia's natural resources. This was done primarily because the EPRDF could count on MIDROC as a foreign investor. The United Nations Conference on Trade and Development once reported that about 60 per cent of the overall foreign direct investment approved in Ethiopia was related to MIDROC.

MEDROC's expansions began with acquisitions of many previous public enterprises – manufacturing branches, state farms, gold mines, and other mineral resources mostly outside of public scrutiny. MIDROC is most commonly associated with land grabs in many parts of Oromia, at the heart of Addis Ababa and Gambella, causing havocs through evictions of millions of households from their ancestral lands.

Other Murky Deals

The contradictions in Ethiopia's business environment are rather perplexing. On the one hand the TPLF dominated regime in Addis Abeba has a very hostile attitude to private domestic investors. Ethiopia has remained at the bottom of World Bank's country ranks in ease of doing business, ranking 146th out of 189 countries in 2015. But EFFORT, METEC and MDROC business empires and their affiliates are exempt from such restrictions and the little private businesses in the country have to survive the three to make a meaningful economic gain.

On the other hand Ethiopia is known for making extraordinary concessions to attract foreign investors, particularly during the last decade. Here is the question – why such officious treatment for foreign investors when private business are forced to eat dirt? The answer lies in the assumption that the government often acts in the interest of domestic cronies – foreign investors are needed to camouflage EFFORT's aggressive expansions. The deals to couple EFFORT with foreign businesses are surrounded by dark secrets; details are unavailable to the general public. Foreign investors have often been lured into joint ventures with party owned or affiliated local companies. The recent US$30 million worth deal between a local pharmaceutical company owned by EFFORT and a foreign company symbolizes that assertion. The overlap between the operations of domestic oligopolistic companies and their foreign counterparts is so much that it is difficult to know where one ends and the other begins.

The recent fall out between the government in Ethiopia and the Karuturi Global Ltd has revealed the murky nature of foreign investment deals in Ethiopia that prompted many to summarize "in Ethiopia, foreign investment is a fancy word for stealing land". In 2010, Karuturi Global Ltd was given a concession to develop 300, 000 hectares of agricultural land in Gambella. However, in Dec. 2015, the deal collapsed when the Agricultural Ministry's land investment agency "cancelled the concession on the grounds that by 2012 Karuturi had developed only 1,200 hectares of land within the initial two year period of the contract." There is a lot more into this fall out than meet the eye, least the fate of the hundreds of thousands of indigenous people who were forced to give up their lands to give way to a deal they know nothing about.

But one of the most unsettling details to emerge out of this fiasco was the claim by Karuturi Global Ltd management that the land was forced upon them by the local authorities despite their insistence otherwise. At first glance this may sound awkward, as if the foreign investor and the Ethiopian authorities switched sides in the process of bargaining. However, for someone who is familiar with the shrewd operations of doing business in Ethiopia it is easy to know why Ethiopian officials were forcing the foreign investor to take 30 times more than it said it could handle. One plausible explanation held by many is that since enough land grabbing had already been done by the cronies during the previous decades, authorities found it prudent to frame a foreign investor as a vehicle to continue land expropriation.

In the wake of a possible persistence of protests by Ethiopians, protesters' targeted attacks against foreign companies operating in Ethiopia may come as sheer anarchic for outsiders. But as long as the people of Ethiopia are kept in the dark as to the nature of the real deals between foreign companies and a government flawed by asymmetrical party coalition (deals that symbolize a life deprived of its means and style),incidents of targeted public outrage against selected foreign companies should not come as a shock.

The same explanation holds true for the land expropriations for flower farms and industrial parks in Oromiya, particularly in the vicinity of Addis Abeba. It is for such reasons that the infamous Addis Abeba Master Plan was formulated, eyeing 20 times more land that would be transformed into wasteful industrial parks all in the name of attracting

foreign investment the nature of it is kept secret from the very people it
greatly affects.

13. Ethiopia's 'Miraculous' Economic Growth: Dancing While Standing Still!

July 19, 2016 (AS)

The 25th episode of "Ginbot 20" was on show in Addis Abeba on May 28th. This is a melodramatic event, an anniversary of the 28th May 1991 when the EPRDF rebel forces ousted the Military regime. Ethiopians have much to celebrate as far as the demise of the *Derge* regime was concerned. Perhaps this is the only element that unites public opinion toward this anniversary.

But May28[th] is celebrated with a mixed feeling. For some it is a "victory day", a military success, a day to remember the lives lost during the civil war, and the dawn of Ethiopia's renaissance. For others, it is a day when all hopes and promises brought about by that victory day have already been shattered one by one; a day that left Ethiopia under the iron fist of a group no less dictatorial than the regime they deposed. Such rare admissions are beginning to be heard even from among critics within the EPRDF inner circles [1].

In order to seek legitimacy, it has been customary for EPRDF to engage the general public by propaganda campaign, often contrasting their achievements in socio-economic progresses with those under their predecessor. At a press briefing he gave to state media on the eve of May 28, Prime Minister Hailemariam Desalegn claimed [2], once again, that the economic policy and the multi-party system introduced by the current regime has brought about tremendous socio-economic progress. He stressed specifically that Ethiopia's agriculture has been "growing at all levels and market oriented farmers were created and these are vital for the advancement of the economic policy of the country".

In this piece, I will focus on Ethiopia's economic success story and examine its validity. I will then highlight broader claims related to multi-party system. Unless stated differently, most data and charts presented in the subsequent sections are taken from the World Bank Development Indicators database.

GDP Growth Rate

The jury is still out on the credibility of Ethiopia's double digit GDP growth rate. On the one hand, government official data have presented double digit growth for more than a decade. The official version has often been reflected in flagship reports regularly published by the multilateral agencies such as the World Bank and the IMF.

On the other hand, analysts have utilized credible empirical evidences to raise serious questions about the validity of the official data. For instance, in its March 2nd 2012 issue, the *Economist* [3] warned that Ethiopia's GDP growth figures cannot be taken seriously:

> Just how sustainable is Ethiopia's advance out of poverty? This is a vexed topic among bankers and others in Ethiopia who hold large wads of birr, the oft devalued currency. Despite hard work by the World Bank, oversight from the International Monetary Fund, and studies by economists from donor countries, it is not clear how factual Ethiopia's economic data are. Life is intolerably expensive for Ethiopians in [Addis Abeba], the capital, and its outlying towns. Some think Ethiopia's inflation figures are fiddled with even more than those in Argentina [4]. Even if the data are deemed usable, the double-digit growth rates predicted by the government of Prime Minister Meles Zenawi look fanciful.

In another piece, published on London School of Economics blog, I have provided compelling empirical evidences to suggest that at least agricultural GDP was substantially inflated. The best way to confirm whether or not the growth figures were factual is to triangulate it by examining other economic variables closely related to it. Now let us shift our attention from growth rate based discussion and anchor the policy debate on change in the size of the economy during the post 1991 period.

GDP Per Capita

It proves useful to begin by examining changes in GDP per capita since it combines changes in the sizes of two variables – economic and demographic.

Real GDP per capita changed from $129 in 1991 to $315 in 2014. "Real" because the influence of inflation is filtered out. Thus, if Ethiopia's GDP was *equally* divided among all citizens, then income of every Ethiopian would have more than doubled between 1991 and 2014. I will return to the likelihood of equitable distribution.

But is the doubling of income per person such a big deal, given what we know about Ethiopia's potential growth? Here I am not talking about abundant national resource endowments. The analysis here is confined to opportunities offered by the exceptionally high rates of capital inflows, the official development assistance and aid (ODA).

Ethiopia received $1.7 and $3.5 billion respectively in 1991 and 2014. The cumulative total inflow was $53.6 billion. Real GDP in 2014 was only $30.6 billion, that is less than two-third of the total ODA. In other words, Ethiopia's GDP is only a fraction of the amount of its cumulative ODA.

A dollar injected into any economy would have a multiplier effect, that is to say "the capacity of new money to initiate chain reactions – generate jobs and hence income as it keep circulating in the economy". There is a ripple effect emanating from it, like a piece of stone thrown onto a still water, causing a motion in some predicable way in all directions. The size of the multiplier would depend on productive utilization.

The World Bank estimates the sizes of such multipliers [5] to range between two and five. Hence, the $53.6 billion should have generated between $107 billion and $268 billion. The sum of Ethiopia's GDP over the entire period comes to about $320 billion. We normally expect ODA to constitute a small fraction of the size of an economy. Above all, ODA is meant to boost GDP, not to replace it. Clearly, there is something seriously bizarre about the way ODA has been utilized in Ethiopia. GDP does not rise even proportionately with ODA, let alone in multiple of it.

In order to put matters in perspective, I would draw a parallel with South Korea which is known for using ODA for recovery from the Korean War as well as to propel itself onto a sustainable growth path. It is estimated that the total amount of ODA [South] Korea received from foreign countries was US$12 billion [6]. As economic policies took effect, however, the dependence on foreign grant assistance lessened. In less than ten years, South Korea's economy grew so rapidly that the United States decided to phase out its aid program to Seoul. Starting from late 1980s, South Korea graduated from recipient to donor status.

This means South Korea achieved so much with less than a fourth of the ODA Ethiopia received. In a nutshell, the size of Ethiopia's GDP (and GDP per capita) should have expanded by a multiple of what has been reported, as miraculous achievement at that!

Structural Transformation

The livelihood of about 85% of Ethiopia's population is supported by agriculture. Economic development in such countries is accompanied with two concurrent changes: the size of GDP, and the composition of GDP. The latter means the structure of the economy changes from predominantly traditional, rural and agricultural to modern, urban and industrial. This is what is called *structural transformation*. The art of devising sound economic development policy lies in balancing these two changes, without necessarily putting one ahead of the other.

EPRDF initially indicated a policy commitment to give priority to the Agricultural sector, when "Ethiopia had formally adopted Agriculture Development Led Industrialization (ADLI) as its development strategy in 1994" [7]. Through ADLI, agriculture was supposed to pave the way for industrialization.

However, enabling agricultural policy instruments such as fertilizer subsidy were withdrawn just three years into the launch of ADLI. Government affiliated companies used "strong-handed promotion of the credit-fertilizer packages… [A]gricultural output continued to fall behind population growth." [7] Agricultural Extension and credit-fertilizer have been extensively used "as a means of control over smallholder producers" [8].

This culminated onto yet another bold program called the Growth and

Transformation Program (<u>GTP</u>) [9]. This involved major departure from the previous policy commitment to small holder agricultural development. Small holder supports have largely become an exercise in trivia e.g. teaching farmers how to sow *teff* in rows! Horticulture and large scale farming have got precedence over small holder farming. However, large scale farming caused incalculable damages to the livelihoods of farming households who are evicted from their ancestral lands.

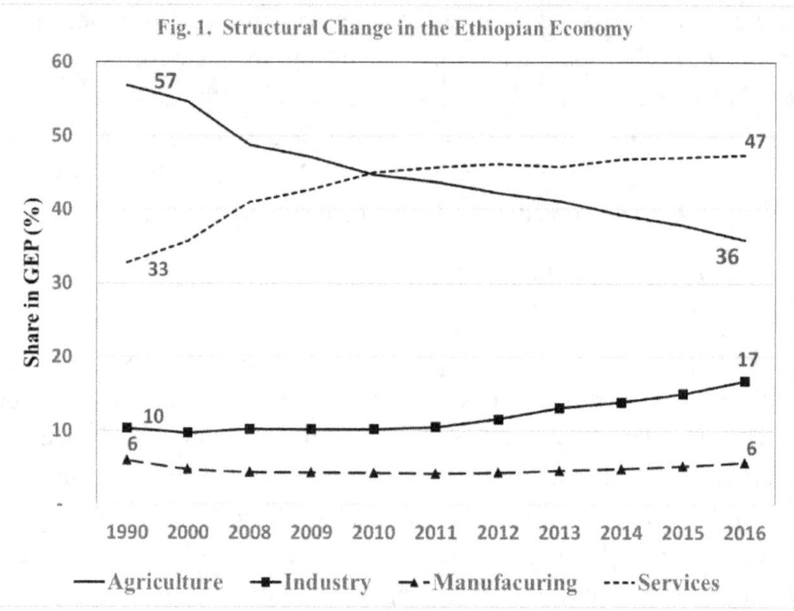

The above chart (Fig.1) displays a litmus test of Ethiopia's economic success story. I plotted the share of various economic sectors in aggregate GDP (1990-2016) (Source: World Bank, World Development Indicators Database). The share of industry increased from 10% to 17% but this is simply due to explosive growth of the construction sector. The share of manufacturing was stuck at around 6% for the entire period.

Agriculture's share was about 60% in 1991 but it dropped to around 40% in 2014. The initial share of services was about 30% in 1991 but now it increased to 40%. The sharply contrasting shapes of the lines give the impression that the service sector expands almost exclusively at the expense of the agricultural sector. Since almost nothing happened to the share of the industrial sector, it follows that any transformation that has occurred is only between agriculture and services. De-industrializing advanced economies can afford to specialize in services, but certainly this should not apply to a traditional economy.

The External Sector

The preceding sections have focused on the structure and performance of the domestic economy. Now I proceed to examining how sectoral policy bias in the domestic economy has adversely affected the external sector. Rhetoric aside, EPRDF has never favored commodity producing sectors, that is why agriculture shrank and industry stagnated.

However, the construction and service sectors have grown considerably as a direct consequence of favorable policy toward them. This is a cocktail of catastrophic policy blunder – promoting non-tradable services (non-exportables) and discriminating against tradable commodities (or exportables). Critically, the sectoral policy bias is inevitable outcome of regional development policy bias, for instance, against the now decaying coffee growing regions such as Jimma, *as discussed in is devaluation of birr the answer to ethiopia's economic troubles* (in this series).

Fig. 2 displays the outcome of these policy blunders (Source: World

Bank, World Development Indicators Database). It shows an ever widening gap between earnings from exports and payments for imports. In 1991, the external sector gap was only $305 million, but it rose to $8.1 billion, a gigantic 27 fold increase. The balance of payment deficit has been growing every year by more than the initial amount. So, the regime has nothing to celebrate as achievements in export promotion.

In addition to generous ODA, Ethiopia has received exceptional treatment in debt cancellations. These assistances and grants should have helped close the external sector gap displayed in Fig. 2. One would not expect a piling up of external debt stocks. The fact is Ethiopia's debt is hitting the roof, as shown in Fig. 3. It is incomprehensible why this happens.

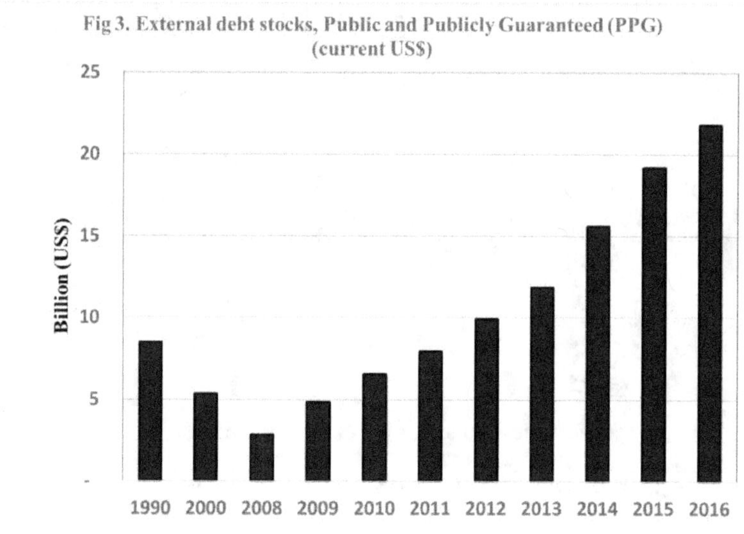

In 1991, the *Derge* regime left behind a debt stock of $8.5 billion. It was thought such a high debt pile was scandalous. The matter seems to have gotten from bad to worse under the EPRDF regime. By 2016, the size of debt stock nearly trebled, currently standing at $22 billion. This constitutes 30% of GDP in current prices.

Income Distribution

At this juncture, it is appropriate to refer back to the nearly two and a half fold real increase in GDP per capita. I have provided tangible evidence to suggest that Ethiopia's GDP could have increased by a substantially greater magnitude if internal and external resources were utilized effectively and efficiently. Be that as it may, it is essential to know to what extent all Ethiopians have experienced fairly balanced and equitable changes in their incomes.

Income distribution has been the least studied aspect of the Ethiopian economy. Of course, there is abundant literature on poverty metrics. But they often rely on household survey data which are conducted under the auspices of government officials. Results from a few thousand persons are, more often than not, hastily generalized to arrive at "amazing and almost miraculous sounding conclusions". For instance, IMF's [10] recent report on Ethiopia concluded: "Unlike other rapidly growing economies, the country has not experienced a significant increase in inequality, as measured by the Gini coefficient, even as poverty reduction occurred at a rapid pace".

However, given what Ethiopians know about their country's situation, it is mind boggling to read such statements from a reputable multilateral agency. In any event, it is not a difficult task to triangulate the issues and establish some balance in the argument. A report compiled by the World Bank in 2005 [11] states that "real wages in Oromia declined by 36% followed by Amhara (31%)." This refers to wages of civil servants.

EPRDF has an explicit policy to keep wages low in all sectors, public or private, in order to attract foreign investment. For instance, in a recent interview [12], PM Hailemariam reiterated that "to achieve our advantage in light manufacturing, we have kept such costs low. This ... starts with government wages. If you make government wages large, it impacts and inflates the market." Perhaps it is fair to say that inflation is the only economic variable that has been persistently growing in double digits in Ethiopia. Now given that the government has such an explicit policy to keep nominal wages low, how can real wage even stagnate or stay at the same level, let alone grow?

The civil servants and other fixed income groups, although their livelihoods have stagnated or worsened due to the wage policy, are actually in a relatively better off positions compared to the 85% of rural farming households. The declining wage of the civil servants supports not just the employee and his/her immediate families in cities but also their extended families often residing in rural areas. The fact that rural farming households depend on their salaried relatives living in cities confirms that actually their income and hence livelihoods are in a worse situation compared to those of their relatives earning fixed income.

This in turn tells us that the lion's share of the cake, per capita GDP whose size more than doubled, must have gone to a tiny section of the population who depend neither on farming nor on wage income. After all, it is reported [13] that "Ethiopia is creating millionaires at a faster rate than any other country on the continent."

Fallacy of Composition

Economic policy discussion on Ethiopia's success story is becoming a philosophical debate in a fallacy of composition. To begin with, for proponents of the EPRDF regime whether or not the success story does actually exist is proving to hinge more on faith than evidence. Although I have not covered it in this piece, the contradictions in Ethiopia's political economy start with the governance system. In addition to "achievements in economic progress", PM Hailemariam stated that EPRDF established a multi-party system as well as "a government structure which accommodates diversity and entertains the rights of nations and nationalities". In fact nothing could be further from the truth.

NPR journalist, Gregory Warner, paraphrased the late PM Meles Zenawi's speech in 2005 and stated that EPRDF [14] waits until the opposition assemble and grow legs, that is establish leaders and constituency. They then cut off those legs and make the head (the leader) float on air with no root to give semblance of multiparty democracy in the country. Continue the same vicious policy over and over until the opposition is fully dismantled. It is by using such diabolically smart tactics that EPRDF "wins" elections. In fact, it is nonsensical to talk about multi-party democracy existing in Ethiopia.

Some overzealous reporters have hailed Ethiopia as "African Lion" [14], presumably to draw a parallel with Asian Tigers. However, one can only draw an analogy with a sick lion which cannot hunt and kill to feed itself, and always on a lookout to scavenge for leftover from other carnivore.

EPRDF officials and some gullible foreign analysts are seriously discussing that the country will join the middle income group by 2025 but manufacturing has barely moved from where it was 25 years go. There are compelling empirical evidences emerging from reviews of progress in GTP I achievements that indicate nothing miraculous can happen in the remaining nine or so years. Similarly, the EPRDF claims a dramatic fall in the poverty rate and improvements in living standards of Ethiopians but there are equally compelling evidences to suggest that the benefits of economic growth must have gone to only a tiny group of elites.

At every "victory day" anniversary, the EPRDF reminds Ethiopians that the country has turned into a paradise. Yet, youth unemployment in Addis Abeba alone is at least around 30% [15], according to a December 2014 research paper by Beshir Butta Dale [2014]. Ethiopia's youth are departing in droves to different parts of the world. At least half a million have migrated to Saudi Arabia [16] in recent years alone. Between 2008 and 2012, about 164 thousand Ethiopians have migrated to the USA [17]. These provide some clues to obtain rough estimates of the total size of labor force that have migrated over the years to different destinations, including other Middle East Countries, South Africa, and Europe, and including those who perished along the way in the deserts and high seas.

In the finale of Francis Spufford's novel, *Red Plenty,* set in the Soviet Union, and referring to Khrushchev's angry remarks [18] while in retirement: "Paradise … is a place where people want to end up, not a place they run from. What kind of socialism is that? What kind of [s**t] is that, when you have to keep people in chains? What kind of social order? What kind of paradise?"

References

[1] Major General Abebe Tekle Haimanot, ‹‹ኢሕአዴግ ቆሟል ወይም ወደኋላ እየነጎደ ነው››, literally meaning "EPRDF at standstill or walking backwards?" Ethiopian Reporter, 29 May 2016

[2] Ginbot 20 paves right path for Ethiopia's renaissance- Premier. Walta info as replicated at
https://www.africanewshub.com/news/5067324-ginbot-20-paves-right-path-for-ethiopias-renaissance-premier

[3] How well is Ethiopia's economy really doing? (Ethiopian economics A peculiar case). The Economist. March 20, 2012. http://www.economist.com/blogs/baobab/2012/03/ethiopian-economics

[4] The McFlation index: Lies, flame-grilled lies and statistics. What do burger prices tell us about the reliability of official inflation figures? The Economist. January 27, 2011. http://www.economist.com/node/18014576

[5] World Bank. World Bank Group and GEF: Leveraging development finance for the benefit of the global environment. October 17, 2016 http://www.worldbank.org/mdgs/documents/FfD-MDB-Contributions-July-13-2015.pdf

[6] History of Korea's ODA. Korea Official Development Assistance. http://www.odakorea.go.kr/eng.overview.History.do

[7] Xinshen Diao 2010. Economic Importance of Agriculture for Sustainable Development and Poverty Reduction: The Case Study of Ethiopia. Paper was first presented to the Working Party on Agricultural Policy and Markets, 17-20 May2010. Reference: TAD/CA/APM/WP(2010)23 http://www.oecd.org/agriculture/agricultural-policies/46378942.pdf

[8] Peter Hazell, Colin Poulton, Steve Wiggins, and Andrew Dorward. 2006. The Future of Small Farms: Synthesis Paper. This document is part of a series of contributions by Rimisp-Latin American Center for Rural Development (www.rimisp.org) to the preparation of the World Development Report 2008 "Agriculture for Development".

[9] National Planning Commission 2015. The Second Growth and Transformation Plan (GTP II) (2015/16-2019/20) (Draft). September 2015 Addis Ababa https://www.africaintelligence.com/c/dc/LOI/1415/GTP-II.pdf

[10] The Federal Democratic Republic Of Ethiopia: Selected Issues. IMF Country Report No.15/326

https://www.imf.org/external/pubs/ft/scr/2015/cr15326.pdf

[11] Mohammed Mussa. Civil Service Employment and Pay in Ethiopia: Challenges for Service Deliveries and Achieving the MDGs. Labor Markets and Employment in Ethiopia and the Emerging Policy Agenda. Joint MOLSA/ILO/WB Technical workshop. December 8, 2005.
http://siteresources.worldbank.org/INTLM/Resources/390041-1134749230121/2034249-1134749273741/Mussa_CivilServPay.pdf

[12] Greg Mills, Ethiopia's Hailemariam Desalegn: Growth has to be shared to be sustainable, The Daily Maverick, 7 June 2016.
http://www.dailymaverick.co.za/article/2016-06-07-ethiopias-hailemariam-desalegn-growth-has-to-be-shared-to-be-sustainable/#.V1mVTzVPj62

[13] David Smith (Africa Correspondent). Ethiopia hailed as 'African lion' with fastest creation of millionaires. The Guardian. December 4, 2013. https://www.theguardian.com/world/2013/dec/04/ethiopia-faster-rate-millionaires-michael-buerk

[14] Gegory Warner. Ethiopia Stifles Dissent, While Giving Impression Of Tolerance, Critics Say. Parallels. June 8, 2016.
http://www.npr.org/sections/parallels/2016/06/08/481266410/ethiopia-stifles-dissent-while-giving-impression-of-tolerance-critics-say

[15] Beshir Butta Dale Unemployment Experience of Youth in Addis Ababa MSc Thesis https://thesis.eur.nl/pub/17474/Beshir-Butta-DALE.pdf, 2014

[16] Ethiopia, Saudi Arabia to Conclude Labour Recruitment Contract. The Ethiopian Herald. Replicated at
http://allafrica.com/stories/201508270774.html

[17] Christine P. Gambino, Edward N. Trevelyan, and John Thomas Fitzwater 2014. The Foreign-Born Population from Africa: 2008-2012. US Census Report Number ACSBR/12-16.
http://www.census.gov/library/publications/2014/acs/acsbr12-16.html

[18] David Michael. Bright Sparkling Speeches. Open Letters Monthly and Arts and Literature Review (Review of Red Plenty by Francis Spufford) May 1, 2011.

http://www.openlettersmonthly.com/bright-sparkling-speeches/

14. Rush for the Exits: Why is Ethiopia's Capital Flight Accelerating?

May 9, 2016 (AS)

A substantial sum of money has been illegally flowing out of Ethiopia during the last decade. What is even more worrying is not just that the levels of out flows are high but also the sizes of illicit capital outflows have been rising at alarming rates. This rather unique pattern has attracted the attention of the general public as well as those of bilateral and multilateral donor agencies.

I will also attempt to put some flesh on the bones of facts presented in the GFI database. I will do so by shedding some light on the political economy context of the illicit capital outflow (IFFs) from Ethiopia.

Stolen Money Trails

The natural starting point is to get a sense of magnitude on the levels and trends. The GFI data is summarized and plotted in Fig. 1. For the time being we focus on the total flows, that is the heights of each bar denoting sizes of annual illicit money outflows. The sum of the blue and red colors gives total amount of money illegally moved aboard from Ethiopia during that year. This ranged from USD $0.4 billion in 2004 to USD $5.6 billion in 2010.

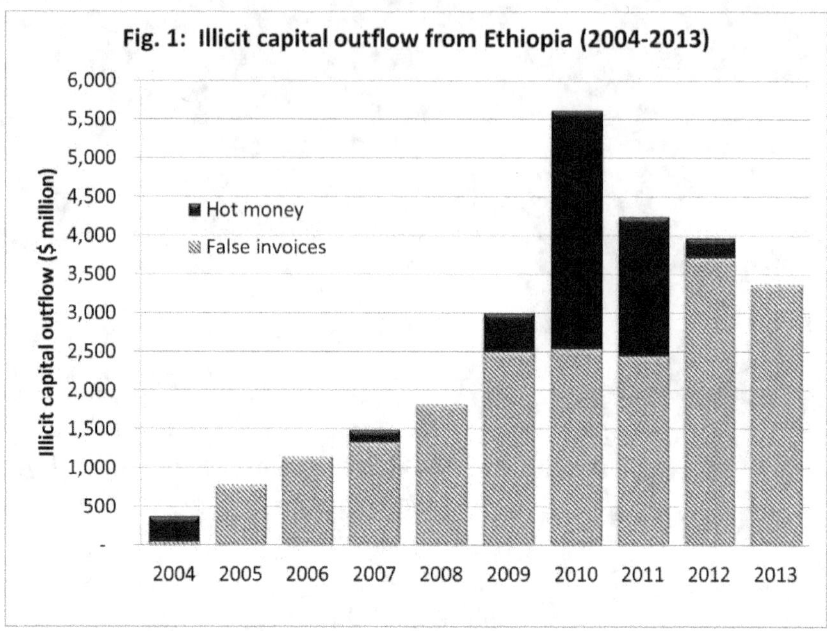

The average annual outflow was $2.6 billion during 2004 and 2013. This is a sizeable sum of money by any standard. For instance, according to estimates reported by the World Bank, the amount of official development assistant (ODA) Ethiopia received in 2010 was $4 billion but total amount of IFFs during that year was $5.6 billion.

This means in 2010 alone Ethiopia's IFFs exceeded the ODA it received that year by $1.6 billion. In other words, Ethiopia's IFFs amounted to diverting the entire aid money of 2010 to foreign banks and then still transfer abroad an additional sum of money.

During the entire period (2004 to 2013) the total amount of money that Ethiopia lost due to IFF was $26 billion. This amounts to stealing nearly $300 per citizen. Alternatively, the size of stolen money was about 11 times the total the amount of emergency aid being sought from donors in the current year to buy cereals from abroad and feed the drought victims.

Potential Culprits

One may wonder – who are the culprits responsible for Ethiopia's economic fraud at such massive scale? The GFI categorizes possible perpetrators into three groups: (a) financial institutions; (b) complicit business counterparts, mainly importers and exporters; and (c) government officials.

In the Ethiopian case, it is reasonable to exclude financial institutions because there is no foreign bank operating in Ethiopia, and the domestic private banks are extremely tightly controlled. Ethiopia's most influential banks, the Commercial Bank of Ethiopia (CBE) and the National Bank of Ethiopia (NBE), are owned and run by the government. Therefore, in the context of Ethiopia it is safe to include (a) under (c).

That is to say Ethiopia's IFF can only be undertaken by importers, exporters or government officials. One would hasten to add that there is a huge extent of overlaps between government officials and big businesses in Ethiopia, since big businesses are highly interconnected with the government and/or they are directly or indirectly owned and run by government officials.

Money Diversion Channels

Now we can shift our attention back to fig. 1 and consider the breakdowns of the IFFs, the individual component denoted by the blue and red sections in each bar. The GFI applies a methodological framework that accounts for two types of illegal movements of money from one country to another.

The first one is export or import trade mis-invoicing. This is measured by using a methodology called Gross Excluding Reversals (GER). This simply mirrors exports by one country with imports of another country and vice versa. For instance, items of imports recorded by Ethiopia should agree with records of exporters to Ethiopia in all aspects – value, quantity and quality.

The second one is various leakages in the balance of payments, measured by using the "hot money narrow" (HMN) approach. The latter one is often referred to as "net errors and omissions" in the balance of payment jargon. For instance, if a donor agency or country recorded $1 million grants to Ethiopia but this does not appear in the records by the authorities in Ethiopia, then the GFI records this as a leakage from Ethiopia's balance of payment.

It is clear from Fig. 1 that the bulk of illicit money transfer from Ethiopia has taken place using trade mis-invoicing, denoted by the blue component of the bar. In 2004, trade mis-invoicing constituted only 14%

of the total IFFs. In 2013, however, this proportion has grown to 100%, the entire IFFs began to be accounted for more and more by trade mis-invoicing. For the entire period under discussion, $19.7 billion (or 76% of the total IFFs) was conducted through trade mis-invoicing. The year 2010 is an exception – diversion of "hot money" dominated in that year; it constituted 55% of the total IFFs.

False Invoices

Trade mis-invoicing can take place in one of the following four ways: over invoicing exports, under invoicing exports, over invoicing imports and under invoicing imports. In Ethiopia's case, the GFI report indicated import over-invoicing is by far the most important method of transferring money abroad. During the period under analysis, about $19.7 billion was transferred abroad through import over-invoicing.

It is critical to understand how import mis-invoicing hurts the Ethiopian economy. This is important in the context of huge public construction projects with substantially large components of imports of machinery and other equipment. For instance, an acquisition of a set of machinery whose real value is $1 million is recorded with inflated invoice of $1.5 million.

The importer allocates project budget at the inflated import value, pays the real value to the supplier and then siphons-off the difference (in this case $0.5 million) and deposits it in a foreign bank account. The real damage to the economy happens in terms of inflated capital expenditure. Perhaps the opportunity large capital projects provide for corrupt officials could be the ulterior motive for the uncontrollable urge to attach such a high priority to large capital projects in economic development strategies.

However, it should be noted that public capital projects are often financed through commercial loans that should be paid back with cumulative interests in years to come. The economic return to capital project would partly depend on the cost consideration at project implementation stage.

The GFI also finds some export trade mis-invoicing in Ethiopia's foreign trade, over-invoicing by $6.5 billion as well as $3 million under-invoicing. In trade based money laundering, the most common types of mis-invoicing are import over-invoicing and export under-invoicing. As noted above, the case of import invoicing has no complications – so much over invoicing has taken place and it explains the bulk of trade based money laundering in Ethiopia. However, the case of export over-invoicing is uncommon.

Export over-invoicing [1] do happen although they are rare, e.g. China's trade with Hong-Kong. Export over-invoicing is required when there is a need to plough back money from abroad and report it as inflated foreign direct investment. This is likely the case with Ethiopia where the authorities have been desperate to report higher foreign investments particularly in the first half of the period under analysis.

Ethiopia's Capital Flights Dwarfs Rest of Developing Countries

It would prove useful to know how bad Ethiopia's IFFs is relative to other countries. Fig. 2 below compares Ethiopia with its neighbors, the rest of Sub-Saharan Africa (SSA) as well as the average of developing countries (DCs). The comparison was done by expressing total illicit money outflow as percentage of GDP. The years are grouped into three intervals. For reasons discussed further below, it would prove useful to contrast pre- and post-2005. Accordingly, I have isolated 2004 and then divided the remaining years into two equal intervals.

This revealed astonishing patterns of illicit money outflow from Ethiopia which starkly contrasted with those for other countries. First, throughout the years Ethiopia's records considerably exceeded those for its two immediate neighbors, Kenya and Tanzania. Second, a comparison of 2004 across the countries shows that Ethiopia's illicit money outflow was way below the Uganda, SSA, and the DCs averages.

Third, the situation changed dramatically from 2005 onwards. Ethiopia outstripped Uganda, and then closed the gap with the SSA average. Fourth, Ethiopia's average annual money outflows between 2010 and 2013 reached 11% of the country's GDP, considerably exceeding the corresponding figures for the other countries – SSA (5%), DCs (4%), Uganda and Tanzania (2%) and Kenya (0.013%). Fifth, it is important to note that illicit money transfers abroad constituted smaller and smaller percentages of GDP for most countries over the years, implying substantial improvements in transparency in their economic management. The situation in Ethiopia sharply contrasts with this reality – illicit money outflow becoming a larger and larger percentage of

Ethiopia's GDP. This indicates transparency in Ethiopia's economic management has gone from bad to worse over the years.

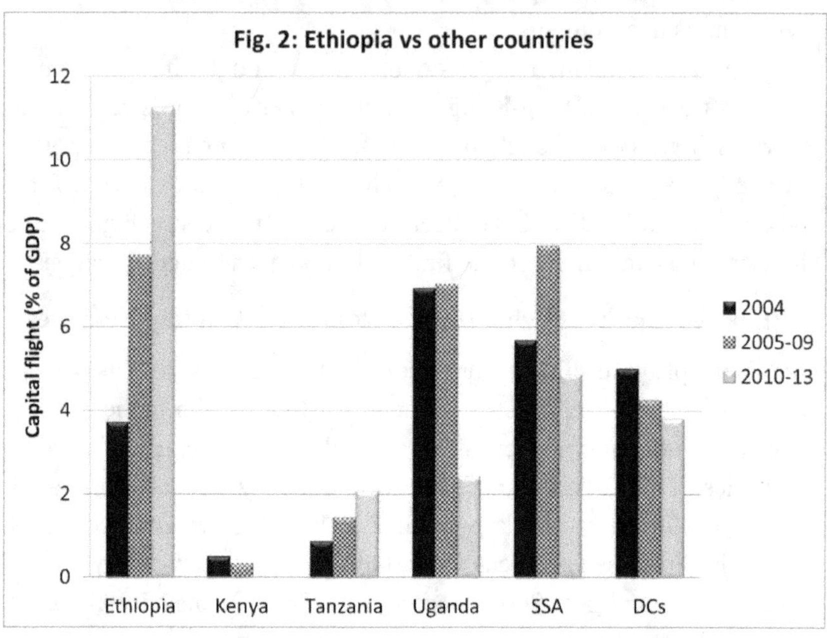

It should be noted that the SSA average is largely driven by money being squandered by oil and other mineral resources exporting countries such as Nigeria and Angola. It is telling to note that Ethiopia, a country not known for exporting substantial mineral resources, is now characterized by illicit money outflow to GDP ratio exceeding that of an average SSA country.

Blind Spots in Accounting for Remittance Flows

The analysis in the preceding sections relied entirely on the Global Financial Integrity (GFI) report. GFI methodology is strictly confined to official records as starting points and then mirrors records at different places and times. Systemic discrepancies between records are then registered as illicit transactions.

Clearly, then the GFI methodology does not account for illicit money flows that take place through financial transactions in informal or black markets. Remittance flows are riddled with black markets in hard currencies. The situation is even worse in the context of Ethiopia, where official hard currency flows are tightly controlled, and hence creating conditions for prevalence of underground currency transactions.

To the extent that remittances are channeled through formal banking or foreign exchange offices, then the transactions get into the balance of payment records. Leakages from the flow are accounted for through the GFI approach called "hot money" discussed earlier.

However, there are strong evidences [2] indicating that the bulk of remittance transfers to Ethiopia actually happen through informal channels, mainly because of better rates and lower costs.

The informal channels may take one of two forms. First, it is common for Ethiopians living abroad to take hard currencies with them every time they visit home and then directly exchange it to birr in local black markets at better rates by avoiding transfer fees. It also happens that they send hard currencies via travellers they trust so that they give it to their relatives, who in turn get it converted in local black markets. The World Bank estimated that 14% of Ethiopians to whom money was transferred from abroad in 2010 got it through travelers. Since the World Bank has not made a reference to money converted at local black markets, it means the total amount of hard currencies entering Ethiopia by informal channels is much higher than the 14% who regularly receive remittances.

Additionally, there is a more sophisticated black market which operates pretty much like the way foreign money transfer services operate, except that these are operated informally by individuals living abroad. As any Ethiopian living abroad can tell, every big city countries with hard currencies has a few black market operators who offer exchanges of foreign currencies to birr with additional incentives, at least two or three birr on top of the going rate that money transfer agencies offer.

I selected a couple of major cities and gathered background information for this piece. The margins offered vary across time and space but the current margin on above Western Union conversion rates were at least one birr per unit of USD equivalents of local currencies in London, Dubai, and Kuwait, excluding foreign exchange office fees charged per transaction. This means Ethiopians living abroad have good enough incentive to look for black market operators rather than sending money through formal channels.

The role of the black market is simply to collect and bulk the hard currencies. Where exactly the collected money goes is anybody's guess. One may hope that importers who face constraints in foreign exchange rationing may smuggle out the hard currency they collected and/or importers may assign agents in foreign countries to collect and bulk hard currencies for them.

In both cases importers may spend the money they bulked on purchasing goods and services that will eventually enter Ethiopia. This is an optimistic scenario since the country may eventually benefit from availability of goods and services in the domestic market, except that the transactions were done informally and the government might have lost some tax revenues.

The upshot of this discussion, however, is that the hard currencies collected from local black markets may get smuggled out and get deposited in foreign bank accounts. Similarly, black market operators residing abroad may also be primarily motivated by a pressing need to convert birr into a hard currency and safely deposit it in a foreign bank account.

It should be noted that the GFI methodology misses out such blind spots in remittance flow accounting, which means Ethiopia's capital flights discussed in the preceding sections is highly likely to underestimate the size of illicit capital flights from Ethiopia. If so much has been done to move money illegally abroad by abusing formal channels, then it is realistic to assume that the informal channels are even more susceptible to abuses by the same group of actors who seem to be in a rush to the exits.

Why the Rush?

At this juncture it is appropriate to pool together different lines of discussions in the preceding paragraphs. The most crucial point here is the timing of dramatic changes in Ethiopia's capital flight. It is clear from the facts presented in this piece that 2005 was a watershed moment in Ethiopia's capital flight history in recent years.

For those who closely follow Ethiopia's political and economic affairs, the fact that dramatic things began to happen soon after 2005 does not come as a surprise.

The general election of that year and the upheavals that followed had seriously shaken self-confidence among the elites who held political and economic power. The possibility of losing power and economic advantages that accrues from it began to be felt starting from that year, when the ruling EPRDF snatched power under murky conditions from the hand of the opposition who claimed they actually won the general election.

This argument is substantiated by the following logical reasoning established in our discussion earlier. In the Ethiopian context there are no foreign banks, and domestic banks are very tightly controlled by the government. Also, there is a great deal of overlaps between interests of big businesses and those of government officials.

In that case, corrupt government officials and their affiliated businesses are the likely culprits for capital flights from Ethiopia at such epic proportions. The fact that rampant corruption has crippled the current government is openly debated in local media and among the elite at official forums. The evidence provided in this piece only corroborates the ongoing public debate.

References

[1] Jake Van Der Kamp. How the export invoicing trick works. South China Morning Post. January 2014.
http://www.scmp.com/business/article/1403214/how-export-invoicing-trick-works

[2] Ethiopia: Remittance Dilemma. Wardeer News. January 5, 2015.
http://www.wardheernews.com/ethiopia-remittance-dilemma/

15. Oromo Protests: Getting the Messages Right

January 25, 2016 (AddisStandard.com)

The most commonly held rallying cry of the ongoing Oromo protest in Ethiopia is "Say No to the Master Plan!" There is a consensus among the protesters and the general public that the "Master Plan", named by some campaigners as the "Master Killer", has just served as a focal point that ignited the widespread discontent in a range of social, political and economic lives of the Oromo who finally went out en masse to express their outrage.

This piece is concerned with effective messaging of the protest. If framed wisely and clearly, messages and slogans can contribute to effective communication between the wider Oromo society in general and, most importantly, with the rest of the Ethiopian people and the international community.

It should be emphasized that the Oromo protest is a spontaneous outburst of rage among the Oromo youth and the general public at large, who had enough of the relentless and systematic oppression and dispossession by the current EPRDF led government in which the Oromo people are not genuinely and meaningfully represented. Since the protest is not centrally organized and coordinated, it is not surprising if the messages are not as sharp as they should.

The "Plan"

The concerns and questions related to the 'Master Plan' can be classified into the following sets of issues and regulations: *The 'Master Plan'*– The request to scrap the 'Master Plan', a technical document that specifies the expansion of Addis Ababa by 20 times its current size, albeit with the ominous prospect of dissecting Oromiya into two parts through a deliberate enlargement of Addis Ababa; and *Evictions and Land Grab* – This follows from (a) the enlargement of Addis Ababa will inevitably get accomplished by evicting hundreds of thousands of farmers and turning pristine farm lands into a massive urban development spaces; and (b) *Urban Development Law*– recently passed by *Caffee* Oromiya, which was rushed through as an urban development law with far reaching implications, essentially obliterating Oromia's right on its urban centers.

If we count slogans that appeared on placards carried at demonstrations in towns and villages of Oromiya as well as solidarity rallies organized by the Oromo diaspora, then perhaps more than 90% of the cases would refer to the 'Master Plan', that is in the sense of (a) above. We witness similar levels of frequent references on social media; for instance, profiles of activists on Facebook often appear with a familiar red-green colored two worded slogan, "Say NO", a shorthand for "Say No to the Master Plan". Matters related to land grab are also referred to during chants by protesters but with less frequency than "Say No" type slogans. As far as I am aware, the "urban development law" has received a very marginal attention during the protest rallies and related discourses.

Unintended Outcomes

There is an unintended consequence of heavy reference to the 'Master Plan' during opposition and solidarity rallies and expert discussions. The presence of the very word 'Plan' in 'Master Plan' seems to have hugely distorted the message. By definition, 'plans' are essentially futuristic. Therefore, any opposition to a planned activity can essentially (and easily) sound as if it is all about opposing something yet to take place. To complicate matters, even in latest press releases by Oromo political groups appear with phrases like "if implemented"; that is to say "if this

Master Plan is going to be implemented".

In rare cases when they report on Oromo protest, the western media often misrepresented Oromo protest as opposition to "development plan", with negative connotation of portrayal as anti-economic development. The EPRDF led government has often projected this image portraying itself as pro-development and Oromo activists as obstacles against its development plans. Even if Oromos put their cases in the best possible way, then I suspect the government would still devise ways to distort it and the Western Media would still be reluctant to provide fair coverage. Such that lack of focus in getting messages right have therefore immensely contributed to the distorted image of Oromo activism, specifically related to opposition to the 'Master Plan'.

The excessive reference to the 'Master Plan' has already caused some misunderstandings and created obstacles to the ongoing Oromo uprising. For instance, government officials have reluctantly indicated their willingness for dialogue. Under pressure they have gone as far as announcing a closure of the Integrated Master Plan Project Office. The US government has provided a lip service to Oromo protest, effectively implying that "what happened is regrettable, but now that the government is willing to talk to you, stop protesting and start engaging with the authorities". Sadly, the US government has yet again given the moral high ground to the government in Ethiopia, whose security forces have already killed more than 80 peaceful Oromo protesters, including a mother who tried to plead and protect her son.

Sharpening

In my view, what is required is simple and straightforward. The messages can get right by doing two things:

Prioritize: I propose prioritization the messages in the following order: oppositions against the general practice of land grab; the Oromiya urban development law; and the 'Master Plan' itself. Meanwhile references to the later have to be kept to the minimum. Land grab, the end result of the 'Master Plan', has to be brought up front and protesters have to be vocal in their opposition to the ill-designed and deceitful regulation rushed through *Caffee* Oromiya. References to the fuzzy, vague and broad "plan" have to be relegated to a third category. However, I believe it should still remain on the placards but with less frequency than it currently appears.

Balance: The message gets clearer if opposition to the 'Master Plan' is unpacked and presented in its time dimension: past, present and future. So far, the misunderstanding emanates from the presence of the word 'Plan' in 'Master Plan', which gave totally wrong impressions that Oromos are protesting a plan that is not yet implemented. It is a known fact that this is not the spirit in which the Oromo protests have taken place. The fact of the matter is the 'Addis Master Plan' has already been implemented. The EPRDF government should therefore be accused and challenged not only for lack of public participation in the preparation of the 'Master Plan' but also for declaring a plan for City development activity which has already been substantially implemented without much say from the general public.

This would mean reframing the message and challenging primarily the implemented component of the Addis Ababa Master Plan. In other words, the focus of the movement should shift from what is yet to happen to what has already happened. This will save the protest from being labeled as a protest led by "imagination" to opposition against incalculable damages and crimes already perpetrated on the Oromo people.

Focusing

The whole purpose of this analysis is to assist with sharpening the messages and messaging in the ongoing Oromo protest. I will conclude by providing rough sketches of the nature of effective messages I would like to see in future rallies. Although I put "Land Grab" as a primary target for opposition, even this would need to be framed in such a way that the message to be conveyed is a great deal more focused and sharper. In the context of Oromiya, "We Oppose Land Grab" is not good enough. Instead *"Lafaa Hattee Deebisi!"* or "Return Stolen Properties!" sounds sharper. I will simply outline a few focal points, and leave the task of coining effective slogans out of them. (of course, that is if my concern is shared with others colleagues).

Compensation– peaceful protesters would need to put across messages that target proper compensation for millions of families that have already been evicted over the last two decades. The justification for this is clear and straightforward. Ill-compensated farmers have legitimate cases to legally hold the authorities accountable for their dispossessed properties. There is no such a thing as bygones are bygones in such matters. In this case, the target has to be proper compensations perhaps over a longer period of time. It is possible to imagine the kinds of settlement that can be reached.

This might include establishing an inquiry that will look into the elaborate scams surrounding property development deals, amount of money collected, and then institute public fund for special compensations that will regularly pay evicted farmers and reinstate their dignities as human beings. Inevitably, such compensation funds can be sustained through property taxes, which in turn force those who unjustly acquired land to pay back in the long run. Such guarantees will save current owners from insecurity in the short term to medium term.

'Master Plan'– The manner in which protesters oppose part of the 'Master Plan' yet to be implemented would need to be reframed. The aspect related to inevitable future land grab will remain as in the current rally but it should not be allowed to overshadow other aspects. However, I think it is important to express opposition to the deceitful merger of Addis Ababa with surrounding Oromiya towns in the pretext of development. Peaceful protesters would need to vocally express their opposition to "merger". The reason is clear; it violates the basic principles of federalism. Something like this would send a strong message: Development Plan Integrations, Yes!; City-Town Mergers, No! It can never be a difficult task to elaborate the underlying reasons for such slogans. It will also remove the unfortunate image of sounding a protest against "development plans". Holding this slogan is like hitting two birds with one stone – a protest against land grab, gerrymandering, and the urban development proclamation. It also gives confidence for others who plan to settle in Oromiya.

16. Ethiopia's Productive Safety Net Program: Chasing Two Rabbits, Catching Neither!

September 8, 2016 (AS)

Prolonged humanitarian assistance and recurrent emergency relief have created a dependency syndrome in Ethiopia. For over four decades, Ethiopian history has been inextricably linked with famine and disaster [1]. The country is often characterized as dependent on foreigners; and although successive Ethiopian governments have actively engaged in disaster risk management, disasters remain at the heart of Ethiopian politics.

In what sounded a very bold move to do away with dependency culture, the Ethiopian government launched the Productive Safety Net Program (PSNP) in 2005. This program has two key elements. First, Ethiopia's humanitarian aid has traditionally been channeled to beneficiaries through a large number of independently operating bilateral and multilateral agencies. However, the financing of the PSNP was designed to create a pool of funds coming from disparate sources and then channel them to target beneficiaries in a coordinated manner. Secondly, the expressions "productive" and "safety net" imply that the program will finance not only "consumption" but also "asset creation" and hence ultimately enhance Ethiopia's food security.

In other words, the PSNP is designed to accomplish one additional objective, asset creation, with the same amount of resource that would have been committed to finance only final consumption of target beneficiaries.

This piece sets out to seek answers to two interrelated questions: to what extent has the PSNP contributed to reduction in Ethiopia's dependency on humanitarian assistance? And has PSNP really achieved its two-pronged objectives? But first I will provide a brief program description and then proceed to its assessment.

PSNP Synopsis

The PSNP is an initiative by the Government of Ethiopia (GoE) to change from ad hoc emergency relief oriented toward welfare to a production inducing development activity. The government designed PSNP in partnership with multilateral organizations, bilateral donors and non-governmental organizations actively engaged in humanitarian assistance. The program did not replace emergency relief, but it supplemented the existing National Food Security Program (FSP).

PSNP has three specific objectives. The first one is *smoothening household consumption* by bridging the gap between production and consumption among chronically food insecure farming household. The second is *protecting household assets*, by reducing asset depletion and hence vulnerability of poor households during droughts. The third objective is *creating community assets* by engaging participants in productivity-enhancing public works. These are reinforced with two principles: *predictability* of flows of funds and *avoiding dependency* by linking transfers to labor services in public works. The program provides Direct Support to households who cannot provide "labor services", mainly the elderly and disabled.

Chronically food insecure households have been identified in famine-prone areas of rural Ethiopia. The program started covering 192 districts and 4.5 million beneficiaries. The size of the program expanded over the years both in geographic coverage and number of beneficiaries – 318 districts and 8.3 million beneficiaries in 2015 [2].

Long Hands

Be that as it may, a cursory look through PSNP's organogram would prompt one to seriously question whether or not Ethiopia is really a federally constituted country. One expects regional authorities to spearhead programs like PSNP, because they are best placed to more quickly observe looming droughts and more effectively manage emergency relief operation.

However, Ethiopia's federal government designed the governance of PSNP in such a way that its long hands would do everything, leaving no room for regional authorities in decision making. The Ministry of Agriculture is assigned the overall responsibility in planning and implementation; the Disaster Risk Management and Food Security Sector is tasked with overall program coordination; the Food Security Coordination Directorate facilitates the day-to-day management and coordination of the PSNP; the Natural Resource Management Directorate provides coordination and oversight of the public works; and the Ministry of Finance and Economic Development oversees financial management, including disbursement of funds according to plans supplied by the MOA.

These federal implementation arrangements are replicated within the eight regions and 318 districts covered by the PSNP. Regional and district bodies are also responsible for multi-sectoral coordination of the public works. One would normally expect that the overall planning and coordination in each region would be assigned to regional governments and then the sectoral ministries would be tasked to provide technical supports. This reality is put upside down – it is the regional states that receive orders from sectoral ministries.

Food Insecurity Worsened

How does the program logic that PSNP would contribute to food production and hence food security would apply in practice? The underlying conflicts in PSNP design can become clear if we look into ways in which the PSNP has actually caused food insecurity to move from bad to worse.

The public works are designed to contribute to environmental improvements, changing the ecology of areas that have suffered recurrent droughts and hence famine over several decades. However, the program designers have grossly underestimated the length of time required for investments in public works to yield fruit. The ultimate benefit from public works comes with long time lags. Environmental regeneration may gradually lead to some change in the microclimate to induce rain so that sustainable local food production would become a reality. It is likely that public works would not induce local food production in any immediate future.

The conflicts in food security objectives over different time horizons were the most fundamental flaws in the PSNP program design. PSNP probably enhances food security in the very long run, but it certainly reduces food availability in the short to medium run. This becomes clearer if we examine the adverse effects of PSNP on food security through re-allocation of agricultural labor. One does not need to be an agronomist to appreciate how any diversion of labor from farming activities can reduce agricultural output.

It is one thing to create employment opportunities for people who remain idle during disaster periods, when farmers could not undertake farming activities because of lack of rain. However, it is an entirely different matter altogether to engage millions of farmers, whose job is food production, with public works even during seasons with favorable weather. Confusing these two conditions seem to have proven a fatal mistake.

It is claimed that attempts have been made to minimize public work during sowing seasons, July to September, by restricting activities to the post-harvest seasons, January to May. However, this only displays astonishing extents of ignorance among program designers about Ethiopian agriculture. Farmers do not just walk to the fields to sow seeds. Land preparation and threshing the soil takes place months before sowing season arrives. Besides, the months immediately after sowing are busy seasons for weeding crop fields.

Farmers would always experience acute shortage of labor during peak harvest or sowing seasons. It is untenable to argue that participants in public works are vulnerable farmers who may have smaller plots and hence may not contribute much to food production. The diversion of farm labor can still cause damage even in this case because it is common in rural areas for the relatively better off farmers to employ local laborers. Community level food production critically depends on a pool of labor locally available.

Here we are not talking about a marginal diversion of labor away from food production. The average number of working days that PSNP participating [3] households have annually spent on public works ranged between 104 in Oromia to 155 in Tigray. Critically, even during sowing season, on average participation in public works were 21 days in 2007 and 31 in 2009.

It is not straightforward to establish the exact number of working days, particularly given the regional variations due to religious and cultural holidays. Elsewhere in the world, the total number of working days in a year is around 220. If we go by this conservative estimate, then it means PSNP beneficiaries have spent 47% to 70% of their labor time on public works. Since the number of program participants is given in several millions, exorbitant agricultural person-days have been diverted from food production every year since the launch of the PSNP. No wonder then the country's food security has worsened.

A further complication in food security issues lie in possible inflationary effects of PSNP. This is related to disturbances to food prices due to induced imbalances between food supply and demand. PSNP inevitably reduced food production. Cash transfers to beneficiary households inevitably turning food sellers to food purchasers. The end result is food inflation. It defies belief that such obvious facts escaped from the attention of the donors who keep pouring billions of dollars on this program.

Welfare Deteriorated

The analysis so far has been confined to country level outcomes of the PSNP program. Now we turn our attention to examining how "beneficial" the program has been to the "beneficiaries". It is useful to look into extents of unfairness in the payments for their labor contribution. For participants in public works, daily wage rate started with birr 6 in 2005 and remained stagnant at that level until 2008, when it increased to birr 8, and finally rising to birr 10 in 2009.[4]

Stagnant nominal wage rate means rapidly declining real wage, given the alarmingly increasing inflation over the years. Given program fund comes in hard currency terms, it is legitimate to anchor wage payments to variations in the value of the local currency with the USD. Between 2005 and 2016, the exchange rate of the birr against the USD declined by 163%, but the wage payment barely moved from its original position.

The above analysis is based on data obtained from program

documents and then used by independent program evaluators. However, if we use survey data and calculate average person-days with total payments for specific years, then we get a different figure. For instance, a survey conducted by IFPRI indicated that daily wage rates varied significantly across the regions, ranging between birr four and seven in 2007 and four and nine in 2009. [3]

The miserably low wage rate paid under PSNP is perhaps a tenth of the prevailing labor market rate in rural Ethiopia. There is an opportunity cost to households supplying labor to the government for public works. This comes not just in terms of missed opportunities to engage in their normal duty as farmers, but also the alternative of supplying their labor to the private sector at the prevailing wage rate. Program participants are highly likely to have experienced incalculable welfare losses.

Program Evaluation Dodged

There is a very strong rationale to subject the implementation of PSNP to some scrutiny through independent evaluation. It is not enough to report the number of people who have had "access" to the program. What would need to be evaluated are: "concrete and measureable" changes in the livelihood of beneficiary households, particularly change in their behavior in terms of seeking humanitarian assistance; and changes in environmental outcomes, visible effects of the program on the natural environments of the districts covered by this program. PSNP is meant to detach Ethiopia from dependency syndrome. The program has been in place for over a decade and it is time to show concrete outcomes indicating that Ethiopia is becoming less and less dependent on humanitarian aid.

However, there has been fundamental flaws in the way PSNP monitoring and evaluation has been approached. Not only is the responsibility of administering and governing PSNP lies in the hands of the Ethiopian government, but also, bizarrely enough, the donor community has effectively left the responsibility of monitoring and evaluation to the Ethiopian government. A Program appraisal document by the World Bank to justify PSNP 4 (2015-2020) stated that: "… impact evaluation surveys will be done using single source selection [5]. The Central Statistics Agency (CSA) is the only agency qualified and capable to undertake such big national surveys in Ethiopia. … [T]he development of the survey methodology is likely to require raw data from several prior CSA surveys, both for selecting sample *Kebeles* and for calculating household sample size. The types of data needed to design the survey are made available only for use in surveys carried out by CSA…. CSA shall be engaged to carry out the baseline and impact evaluation surveys under PSNP 4."

CSA is a government agency and its staff would have a vested interest in collecting and organizing information to show "success". CSA would collect data from civil servants working with branches of sectoral ministries at different levels in PSNP governance structure. The assessment of staff promotions would strictly depend on their ability to successfully implement programs like PSNP. Therefore, regardless of the extent of sophistication in survey design, the content of information collected by CSA is bound to be biased toward success. What matters is who has the power to influence the way data is collected and organized, not who would analyze the data and write reports. PSNP needs genuinely independent and impartial program evaluators who would handle the process of information collection, organization, analysis, and interpretation.

Dependency Syndrome Aggravated

In the absence of credible monitoring and evaluation mechanism, we resort to using deductive methods to infer the extent to which PSNP has led to reduction in Ethiopia's dependency on humanitarian aid. This can be assessed in a very straightforward manner – by examining key indicators such as changes in humanitarian aid metrics – year-on-year changes in the number of people dependent on humanitarian aid, geographical coverage, and sizes of funds.

PSNP was launched in 2005 with USD \$203 million budget, supporting 4.5 million target beneficiaries in 192 districts [4]. The program has steadily expanded over the years with the number of beneficiaries reaching 7.6 million in 2012 and 8.3 million in 2015_[2]. Similarly, annual program budget averaged around \$310 (2005-2009) and \$460 (2010-2014). The corresponding figures for PSNP 4 (2015-2020) is planned to be more than double the amounts at the launch of PSNP – number of beneficiaries further rising to 10 million and budget moving up to a whopping \$720 per annum [6].

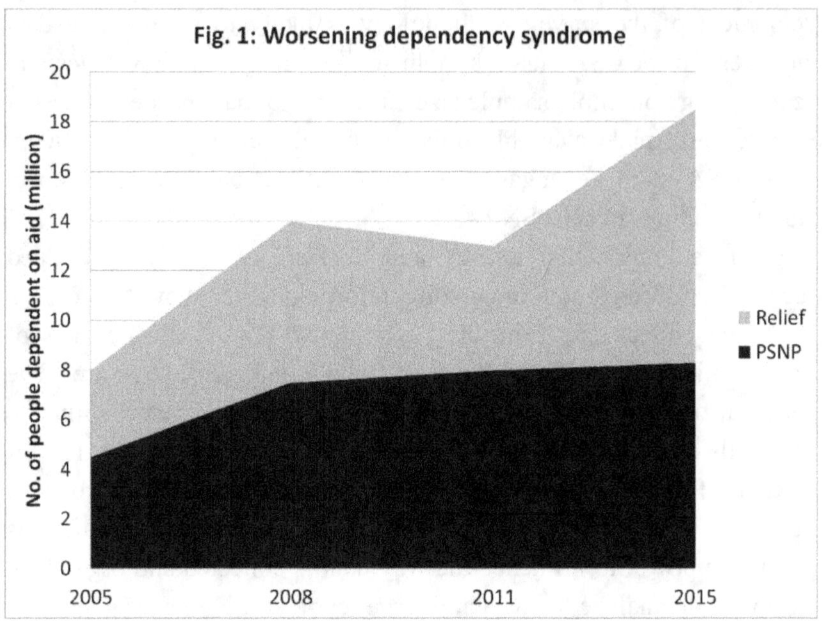

Has emergency aid declined since the launch of PSNP? Fig. 1 indicates that there is no sign of ad hoc emergency aid falling [7]. If anything the situation has gotten worse over the years [8]. In 2005, the number of people relying on humanitarian assistance was about 8 million (PSNP and relief were 4.5 and 3.5 respectively). These figures rose to 8.3 million and 10.2 million respectively in 2015. In other words, the number of PSNP dependency has doubled while that of relief dependency tripled.

In a PSNP assessment study published in 2013, Desalegn Rahmato of Forum for Social Studies compared year-on-year changes in emergency fund requests and actual donations between 2005 and 2011 [9]. The receipts were on average only 1% of the total funds it requested. This means the authorities have displayed an insatiable appetite for aid money. This totally contradicts the spirit with which the PSNP was launched.

Back to Square One

At PSNP design stage there were intense debates and significant disagreements among the donor community on the basic principles of the Safety Net Program. It was reported that "the most prevalent debate centered on whether the safety net should be primarily *protective* or *productive* [4]. Some donors opposed the idea of a productive safety net that forced poor people to labor on public works projects, while the Government opposed unconditional social transfers out of concern that this would create disincentives for households to improve their livelihoods and ultimately foster dependency on external assistance," according to a WB document.

The Ethiopian government seems to have forced the donor communities to give in. There was a hidden political ploy behind a façade of Ethiopian government's "steadfast commitment" to shift from "protective" to "productive" humanitarian aid. Desalegn Rahmato concurs with Human Rights Watch (2010) report that the Ethiopian government used PSNP to reward its supporters or punish those who rally behind the opposition. It is highly likely that the Ethiopian government's motivation to initiate the PSNP was to use it as a political weapon. It would prove useful to remember the timing of the PSNP launch – 2005, a watershed year in Ethiopia's political history during the EPRDF era.

At the time, donors resolved to stop providing development aid to the Ethiopian government due to the debacles in the aftermath of the general election. However, donors declared they would continue to provide emergency relief aid to save lives when disasters occur. It should be recalled that the ominous prospect of development aid drying up infuriated the EPRDF regime, who suddenly shifted to an aggressive mode. This was expressed in terms of banning local NGOs from using donor funds and restricting the operations of foreign NGOs, that is to say a pre-emptive strike that made "protective" aid unworkable.

PSNP was simply a variant but scaled up version of such actions, with which the Ethiopian authorities intimidated multilateral and bilateral donors to allow "productive" or development aid by other means. Clearly, donors were caught between a rock and a hard place. It was clear that the Ethiopian authorities would not budge on their position, even if that would mean lives would perish. Consequently, donors had to yield to the demands of the Ethiopian government, effectively handing over aid money and letting the authorities use it more or less unconditionally. That is how PSNP funds have begun to be used as a source of financing wages and salaries of Ethiopia's bloating civil service. The double-pronged strategy to simultaneously achieve "protective" and "productive" goals using PSNP funds was nothing more than a window dressing.

References

[1] Sue Lautze, Angela Raven-Roberts and Teshome Erkineh. Humanitarian governance in Ethiopia. Humanitarian Practice Network (HPN), July 2009 http://odihpn.org/magazine/humanitarian-governance-in-ethiopia/

[2] World Bank. Building Resilience, Creating Sustainable Solutions to Food Insecurity February 3, 2016. http://www.worldbank.org/en/news/feature/2016/02/03/building-resilience-creating-sustainable-solutions-to-food-insecurity

[3] IFPRI/EDRI. Ethiopia Strategy Support ProgramII (ESSPII) Evaluation Of Ethiopia's Food Security Program: Documenting Progress in the Implementation of the Productive Safety Nets Programme and the Household Asset Building Program ESSP II EDRI Report http://essp.ifpri.info/files/2013/05/ESSPII_EDRI_Report_PSNP.pdf

[4] World Bank. Ethiopia - Designing and implementing a rural safety net in a low income setting : lessons learned from Ethiopia's Productive Safety Net Program 2005-2009. January 2010. http://documents.worldbank.org/curated/en/247601469672211732/Ethiopia-Designing-and-implementing-a-rur

[5] World Bank. Ethiopia - Third Adaptable Program Loan Productive Safety Net Project (English). Sept 2009. http://documents.worldbank.org/curated/en/2009/09/11185686/ethiopia-third-adaptable-program-loan-productive-safety-net-project

[6] Ethiopia Productive Safety Net Program phase 4 (PSNP 4) https://assets.publishing.service.gov.uk/government/uploads/system/uploads/attachment_data/file/575366/Ethiopia-PSNP4-Dec-2016.pdf

[7] Courtenay Cabot Venton, Tenna Shitarek, Lorraine Coulter, Olivia Dooley. The Economics of Early Response and Resilience: Lessons from Ethiopia. May 2013
https://www.gov.uk/government/uploads/system/uploads/attachment_data/file/226157/TEERR_Ethiopia_Report.pdf

[8] FEWSNET. Ethiopia: Drought - 2015-2018.
http://reliefweb.int/disaster/dr-2015-000109-eth

[9] Dessalegn Rahmato, Alula Pankhurst, Jan-Gerrit van UffelenFood Security, Safety Nets and Social Protection in Ethiopia.
http://www.africanbookscollective.com/books/food-security-safety-nets-and-social-protection-in-ethiopia

17. History Repeating Itself in the Horn of Africa: is the Crime in Darfur Being Replicated in Eastern and Southern Oromia Regional State of Ethiopia?

April 10, 2017(AS)

It is saddening to witness repetitions of similar tragic events in history. Recurrences of such dreadful events can even sound farcical when they happen in a very short span of both time and space. This is exactly what is currently happening in the Horn of Africa. It is barely over a decade since the height of the Darfur genocide. One would hope that the international community has been well informed to avoid repetition of Darfur like tragedy anywhere in the world. However, it is depressing to observe that the Darfur crisis is in the process of being replicated in Ethiopia.

In this piece, I will explain how the scale of the crisis unfolding in Ethiopia's Eastern and Southern regions (and those brewing up in other regions) can have a potential to dwarf the Darfur crisis. The Janjaweed militia (in the case of Sudan) and the so-called Liyyu police (in the case of Ethiopia) are the catalysts for the crisis in their respective regions. For this reason, I will focus my analysis on explaining missions and functions of these two proxy militias.

Sudan's Janjaweed – Devils on Horseback

In order to draw a parallel between the Darfur and Eastern Oromia, it would prove useful to recap the Janjaweed story. *Janjaweed* literally means devils on horseback presumably because the Janjaweed often arrived riding horses while raiding and wreaking havoc in villages belonging to non-Arab ethnic groups [1].

The origin of Janjaweed is rooted in a long established traditional conflict primarily over natural resources such as grazing rights and water control among the nomadic Arabized and the sedentary non-Arabized ethnic groups in Chad and Sudan. The Janjaweed militia were initially created as a *pan-Arab Legion* by the late Mohammed Gadafi in 1972 to tilt power balance in favor of the Arabized people of the region [1].

The key point to note here is that the origin of the Janjaweed as well as the conflict between Arabized and non-Arabized people in the region long predates the Darfur crisis which started in 2003.

The beginning of the Darfur crisis signified a confluence of the traditional conflict between ethnic groups with another strand of conflict in the region – the wider conflict between Sudanese national army and regional liberation movements, the Justice and Equality Movement (JEM), and the Sudan Liberation Movement/Army. The latter was still fighting to liberate what has now become South Sudan. In 2003, the government of Sudan encountered setbacks in its military operations against JEM and SPLA.

In its desperate attempt to overcome failures in military front and also cover up for its planned ethnic cleansing in Darfur, the Al-Bashir government applied divide and rule tactic, thereby merging the two strands of the conflicts into one. This was accomplished by organizing, training, arming and providing all necessary logistical support to the Janjaweed militia of the Arabized ethnic group in Darfur. This was how Al-Bashir's government has engineered ethnic cleansing and undertaken genocide in Darfur with a brutal efficiency, using the Janjaweed as a proxy militia group.

The number of people killed in Darfur was estimated to range between 178,000 to 462,000 [2]. Human rights groups have documented staggering number of rapes and mass evictions and destructions of livelihoods of millions of people in the region.

Ethiopia's Liyyu Police – Devils on Armored Vehicles

"Liyyu" is an Amharic expression to mean "special", so Liyyu police denotes a "special police". If the Janjaweed are devils on horseback, then Liyyu police can be described as demons maneuvering armored vehicles. It is instructive to examine why, where, and when the regime in Addis Ababa has created Liyyu police.

The Liyyu police was created in 2008 in the Somali People's Regional State of the ethnically constituted federal government of Ethiopia [3]. It is important to note that like any other regional state, the Somali Regional State (SRS henceforth) has a regular police force of its own. But why was a special police required only for SRS?

The key point is to recognize that Liyyu police is nothing but only a variant of the usual proxy politics that has riddled Ethiopia's political affair during the ruling EPRDF era. This special force has no separate existence and no life of its own as such but it is just a proxy militia purposely created to cover up for human right abuses that was being perpetrated by Ethiopia's National Defense Force (ENDF) but also planned to be intensified in its battles against the Ogaden National Liberation Front (ONLF).

The armed wing of ONLF, the Ogaden National Liberation Army (ONLA), has been engaged in armed conflict with ENDF for many years. This conflict reached a turning point in April 2007 [4], when the ONLA raided an oil field and killed 74 ENDF soldiers and nine Chinese engineers. This was followed by frequent clashes between ONLA and ENDF. The conflicts have led to gross human rights violations in the region at a scale unheard before. In its report of early 2008, the *Human Rights Watch* accused the ENDF for committing summary executions, torture, and rape in Ogaden and has called for donors to take necessary measures to stop crimes against humanity.

In an article entitled "Talking Peace in the Ogaden: The search for an end to conflict in the Somali Regional State (SRS) in Ethiopia", author Tobias Hagmann observes that the creation of Liyyu police is essentially "indigenization of confrontation" [6]. In other words, the government in Ethiopia established Liyyu police to create a façade that human rights violations in Ogaden and its neighboring regional state are "local conflicts".

This was done pretty much in similar fashion with Sudanese government that resorted to countering freedom fighters in Darfur through the Janjaweed militia. However, unlike the Janjaweed which were already in place, the government in Ethiopia had to assemble the Liyyu police from scratch, applying doggy recruitment methods, including giving prisoners the choice between joining Liyyu police or remaining in jail. The founder and leader of Liyyu Police was none other than the current President of SRS, Abdi Mohammed Omar, known as "Abdi Illey", who was security chief at the time [7].

The size of Liyyu militia is estimated to have grown considerably over the years, currently standing at approximately around 42,000 [8]. However, any debate over the size of Liyyu police is essentially a superfluous argument, given that there is a very blurred line between ENDF and Liyyu police. After all, it requires an expert eye to distinguish between the military fatigues of the two groups.

It has been proven time and again that ENDF soldiers often get engaged in military actions disguised as Liyyu police by simply changing their military uniform to that of Liyyu police. In fact, it is a misnomer to consider Liyyu police as a unit separately operating with different military command structure within the Ogaden region. For all intent and purposes, if we ignore niceties, the Liyyu police is a battalion of Ethiopia's army operating in the region.

Fomenting Inter-Ethnic Conflict

Liyyu police is a special force with a dual purpose. The first purpose has already highlighted Liyyu as a camouflage for atrocities being committed by ENDF in the SRS, to relegate such atrocities to a "local affair", as if it is internal conflict between Somalis themselves.

Liyyu's second purpose is to aggravate the already existing traditional conflicts between Somalis and Oromos over pasture and water resources. ONLA in Ogaden and Oromo Liberation Army, OLA (the military wing of the outlawed Oromo Liberation Front – OLF) have frustrated the Ethiopian army for decades. While OLA has had support all over Oromia, it has traditionally been most active in Eastern and Southern Oromia – Oromia's districts bordering with the SRS.

Therefore, the EPRDF government realized that it could ride on existing traditional conflicts through a proxy militia to fight two liberation fronts. This was carbon copy of how things were done in Darfur, indicating how dictators learn from each other. Except that the EPRDF had to create Liyyu police from scratch, it acted in similar fashion with the way the Bashir government used the Janjaweed militia in Darfur.

Oromo and Somali herdsmen have traditionally clashed over grazing and water resources but such conflicts have always short-lived due to effective conflict resolution mechanisms practiced by local elders on both sides. These conflict resolution systems have evolved over centuries of peaceful coexistence between the two communities. The EPRDF government's divide and rule strategy has long targeted to change this equilibrium, and exploit the existing conflict to its advantage.

Conflicts have traditionally arisen when herds arrived at water holes, leading to confrontations as to whose cattle get served first, essentially a conflict over "resource use", rather than "resource ownership". Conflicts flare up often among the youth but they were immediately put under control by the elders. Besides, each side are equally equipped with simple tools such as traditional sticks or simple ammunitions, so there has always been power equilibrium. But the regime sought an effective means of aggravating these conflicts by transforming them in to a permanent one.

Such manipulation of the situation was done essentially in two ways. First, supplying deadly modern military equipment, training and military logistics to Liyyu police, thereby destabilizing the existing power balance. Second, and critically, by changing the nature of the conflict from "use rights" to "ownership" of the resource itself. The conflicts were engineered to be elevated from clashes between individual members of communities to that between Somali and Oromo people at a higher scale.

The seeds for conflicts were sown in the process of redrawing borders along adjacent districts of the Somali and Oromia regional states. In this process, the number of contested *Kebeles*, the lowest administrative units in Ethiopia, were made to suddenly proliferate. Over a decade ago, the number of such contested *kebeles* already escalated to well over 400 [9] . In order to resolve disputes between the two regional states, a referendum was held in October 2004 in 420 *kebeles* along 12 districts or five zones of the Somali Region.

The outcome of the referendum was that Oromia won 80% of the disputed *kebeles* and SRS won the remaining *kebeles*. Critically, regardless of the outcome, severe damage was already done to durable good-will in community relationships due to purposeful manipulation of the process by the regime in Addis Abeba before, during and after the referendum [10].

Once the referendum results were known, all the dark forces bent on divide and rule needed to do was to nudge the Somalis to claim that the vote were rigged during the referendum and hence they should aim to get their territory back by other means, that is to say by force and the Liyyu police was created to do the job.

Since it came into existence, Liyyu's operations have often overlapped but with varying degrees of intensities across its dual-purposes. During its first phase, Liyyu police focused on operations within Somali region. These operations had much less to do with fighting ONLA but raiding villages and drying up popular support base of the ONLF, in the process committing gross human rights violations at a massive scale. Human rights organizations have widely documented [11] arbitrary detentions, extrajudicial executions [12], rapes, tortures and ill-treatment of detainees in the region.

Over the years, however, Liyyu's operations have increasingly focused on the second pillar of the proxy militia's mission – cross border raids into Oromia. However, Liyyu's frequent raids into Oromia have not received enough attention from human rights organizations and hence atrocities committed by this proxy militia on Oromo communities over a decade or so has not been well documented. The authorities in Addis Abeba, who have purposefully sown seeds of conflict to aggravate traditional clashes, have often deliberately misreported Liyyu Police raids as "the usual fights" between Oromo and Somali herdsmen but nothing could be further from the truth.

In a desperate attempt to gain popular support from the Somali people, the Liyyu police military adventures have been conducted in the name of regaining territory the SRS lost to Oromia during the referendum of 2004. The evidence one could adduce for this is that every time Liyyu Police encroached into Oromia and occupied a village, they would immediately hoist the Somali flag [13] as a sign of declaring that territorial gains.

The proxy militia has done so after attacking and killing large number of civilians and displacing thousands of households in numerous districts in Eastern Oromia [14]: Qumbi, Mayu Mulluqe, Goohaa, Seelaa Jaajoo, and Miinoo. Liyyu Police overrun the town of Moyale in Southern Oromia resulting in the death of dozens of people and forcing tens of thousands to flee to Kenya. It was reported [15] that during an attack on Moyale town in Southern Oromia "the 4th army division [of ENDF] stationed just two miles outside the town center watched silently as the militia overrun the police station and ransacked the town. Then the militia was allowed safe passage to retreat after looting and burning the town while administrators of the Borana province who protested against the army complacency were thrown to jail."

Alliances and Counter-Alliances

The Oromo Peaceful protests erupted on 12th November 2015 [16] and then engulfed the nation, spreading to all corners of Oromia like a forest fire. Oromo Protests ignited Amhara resistance, and then ended up with Oromo-Amhara alliance. It became commonplace to see solidarity slogans on placards carried by protestors both in Amhara and Oromia. It should be noted that Oromo and Amhara population constitute well over two-third of Ethiopia's population.

It was historical acrimony and rivalry between these two dominant ethnic groups which provided a fertile ground for the divide and rule strategy so intensely practiced by the current regime which is dominated by the TPLF, the Tigrean People's Liberation Front. The Tigre ethnic group account for less than 6% of Ethiopia's population.

The Oromo-Amhara solidarity sent shock waves among the Tigrean ruling elites [17]. The Oromo Protest, Amhara Resistance and other popular protests elsewhere in Ethiopia exposed the fake nature of the coalition in the ruling party, the Ethiopian People's Revolutionary Front (EPRDF). It has always been an open secret that EPRDF essentially means TPLF (the Tigrean People Liberation Front).

The remaining parties, especially the OPDO (Oromo People's Democratic Party) was cobbled up in haste from prisoners of war when TPLF was approaching Addis Ababa to control power by ousting the military junta back in 1991. However, even the so-called OPDO – lately joined by the Amhara National Democratic Movement (ANDM) – felt empowered by the popular protests in their respective regions sending a clear sign that TPLF was about to be left naked with its garbs removed.

Now that the Tigreans realized that they cannot reply on dividing Oromo and Amhara any more, they resorted to another variant of divide and rule – fostering alliance between minorities to withstand the impending solidarity between the two majority ethnic groups. This strategic shift was elucidated by two most senior TPLF veterans, Abay Tsehaye and Seyoum Mesfin, in their two-part interview [18] conducted (in Amharic) with the government affiliated Fana Broadcasting Corporation.

The TPLF-dominated-EPRD's new strategy was to present the Oromo-Amhara coalition as a threat to the minority ethnic groups, such as Tigre and Somali. The regime has already experimented pitting minority against majority at different scales: Tigreans against the rest of Ethiopians at national scale, Somali against Oromo at regional scale, and many more similar fabricated divisions at regional and local levels in many communities across Ethiopia. What is new is the fact that these two relatively separate strands are explicitly brought together and extensively implemented at national scale.

In addition to the interview cited above, one can adduce more evidences to illustrate the new machination by the Tigre and Somali political and security alliance. For instance, there was an incidence in which Amhara popular uprising caused some ethnic Tigreans to get relocated from the Amhara regional state. What happened next raised eyebrows of many observers: Abdi Mohamoud Omar [19], SRS President who rules his people with iron fist, declared his cabinet's endorsement to "donate 10 million birr for displaced innocent Ethiopian people [Tigreans] from Gondar & Bahir Dar cities of the Amhara regional state".

Further evidence regarding the maneuvering of minority alliance with deadly intent comes from Aigaforum, a TPLF mouthpiece. In an article entitled "Liyyu Police: The Savior" [3], the website came up with the following jumbled up assertion: "they [Liyyu Police] are from the people and for the people of Somali region; to protect the honor and dignity of their own people and overall Security of the region, and Ethiopia at large. This special force has a mandate primarily to protect the people of [the] region, to secure and stabilize the aged conflict in Somali region of

Ethiopia. This Special force is not like a tribal militia from any specific clan or sub-clan in the region, rather they are holistic and governmental arms —who are well screened, registered and recruited from *kebeles* and *woredas* and trained [as per the] standards [of] Ethiopian military training package and armed with modern military equipment. Besides being regional state special forces; they are part and parcel of Ethiopian arm[y]."

In an overzealous effort to glorify the devilish proxy militia, aigaforum inadvertently exposes TPLF by admitting that actually Liyyu Police is part and parcel of the national army, a fact the TPLF politicians have never admitted in public.

Towards Full-Scale Atrocity?

The alliance between Tigre elites and Abdi Mohammed Omar's cabinet got manifested in the transformation of Liyyu police's mission from sporadic military excursions to full scale invasion of Oromia. This started by deploying Liyyu police in Oromia to attack and disburse peaceful protestors. For instance, based on eye witness accounts Land-info [8] reported that starting from January 2016 Liyyu Police was being used against Oromo demonstrators in many locations, including in Dire Dawa and Bededo.

By the third quarter of 2016, popular protests did not only intensify but literally covered most parts of the country. However, protests that were inherently peaceful were transformed into confrontations between the protestors and the security forces because the latter have already mowed down the lives of hundreds of innocent civilians during the previous months. In a desperate attempt to hang onto power, the TPLF dominated regime enacted a State of Emergency (SoE) on October 8, 2016 [21].

An essential component of the SoE is securitization of many regions and transport corridors in Ethiopia. Particularly, Oromia, the birth place of the latest popular protest, was literally converted into a "high security prison" and Oromos were effectively "put under house arrest". Oromia's regional government was made redundant, being replaced at all levels by Military Command Posts, a form of local and regional government by a committee of armed officers. This was exactly the way it has been for the most part of the previous two decades except that the SoE signaled a temporary move to direct control by the military, abandoning the all too familiar indirect controls through puppet civilian parties such as OPDO.

Soon after the SoE was enacted, Abdi Illey declared an all-out war and the Liyyu Police was unleashed on all fronts along the Oromia and SRS boundary, stretching over a total of close to 1200 km. According to information from the Oromia Regional State, the 14 districts affected in the latest wave of Liyyu Police invasion are: Qumbi, Cinaksan, Midhaga Tola, Gursum, Mayu Muluqe and Babile in East Hararghe; Bordode in West Hararghe; Dawe Sarar, Sawena, Mada Walabu and Rayitu in Bale; Gumi Eldelo and Liban in Guji; and Moyale in Borana.

It is highly significant to note that there is at least 500 km "as the-crow-flies" distance between Qumbi (extreme North East) and Moyale (extreme South West). Therefore, the sheer number of districts affected, the physical distances between them, and the simultaneous attacks at all fronts indicate that Liyyu's latest invasion of Oromia is a highly sophisticated and coordinated military adventure which can only be understood as planned by the TPLF-dominated regime's military central command.

The SoE was enacted with explicit intention of laying information blackout all over Ethiopia, particularly in the highly securitized Oromia Regional State. For this reason, it is difficult to obtain reliable estimates on victims of Liyyu's invasion of Oromia. Human Rights Watch (HRW) [20] has been receiving reports that dozens of casualties have been, including many civilians in Oromia but "[R]estrictions on access have made it difficult to corroborate details." Locals indicate [21] that Liyyu police have so far killed large numbers of civilians.

Oromo civilians have given up with the hope of getting any meaningful protection from ENDF, given that by now it has become an open secret that the latter is complicit in the invasion. Consequently, in a desperate act of survival, Oromos have organized a civilian defense force. Based on incidents of confrontation between Liyyu Police and Oromo civilian defense force around 23rd February 2017 in Southern Oromia, the Human Rights League for Horn of Africa (HRLHA) reported about 500 people were killed, over 200 injured [22].

If so much destruction has happened in a few days and few districts, then it is possible to imagine that wanton destructions must have been happening during several months of Liyyu police's occupation in all districts across the long stretch along the Oromia-Somali region boundaries. Opride, an online media, reported: "Mothers and young girls have been gang raped, according to one Mayu resident, who spoke to OPride by phone [13]. He said the attacking Liyu Police were fully armed and they moved about in armored vehicles brandishing machine guns and other heavy weapons. They stole cattle, goats, camels and other properties."

Publicity and Accountability

When it comes to publicity and awareness, Darfur and Eastern Oromia can only be contrasted. Although it did not lead to avoiding large-scale atrocities, the international community got involved in the case of Darfur at much early stage of the crisis. On the contrary, it is well over a decade now since Abdi Illey's Liyyu police began rampaging in Ogaden as well as Oromia but the international community has chosen to turn a blind eye to the regional crisis, which has gained momentum and now nearly getting out of control.

Perhaps the reason gross human rights violations by Liyyu Police has been ignored or tolerated by the international community lies in the fact that some donors have been directly implicated in financing and supporting [23] the paramilitary group. For instance, the British Press has repeatedly accused DFID for wasting UK tax payer money on providing training to the Somali Liyyu Police [24]. Similarly, there are evidences to suggest that the notorious proxy militia has also been funded by the US government [25]. It is no wonder then that the UK, US, and the rest of the international community have ignored for so long the unruly Liyyu Police's military adventures in Ogaden and Oromia.

Last week, the HRW released a report entitled Ethiopia: No Justice in Somali Region Killings [7]. This report is timely in raising awareness of the general public as well as drawing the attention of authorities in the UK and the US, who are most directly implicated with financing the militia group. However, I would hasten to add that what has been lacking is the political will to act and curb the activities of Liyuu police. Starting from 2008 the HRW has released numerous similar reports but this did not stop the atrocities the paramilitary group is committing from escalating over the years.

The HRW's report asserting that "Paramilitary Force Killed 21,

Detained Dozens, in June 2016", indicates that the report is anchored on an incident that happened in SRS about ten months ago. Although the focus of the report was on the particular incident in SRS, it has also highlighted Liyyu Police's latest atrocities in Oromia. As indicated in the report, the SoE related movement restrictions means the HRW had to release the report on the incidence in SRS with ten months delay.

Clearly, HRW and other human rights organizations could not undertake any meaningful independent assessment on the damages caused by the latest invasion into Oromia. The point here is that while HRW has been grabbling with conducting inquiries into a case in which dozens of people were killed or detained in SRS in mid-2016, Liyyu police has killed and abducted hundreds in Oromia since the start of 2017.

The TPLF dominated EPRDF regime in Addis Abeba has long started sowing the seeds of divide and rule strategy coupled with deliberate acts of fomenting conflicts between different communities. The motivation is pretty clear –it is an act of survival, a minority rule can sustain itself only if it turned other ethnic groups against each other. The case of Liyyu Police and its latest invasion of Oromia fits into that scheme.

If not addressed timely and decisively, Liyyu Police's invasion of Oromia has a potential to turn into a full-blown atrocities that is likely to dwarf what happened in Darfur. Clearly, the tell-tale signs are already in place. Genocide Watch [26], the international alliance to end genocide, states that "Genocide is always organized, usually by the state, often using militias to provide deniability of state responsibility (the Janjaweed in Darfur.) Sometimes organization is informal (Hindu mobs led by local RSS militants) or decentralized (terrorist groups.) Special army units or militias are often trained and armed. Plans are made for genocidal killings."

In Ethiopia, this situation on the ground is rapidly changing and it requires an urgent response from the international community.

References

[1] Janjaweed. https://en.wikipedia.org/wiki/Janjaweed

[2] Olivier Degomme and Debarati Guha-Sapir Patterns of mortality rates in Darfur conflict. Volume 375, ISSUE 9711, P294-300,

January 23, 2010. DOI:https://doi.org/10.1016/S0140-6736(09)61967-X

[3] Ahmed Deeq Hussein. Liyu Police: The Savior. http://aigaforum.com/article2016/Liyu-Police.pdf

[4] Raid on Abole oil exploration facility. https://en.wikipedia.org/wiki/Abole_oil_field_raid

[5] Human Rights Watch. Ethiopia: Army Commits Executions, Torture, and Rape in Ogaden. Donors Should Act to Stop Crimes Against Humanity. June 12, 2008. https://www.hrw.org/news/2008/06/12/ethiopia-army-commits-executions-torture-and-rape-ogaden

[6] Tobias Hagmann 2014. Talking Peace in the Ogaden: The search for an end to conflict in the Somali Regional State in Ethiopia. London: Rift Valley Institute.

[7] Human Rights Watch. Ethiopia: No Justice in Somali Region Killings. April 5, 2017. https://www.hrw.org/news/2017/04/05/ethiopia-no-justice-somali-region-killings

[8] Query response Ethiopia: The special police (Liyu Police) in the Somali Regional State. June 2016. http://www.landinfo.no/asset/3404/1/3404_1.pdf

[9] Jon Abbink, Tobias Hagmann (eds.) 2013. Reconfiguring Ethiopia: The Politics of Authoritarian Reform. London and New York: Routledge

[10] Oromia Region. https://en.wikipedia.org/wiki/Oromia_Region

[11] Graham Peebles. Under darkness in the Somali region of Ethiopia. April 2013. http://www.redressonline.com/2013/04/under-darkness-in-the-somali-region-of-ethiopia/

[12] Human Rights Watch. Ethiopia: 'Special Police' Execute 10: Investigate Paramilitary Abuses, Permit Access to Closed-Off Somali

Region. May 2012. https://www.hrw.org/news/2012/05/28/ethiopia-special-police-execute-10

[13] Liyu police raids in Oromia testing Ethiopia's semblance of calm. Opride.com. March 5, 2017. https://www.opride.com/2017/03/05/liyu-police-raids-oromia-testing-ethiopias-semblance-calm/

[14] Oromo: Militia Attacks Villages In Eastern Oromia. Jan 18, 2013. http://unpo.org/article/15380

[15] Ethiopia: Militia Attacks Villages In Eastern Oromia. Ethiopiatimes. January 18, 2013. https://ethiopiantimes.wordpress.com/tag/liyu-police/

[16] Oromo protests: defiance amidst pain and suffering. Addis Standard, December 16. 2015. http://addisstandard.com/oromo-protests-defiance-amidst-pain-and-suffering/

[17] VOANews. Ethiopia Protests Highlight Growing Solidarity Between Oromia, Amhara Regions http://www.voanews.com/a/ethiopia-protests-oromia-amhara-regions/3457240.html

[18] Abay Tsehaye and Seyoum Mesfin on Current Issue Part 1 Sep 2016 (Video Archive) https://www.youtube.com/watch?v=PKf3e-fsXgQ

[19] Ahmed Deeq Hussein. Why Do We Justify the 10 Million Birr Donation to Displaced Innocent Tigriyans by the Ethio-Somali Region. Awuramba Times. September 5, 2016. http://www.awrambatimes.com/?p=15349

[20] Human Rights Watch. Legal Analysis of Ethiopia's State of Emergency. October 30, 2016 https://www.hrw.org/news/2016/10/30/legal-analysis-ethiopias-state-emergency

[21] Despite nationwide state of emergency, several border

incursions leave more than 100 dead in east and south east Ethiopia. Addis Standard March 3, 2017. http://addisstandard.com/news-despite-nationwide-state-emergency-several-border-incursions-leave-100-dead-east-south-east-ethiopia/

[22] HRLHA War Human The Ethiopian Government is Plotting a War Among the Nations and Nationalities in Ethiopia. February 27, 2017. https://ademmisoma24.wordpress.com/2017/02/27/hrlha-war-human-the-ethiopian-government-is-plotting-a-war-among-the-nations-and-nationalities-in-ethiopia/

 [23] British aid 'to fund Ethiopian paramilitaries' accused of rape, murder and torture. The Daily Mail, January11, 2013. http://www.dailymail.co.uk/news/article-2260882/British-aid-fund-Ethiopian-paramilitaries-accused-rape-murder-torture.html

[24] Ben Quinn. UK tenders to train Ethiopian paramilitaries accused of abuses. The Guardian, January 10, 2013. https://www.theguardian.com/world/2013/jan/10/ethiopia-forces-human-rights-funding

[25] Ali Mohamed. Ethiopia: it is time to stop the reign of terror of the Liyu Police. The Hill. June 28, 2016. http://the hill.com/blogs/congress-blog/foreign-policy/285060-ethiopia-it-is-time-to-stop-the-reign-of-terror-of-the

[26] Gregory H. Stanton, President, Genocide Watch. The 8 Stages of Genocide
http://www.genocidewatch.org/genocide/8stagesofgenocide.html

18. Mo Ibrahim Foundation's Report on Ethiopia's Unemployment: Alternative Facts?

April 28, 2017(OP)

In a recent report entitled Africa at a Tipping Point[1], the Mo Ibrahim Foundation presented Ethiopia as the brightest spot – an African success story in maintaining low and stable youth unemployment rate. The report was then rehashed [2] by Quartz Africa reporter, Lynsey Chutel, as "youth unemployment is a problem all over Africa, except for one country" – Ethiopia. The Mo Ibrahim Foundation (MIF) maintained that:

> While the continent's general unemployment and youth unemployment rates were 8 percent and 13 percent in 2016, these figures were significantly lower in the case of Ethiopia (5.7 percent and 8.1 percent, respectively).

The rosy assessment in the MIF report has raised eyebrows of many observers who are familiar with the dire state of youth unemployment in Ethiopia. The report does not only contradict the official storyline but it is also factually flawed. In this piece, I will present a comprehensive and consistent set of data on Ethiopia's unemployment and then indicate the extent to which the MIF report has misrepresented and misinterpreted data on Ethiopia's youth unemployment.

Contradictions

Ethiopian authorities must be the ones most baffled by the MIF report.

High youth unemployment has been a topical storyline of the Ethiopian government in recent months, particularly in the context of addressing the ongoing upheaval in the country. Ethiopia has been rocked by popular protests over the past two years. Protests in the populous Oromia region, which began around April 2014, have also expanded to the Amhara region. Whereas the protests are rooted in a wide ranging political and economic discontents, authorities in Addis Ababa have squarely put the blame on the intolerably high youth unemployment. Therefore, MIF's findings are at odds with the Ethiopian government's own reports and assessments over the last 12 months.

One does not need to be a seasoned statistician or researcher to know Ethiopia has been suffering from high youth unemployment. It is enough to look at the large exodus of its youth, who are prepared to take unimaginable risks– walking across the Sahara desert and confronting high seas in the Mediterranean or the Red Sea to reach Europe or the Middle East.

The migration of Ethiopia's youth to Yemen continues unabated years after that country was plunged into civil war. The European Union has an ongoing agreement to fund local job creation across Africa to stem the flow of refugees to Europe. Ethiopia is one of the countries that EU has identified for this purpose.

Besides, the MIF report flies in the face of everything we know about unemployment in Ethiopia. It does not only contradict the official story line, but it also utterly lacks common sense. Far from being exceptional, Ethiopia actually has unemployment rate that is worse than Sub-Saharan Africa average.

The MIF researchers claim that Ethiopia is an exception in that the country's unemployment rate — both for the youth as well as general — are much lower than most other African countries. But it is not clear from where all these assertions emerge. On page 18 of the report, the International Monetary Fund (IMF) and International Labor Organization (ILO) are cited as data sources for generating a chart that was presented, indicating "smooth and stable" unemployment rate, between 5 and 6 for general unemployment, and between 7 and 8 per cents for youth unemployment. Importantly, this is presented as an "exception" by African standard. It is useful to say a few words about the data sources here. First, IMF_does not publish much data on African unemployment, one can find data for only six African countries, and Ethiopia is not one of them. In that case, the MIF report must have replied only on data obtained from ILO database.

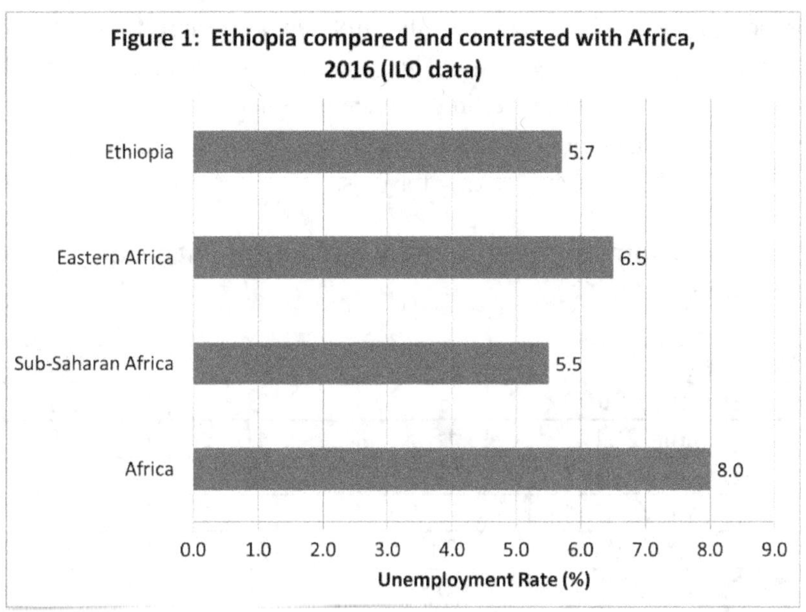

I will return to youth unemployment but for a moment let's focus on overall unemployment rate. I constructed Figure 1 (above) from the same ILO database. Ethiopia's overall unemployment was 5.7 percent in 2016 as reported by MIF. But MIF's assertion that Ethiopia is an exception is totally off mark. The African average is 8 percent, which means Ethiopia is very close to the regional average. Importantly, Ethiopia's average unemployment rate is slightly higher than the Sub-Saharan African average of 5.5 percent, but only slightly lower than the East African average. In fact, if we exclude Kenya, Ethiopia's unemployment is much higher than the Eastern Africa average. Therefore, the MIF report on Ethiopia is factually wrong. In other words, the right figure is used but it is wrongly interpreted and presented.

The Rural-Urban Divide

It is useful to deal with preliminary conceptual issues before we can discuss youth unemployment. In a developing economy, it does not make much sense to discuss *open unemployment in rural areas*. In fact, in development economics there is a different category of unemployment for it – *disguised unemployment*, or *underemployment*. Disguised unemployment simply means that people in rural areas, who are in working age group, mostly have something to do but a significant proportion do not have activities that fully engage them. In other words, they are employed only some of the times. So they are unemployed in some ways. However, that kind of unemployment is often hidden, since people do not have job centers to which they go and register themselves and declare that they are looking for jobs.

Table 1. Unemployment rate by age and location (selected African countries)

All ages (15+)	National	Rural	Urban
Ethiopia 2005	**8**	**3**	**21**
Namibia 2014	18	16	20
Ethiopia 2013	**5**	**2**	**17**
Zimbabwe 2011	5	1	15
Naigeria 2010	21	24	15
Zambia 2008	5	1	12
Malawi 2013	6	5	11
Uganda 2012	4	3	9
Tanzania 2014	2	1	5
Togo 2011	2	1	4
Youth (15-29)			
Ethiopia 2013	**7**	**3**	**23**
Ethiopia 2005	**4**	**1**	**19**
Sudan 2008	22	25	20
Egypt 2012	16	13	20
Malawi 2012	8	7	17
Tanzania 2005	6	2	17
Togo 2012	8	3	16
South Sudan 200	17	17	16
Zambia 2008	4	1	14
Uganda 2013	5	12	8

Sources: Ethiopia 2013: CSA 2014; Otherwise ILOSTAT

Unfortunately, it appears that novice researchers and policy practitioners applied the same concept of unemployment designed for economies such as UK, EU, and US to developing economies and then built it into the ILO labor force surveys. In Europe or the US, regardless of whether one is living in rural or urban areas, any working age person actively seeking jobs would register to seek some kind of job seekers allowances. Such systems are non-existent in economies like Ethiopia. In such circumstances, any discussion of unemployment should focus on urban unemployment, where job seeking can at least be more easily observed, even if not registered. Now, let us look at the details of unemployment in Ethiopia, classifying this joblessness by age, rural, and urban categories.

In order to facilitate comparison with Ethiopia, unemployment data for selected African countries is presented in Table 1. Except for *Ethiopia 2013*, data presented in the table are all compiled from the same source – ILO. Except for Ethiopia, although labor force data are not consistently available for all years, recent year data is available for latest years for most countries.

Ethiopia is the odd one out in that its data for rural and urban unemployment is available only for 2005. Hence, it is important to present data for another (latest) year for Ethiopia. This is done by relying on Ethiopia's Central Statistical Agency, (CSA 2014 [3], and *Analytical Report on the 2013 National Labor Force Survey, Summary Table 6.1 Unemployment Rate by Age group, Place of Residence and Sex, Country – Total 2013*). Since Ethiopia's data is presented for two years, which are 8 years apart, it is reasonable to compare them with data from the other countries.

In Table 1, data for both the all age and the youth unemployment groups are sorted by *urban unemployment* in *descending order*. This reveals some interesting facts. Starting with the all age group, Ethiopia is the worst in terms of urban unemployment: it ranks first with 21 percent in 2005 and third with 17 percent in 2013. In youth unemployment, a central point in the MIF report, Ethiopia's data for 2005 as well as 2013, rank first and second. *In fact, Ethiopia's urban youth unemployment has gotten worse, increasing from 19 percent in 2005 to 23 percent in 2013.*

Again, it does not make much sense to dwell on comparing rural unemployment, and by extension national unemployment, since unreliability of rural unemployment would logically make national unemployment figures unreliable. The latter is an average of rural and urban unemployment rates. Even if we consider rural data, Ethiopia still cannot be an exceptional case as MIF claims, since rural unemployment figures for Zambia, Tanzania, and Togo are about the same with that of Ethiopia.

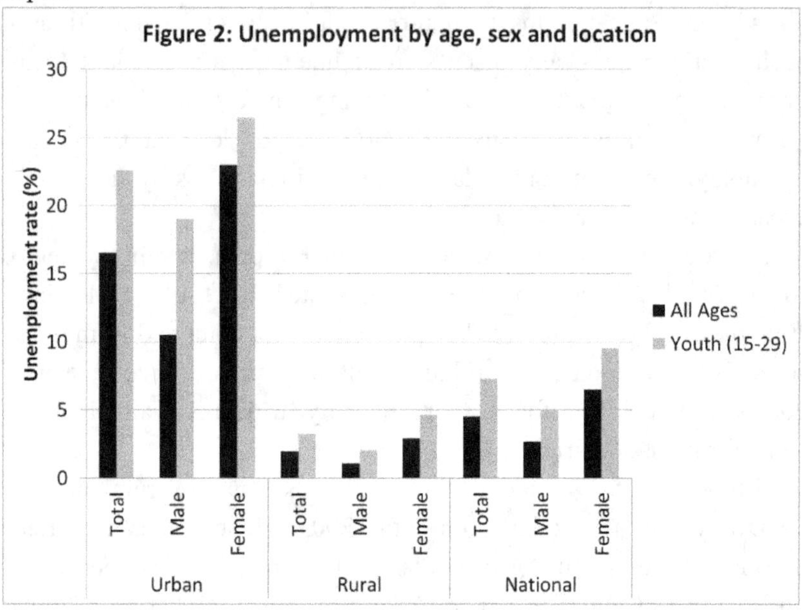

The Gender Imbalance

A closer look at Ethiopia's unemployment data is even more revealing. Figure 2 displays the gender dimension, in addition to the urban-rural divide displayed in Table 1. It is important to pay attention to the urban unemployment with its gender dimension. It is by far the most reasonable barometer of unemployment in Ethiopia, and any other developing economy for that matter. As shown in Figure 1, in 2013, total urban unemployment for all ages and the youth were 17 percent and 23 percent respectively.

Now let's look at the disaggregation of these rates across gender dimension. Urban male unemployment rates were 11 percent and 19 percent, while the corresponding figures for the young female were 23 percent and 26 percent. This means that one out of four working age young girls in urban Ethiopia looked for jobs but found none. The figures reported on rural unemployment rate can by no means be taken seriously.

CSA reports 2 percent unemployment (all working ages, 15+) and 3 percent (for the youth). Even female youth unemployment in Ethiopia's rural areas is reported to be 5 percent. These are not only fancy numbers but also irresponsible way of presenting facts.

Projected, Not Actual

It is established that the conditions of Ethiopia's unemployment is not as rosy as depicted in the MIF report. That Ethiopia's general unemployment rate in 2016 was reported as 5.7 percent in the ILO database is accurate but the MIF report misrepresented and misinterpreted this figure by stating that Ethiopia was an exceptional, success story. The country is not an exception, in fact it performs slightly worse than the Sub-Saharan African average. Facts about youth unemployment rate are completely distorted in the MIF report.

As discussed earlier, one struggles to get a satisfactory and consistent labor force data on Ethiopia in the ILO database. In fact, Ethiopia's labor force data is among the least frequently updated. It has been more than 12 years since Ethiopia submitted its labor force data to ILO. This raises the question: If Ethiopia's data is that much outdated, where did the figures in ILO database come from? This includes the 5.7 percent rate presented in in the MIF report.

When countries do not update their database, ILO uses a model to project and fill the gaps. The bulk of labor force statistics we read in ILO database are not actual but only projected figures. It is an unsound and strange projection for lots of years, relying on very few data points.

Ethiopia's socio-economic data is perhaps the most thoroughly manipulated in the world. In order to substantiate double digit growth all variables have to be systematically adjusted. Labor force data is among those that receive the most "severe treatment." After all, the best way to inflate GDP growth is to assume that the largest proportion of working age population is gainfully employed (that is to say unemployment is low), and hence everyone is engaged in creating material wealth.

In other words, GDP inflation amounts to declaring as if unemployed persons are actually receiving monthly wages. By accepting and endorsing Ethiopia's inflated GDP, donors and other members of the international community, like MIF, have taken a morally and ethically corrupted position, effectively being complicit in a cruel act of saying to the millions of unemployed Ethiopians: "go hungry, we won't recognize or validate your unemployment."

Ethiopian authorities appear adamant to hide the facts presented in figure 2, particularly, the *unrealistically* low rural unemployment. Urban unemployment itself is likely to be underestimated, but the official rural unemployment is rather laughable. But, for Ethiopian leaders, if rural unemployment is grossly underestimated, it pulls down the overall unemployment. The more "rural" a country is the larger influence the rural figures would have on the national average. Ethiopia is among the least urbanized countries in the world. With only 17 percent of the population living in urban areas, Ethiopia's ranks 196th out of 223 countries [4].

Yet using the dodgy 2013 official statistics (Figure 2), although urban youth unemployment was relatively high (23 percent), national (average) youth unemployment became only 7 percent simply because rural youth unemployment was reported as 3 percent. It is this fact that the authorities are uncomfortable with to frequently report the country's latest labor statistics. Instead, they found it convenient to report only the national average, hiding the embarrassingly low rural unemployment.

Saying the Right Thing for Wrong Reason

The Ethiopian authorities have become adept at churning out unrealistically low socioeconomic statistics. Unemployment figures are no exceptions. At the same time, they have the audacity to come out and declare unemployment in general and youth unemployment in particular as the most severe challenges and threats to Ethiopia's stability and security. But how can we explain this inconsistent position of the government in Ethiopia?

Authorities in Addis Ababa have perfected the art of deception over the years. They know very well that there is enough pool of gullible analysts around, like the MIF researchers, who do not take enough time to bring together different arguments and establish consistency. They run away with some headlines and arrive at hasty generalizations. And the regime in Addis Ababa has found this rather rewarding. After all, Ethiopia's current image as Africa's fastest growing non-oil economy was gained through statistical lies that got propagated, recycled in various global databases and became the basis for existing "knowledge" on Ethiopia.

The regime in Addis Ababa appears to have recognized that they do not even need to be consistent with their statistical lies. As such, when a few opportunities arose around unemployment, authorities could not resist the temptation to indulge in some inconsistencies.

The first opportunity was the EU pledge [5] to fund youth employment schemes in African countries in order to stop the exodus across the Sahara and the catastrophic incidences of death in the Mediterranean Sea. Sure enough Ethiopia became a beneficiary [6]. EU never bothered to check the official statistics, perhaps because they knew Ethiopia is a high unemployment country.

The second motivation for the authorities to depart from the previously held storyline and shift to high youth unemployment rhetoric was to distort the cause of the ongoing popular uprising in Ethiopia, which erupted in central Oromia and then spread to all corners of the country. The root causes of the Oromo protests and Amhara resistance are severe political repressions, multifaceted economic injustices and rampant corruption. In a desperate attempt to hang onto power indefinitely, the Ethiopian regime has framed the debate surrounding popular protest as an economic policy problem, narrowing this even further to an *exogenous* demographic phenomenon, the youth bulge, which in turn resulted in high youth unemployment.

"Youth bulge" is a convenient way to refuse taking responsibility even for the economic malaise. So the Ethiopian government is effectively externalizing the real causes of the popular uprising. If the officials in Addis Ababa framed the issue this way, then that is understandable, it is a matter of survival for them.

However, it is perplexing to observe the international community following suit and discussing Ethiopia's troubles in a manner the authorities framed it for them, effectively avoiding the real sources of the crisis. It is even more baffling when the Mo Ibrahim Foundation gets entangled in this quagmire.

The organization has a reputation of working to promote democracy in Africa. In a bizarre twist, this deeply flawed assessment puts the foundation in a rather contradictory position, being complicit with a dictatorial regime that stayed on power for 26 years ruling with an iron-fist, and now doing everything it can to indefinitely clutch on power.

References

[1] Mo Ibrahim Foundation. An Ethiopian success story: Agriculture.
http://mo.ibrahim.foundation/news/2017/ethiopian-success-story-
agriculture/

[2] Lynsey Chutel. Youth unemployment is a problem all over
Africa, except for one country Quartz Africa, April 12, 2017.
https://qz.com/952175/youth-unemployment-is-a-problem-all-over-
africa-except-in-ethiopia/

[3] Central Statistical Authority (Ethiopia)
http://www.csa.gov.et/index.php/survey-report/category/34-nlfs-2013

[4] Urbanization by country.
https://en.wikipedia.org/wiki/Urbanization_by_country

[5] EU. International Cooperation and Development: Building
partnerships for change in developing countries. Ethiopia.
http://ec.europa.eu/europeaid/countries/ethiopia_en

[6] EU. Emergency Trust Fund For Africa. Ethiopia.
https://ec.europa.eu/europeaid/regions/africa/eu-emergency-trust-
fund/horn-africa_en

19. Devaluing the Birr: Doing the Same Thing over and over Again and Expecting a Different Outcome!

October 20, 2017(AS)

At the opening of Ethiopia's parliament on 9th October 2017, Ethiopia's President, Dr. Mulatu Teshome, stated that earning foreign exchange has become a matter of life and death for Ethiopia. Apparently he was hinting that devaluation of the birr was about to take place. Sure enough, devaluation happened – a day later! The National Bank of Ethiopia (NBE) announced its decision to depreciate the value of the birr by 15% with immediate effect [1]. This sequence of events clearly indicated that Ethiopia is in desperate need of hard currency. It sounds the authorities are panicking because the country's foreign exchange reserve has been rapidly depleting.

Ethiopia's decision to devalue the birr brings to mind Albert Einstein's definition of insanity: doing the same thing over and over again and expecting a different outcome. I thought the EPRDF regime has done it more than enough number of times to know that the country would not achieve any economic gain by devaluing the currency. It was time the authorities do something else to address Ethiopia's economic malaise.

In a two part piece, Is devaluation of birr the answer to Ethiopia's economic troubles? and Ethiopia's trade data and the effect of devaluation on import prices (both in this series), I have previously covered the basics of devaluations, why it is necessary and how it works, specifically the political economy context of devaluations in Ethiopia. Hence, in this piece, I will limit my analysis to evaluation of the policy targets of the latest devaluation by relating it to achievements from the previous one. I will start by highlighting statements the authorities have put forward to justify depreciation of the birr.

Rationale – Official Version

Secrecy is a permanent feature of the authorities in Addis Ababa. Major decisions that most certainly will affect the livelihoods of tens of millions of Ethiopians get passed without any public debate, and the latest decision to devalue the birr is no exception. According to local media reports, the decision to devalue the birr was announced by Yohannes Ayalew, vice governor and chief economist at the NBE, "at a press conference where only the state media was invited to attend."[2]

Ironically, the National Bank of Ethiopia (NBE), the government body that announced this decision, did not even bother to put out any document for public record. I expected such a record to appear on NBE website, where I looked for further information on official version of the rationale for the decision to devalue the country's currency. Even the press statement or even a rehashed version of what was broadcast in the government media did not appear even as a "news items" listed on NBE's website.

But, two separate policies were coupled into one policy package in the announcement of the devaluation. First, the birr was devalued by 15%, raising birr per USD to 26.91. This is supposed to stimulate exports, discourage imports and hence reduce trade deficit. Second, in order to ease inflationary pressure, the authorities have raised interest rate (by 2% to 7%).

Let me separately examine the two elements in the policy package using Ethiopia's own experience and by addressing what happened to the two target policies after the previous devaluation in 2010, when the birr was devalued by 17%? [3]

Inflation

It is useful to remind ourselves where the link between devaluation and inflation begins. Post devaluation inflation pressures begin to build up through two channels.

First, devaluation makes the domestic currency cheaper in the foreign exchange market. Now that the birr is cheap, foreigners would buy Ethiopia's goods at a cheaper price than before, hence export competitiveness improves. The latter simply means the quantity of export goods foreigners demand will rise. If there is already a stock of exportable goods then more goods will be sold in the world market. The decrease in the stockpile of goods or the new orders will stimulate producers of exportable products, and hence they will engage in expanding their activities, which means more investment expenditure will take place. Payments for salaries or other supplies will mean new money will enter circulation and hence inflationary pressure builds up. Fig. 1 presents Ethiopia's *consumer price index Inflation [4]*, CPI (with 2010 = 100). The bar over 2010 is shaded in red to indicate that Ethiopia's birr was devalued in that year, by 17%.

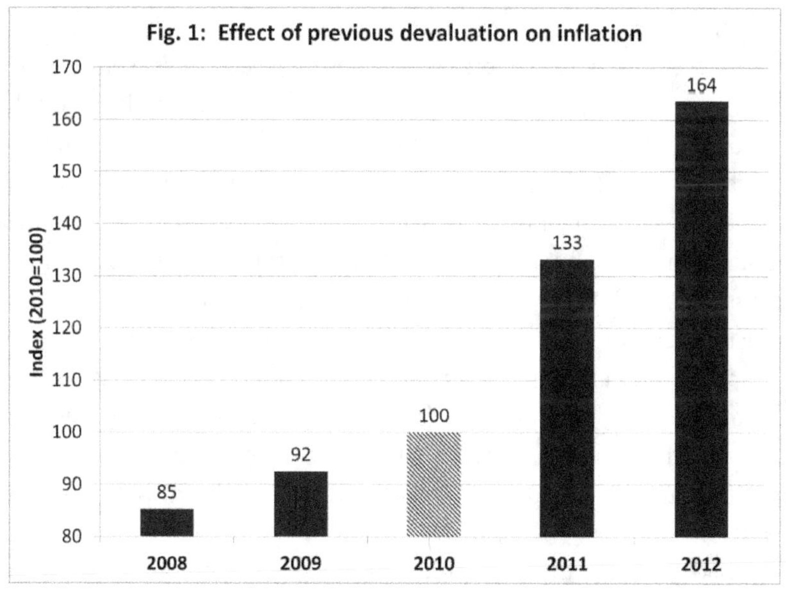

Second, and more straightforward, is the price increase coming through imports. Devaluation makes imports expensive in domestic markets. Prices of new orders for imports or even those that were already imported and currently in stock will immediately translate to an increase in their prices, at the very least by the rate of devaluation. Inevitably, one way or the other, devaluation will trigger an upward inflationary pressure.

In two years preceding the devaluation, inflation was rising at much slower pace compared to the post devaluation year. The CPI rose only by 7% between 2008 to 2009 and then 8% between 2009 and 2010. The 2010 devaluation caused massive increase in inflation; it immediately rose by 33 points in 2011 and then by 32 points in 2012. This figures are taken from the World Development Indicators database, which is likely to be a highly conservative estimate. It was further reported in local press that the 2010 devaluation has resulted in about 40% increase in inflation.[3]

Normally devaluation is not coupled with an interest rate hike, but the authorities in Ethiopia seem to implicitly admit that the situation was not so normal in Ethiopia so they had to resort to an unusual measure. Apparently, they were worried that large increase in inflation may result from the latest round of devaluation, again, so they seem to preempt it by raising the interest rate. There are two strange things in this saga.

First, a two per cent increase in interest rate is just a drop into an ocean, it cannot stop a powerful inflationary pressure, the kind of which the country had previously experienced. After all, the rates of devaluations are about the same, and inevitably inflation is likely to rise by about the same magnitude as before. Surely, the authorities are aware that this is the case, but they are just trying to find shortcuts by giving the impression that they have done something to stop inflation. For instance, the last devaluation was accompanied by some adjustments to salaries, e.g. for civil servants. This one is a quiet affair, no hint of possible salary adjustments. If civil servants ask for one, then the government would have a readily available answer – "look, we have increased interest rates and inflation won't happen", a dishonest way to address a legitimate public concern.

Second, perhaps the authorities are unaware about contradictions or conflicts in their policy package. As noted above, the potential effect of devaluation on export promotion can be realized if and only if economic activities on export productions expand. This requires investment but interest rate increase is likely to work against investment expansions in exports production. While currency depreciation tends to stimulate exports, interest rate increase as well as increases in prices of intermediate and capital goods imports become powerful disincentives against investment.

In any event, even without creating additional hurdles in the way of export producing sectors, the benefits from devaluation would be realized only in the long run. Inevitably, devaluation would have contradictory effects in the short run. It would take time for investment decisions to be made and actual investments to take place. Given this situation, the authorities were expected to reduce interest rate to encourage economic activities, rather than doing the exact opposite.

Exports

It is appropriate to examine the likelihood that devaluation of the birr would lead to exports growth. Let's see the extent the previous devaluation has stimulated exports. Ultimately, whether or not devaluation has succeeded would depend on the effect on trade deficit, which is given as sum of earnings from exports minus expenditure on imports.

Let's bear in mind that export growth by itself is not enough to indicate success with devaluation. Since devaluation will make imports more expensive, then increase from exports should more than compensate for the inevitable increase in expenditure on imports . In a nutshell, although devaluation is often discussed as a means of encouraging exports, the ultimate policy target is improvement of trade deficit.

We are mainly interested in observing differences in the patterns of relationships between the three variables before and after 2010, the year of the previous devaluation, marked by the broken vertical line. Export revenues have increased from $2 billion in 2010 to $6 billion in 2014. Since the eruption of Oromo Protests, which eventually triggered the protest in Amhara regional state, export revenues have sharply declined and fell back to $2 billion in 2016, exactly where it was in the year of previous devaluation.

Note that these figures are given in nominal terms that is to say without taking the effect of inflation into account. The cumulative change in general price level (CPI) from 2010 to 2016 was 2.24; on average there has been more than two-fold increase in prices of goods and service in just six years (2010-2016). Therefore, in real terms Ethiopia's export revenues in 2016 was less than 50% of the amount earned in 2010.

On the other hand, expenditure on imports have sharply increased from $9 billion in 2010 to $26 billion in 2015, nearly a three-fold increase. The sluggish growth in export earnings and rapid growth in expenditure on imports means Ethiopia's current trade surplus has deteriorated, rising from about $6 billion in 2010 to $17 billion in 2016, again nearly three-fold increase. Fig. 2 presents Ethiopia's exports, imports and trade deficit over 20 years period[5].

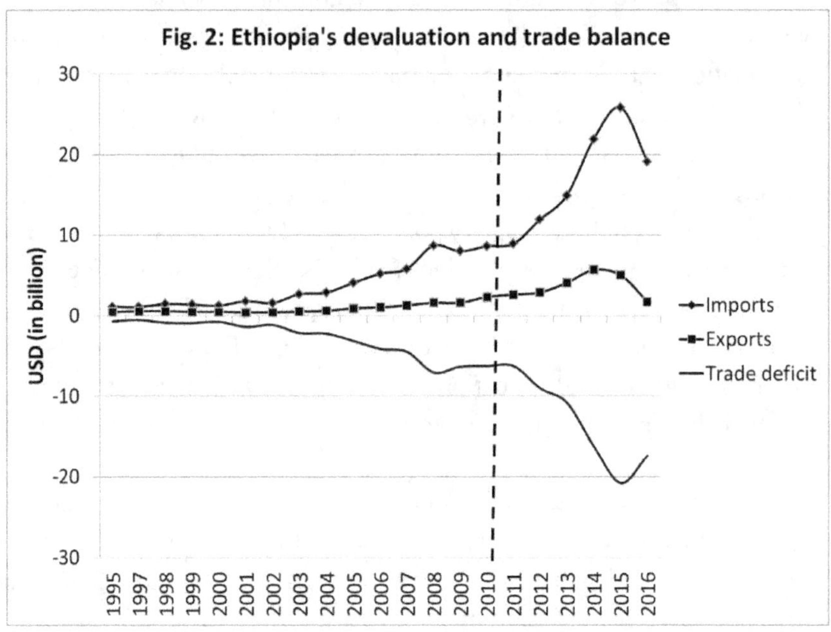

Why doesn't Ethiopia's export respond to devaluation? The answer is clear and straightforward. It would be a gross understatement to say that the authorities do not do anything to stimulate export production. In fact, oddly enough, existing policies do actively discriminate against Ethiopia's mainstay of exports such as coffee, through regional and sectoral bias as noted *in "is devaluation of birr the answer to ethiopia's*

economic troubles?" (in this series). The current export policy is to encourage a pocket of new export sectors, but their contribution to overall exports growth is a drop into an ocean.

Why have expenditure on imports undergone such an explosive growth? Devaluation is an act of deliberately making imports expensive in the hope that high prices will discourage uses of imported products. However, Ethiopia's imports are mostly essential items, necessities, such as petrol, intermediate inputs for manufacturing, and fertilizer for agriculture, among others. Importantly, proliferation of large public infrastructural projects means the very government which tries to discourage imports is actively engaged in importing capital goods at massive scale. Therefore, devaluation would not cause reduction in quantities of goods Ethiopia imports, but it just makes imported items unnecessarily more expensive.

The discrepancies between trade *value* and *quantity* would have far reaching implications. Welfare changes happen in response to changes in quantities of goods and services consumed, rather than their values. Exports are made cheaper, earnings from total exports do not grow that much, but most certainly the quantity of goods exports might have increased by significantly larger proportions than what exports in value terms would imply. There is some opportunity cost for scarce resources utilized to produce the additional goods unnecessarily made cheap and exported to earn about the same export revenue as before devaluation. On the other hand, households or businesses pay more for the same quantity of consumer or capital goods imported.

Targeted Beneficiaries

The analysis so far has been confined to aggregate variables – inflation, exports, imports, and trade deficit. These tell us the effect of devaluation on the country's economy, what is likely to happen to an average Ethiopian in the post devaluation period? Fig. 1 and 2 imply on average Ethiopians are likely to suffer. However, we know averages reveal something important but they do hide really essential elements. For this reason, we need to unpack the figures.

The bottom line is that the authorities are not as oblivious to the disastrous outcomes of devaluation as we might think, it is just a matter of isolating the target groups, whom the government targets to benefit at the expense of others. We need to shed some light on the distributional effects of devaluation, how differently various communities in Ethiopian are likely to be affected.

This requires using a specific category of trade data. For instance, aggregate exports revenue plotted in Fig. 2 does not reveal exports by type of products or their destinations. Ethiopia's bilateral trade by product groups is likely to reveal beneficiary groups. For this purpose, I use Ethiopia's exports to USA.

Fig. 3 is plotted from US trade statistics [6], where details of imports by country and types of products are available. The chart presents average annual exports growth rates by product groups for the years between 2011 and 2016, the post devaluation years. This shows sharply contrasting exports situations.

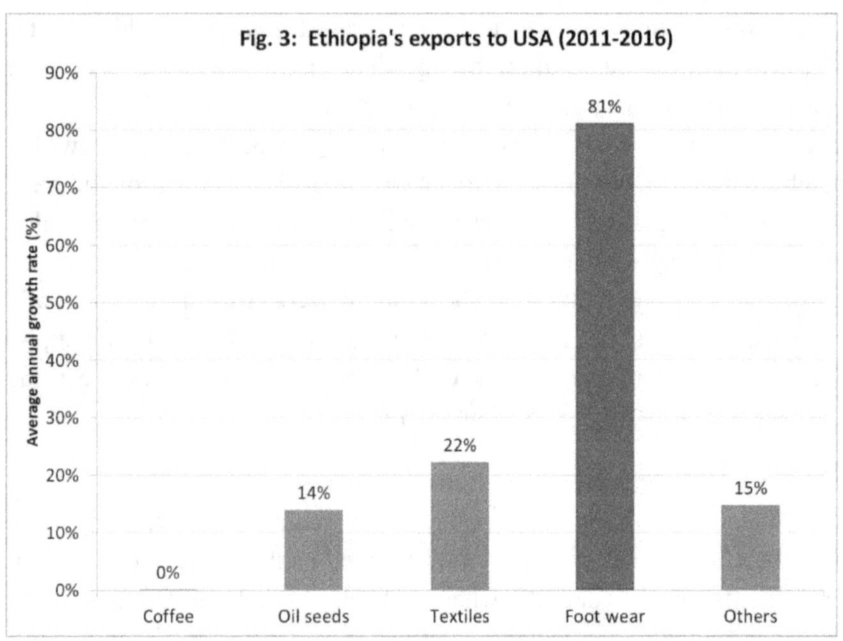

On the one hand, the USA has traditionally been one of the major destinations of Ethiopia's coffee exports. In recent years, however, coffee exports to USA experienced near zero growth. In sharp contrast, footwear exports to USA has grown by a whopping 81% per year; that is to say footwear exports in one year being nearly double of the amount a year before. Textile and oil seeds have also experienced modest growth rates, on average by 22% and 14% per year respectively.

This brings us to the crust of the matter, the core of Ethiopia's political economy of government policy during the EPRDF era. Take for example coffee growers – they are the marginalized farmers. On the other hand textile has become a budding manufacturing sector largely dominated by foreign businesses through the construction of industrial parks.

Let's take one example of footwear products. I would digress a bit at this point. Late in 2016, the Ethio-Chinese connection in footwear production made headlines in mainstream media, moving to prime time broadcasting in USA [7]. What caught media attention was the specific case of a "decision" by the footwear producer, Huajian Group, to relocate to Ethiopia. The reason was that the Huajian Group has been supplying Ivanka Trump's fashion business with shoes branded in her name.

Apparently it was thought the Huajian Group's link with the dictatorial regime in Addis Abeba would be damaging to the Trump administration. The headlines in the USA coincided with the height of widespread protests, when peaceful protesters in Oromia and Amhara regional states were gunned down by Ethiopia's security forces in their several hundreds. Little did the media know that the Huajian Group was already in Ethiopia for a few years before the case was made into headlines in the USA.

I have two reasons to choose 2011 (in Fig. 3) as a start year in calculating the growth rates. First, 2011 was a year following the previous devaluation, a time frame we would expect to see devaluation having effects on exports. Second, it was in 2011 that the Chinese footwear producer, Huajian Group, decided to relocate or expand operation in Ethiopia. The group has already been using Ethiopia as an export platform to access the US market.

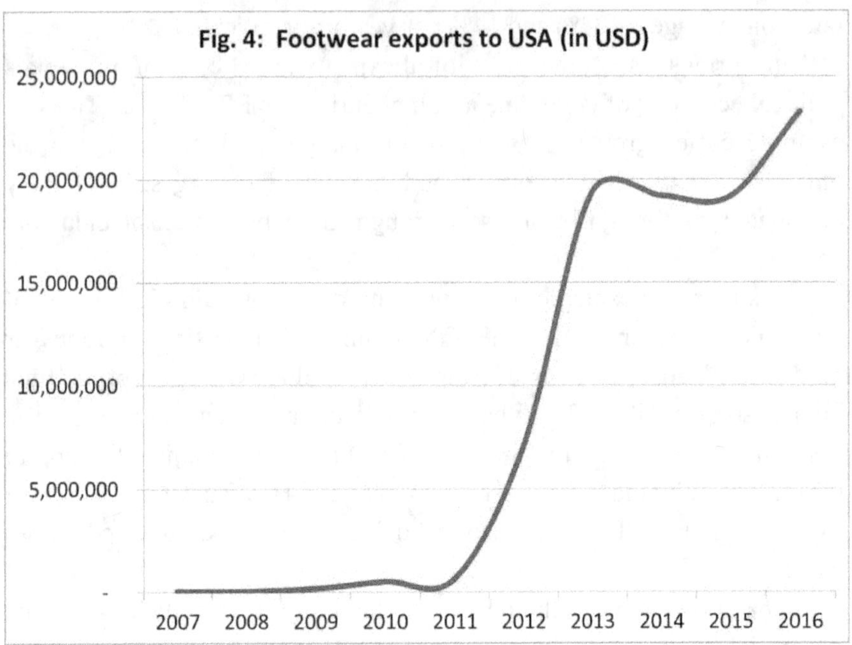

The red bar in Fig. 3 and the line chart in Fig. 4 above measure Huajian Group's exports of footwear to USA by using Ethiopia as an export platform. Huajian's entry in Ethiopia was followed by an explosive growth of footwear exports to USA – a 2,846% growth rate in just two years between 2011 and 2013, nearly a 30-fold increase.

It is highly significant that Huajian entered Ethiopian in a big way just one year after the year of the previous devaluation. It is possible that authorities in Ethiopia have undertaken the 2010 devaluation primarily to entice Huanjian to invest in Ethiopia, although devaluation also benefited other crony domestic and foreign firms.

The preceding sections established that the latest devaluation is likely to harm most producers and producers in the Ethiopia except for very a few domestic and foreign businesses, who are likely to come out as net beneficiaries, as it was the case with the previous devaluation.

AGOA

The most outstanding story emerging from discussions in the preceding section is the eye catching success story of footwear exports, which essentially is Huajian's exports, at least so far. I have chosen exports to USA for a reason – in addition to providing specifics on bilateral trade on product by product basis, this will also reveal additional information on types of producers that have benefited from the special privilege the USA offered to poor African nations through AGOA (The African Growth and Opportunity).[8]

It is appropriate to ask two interrelated questions and try to seek answers for them: (a) Is the Chinese giant footwear manufacturer using the AGOA privilege? (b) if yes, then would that be a misuse and abuse of the AGOA scheme by the Ethiopian government? Fig. 5 below provides a clear answer for the first question. Textiles and footwear have got 55% and 42% of total exports of Ethiopia to USA through AGOA privilege, leaving a margin of 3% for the rest of Ethiopia's poor and marginalized producers. So, yes, the Huajian Group has utilized the AGOA privileges that the USA government extended to Ethiopia, and perhaps that is the main reason the firm had relocated to Ethiopia in the first place.

One does not need to go through the myriads of AGOA legislation to establish whether or not Ethiopia has been abiding by the AGOA eligibility criteria. It would suffice to say a few words regarding Ethiopia's surrender to the Huajian Group, a special privilege the US government extended to Ethiopia to lift small producers out of poverty. It is clear from the forgoing analysis that Ethiopia's poor producers are not benefiting from AGOA. One of the AGOA eligibility determinations criteria is stated as "protection of internationally recognized worker rights"[9]. According to a report by Bloomberg [10], Huagian pays only $40 per month to Ethiopian workers, about a tenth of the wage rate in China. This is the most degrading and unethical wage rate anywhere in the world.

There has to be some value-addition criteria that needs to be observed to ensure that giant foreign investors such as the Huajian Group do not expropriate all the benefits accruing from market access privilege through AGOA. For instance, if a pair of shoes is exported to the US and brought in, say $100 as export revenues to Ethiopia, then how much of it is remitted to China, directly or indirectly, and what proportion remains in Ethiopia?

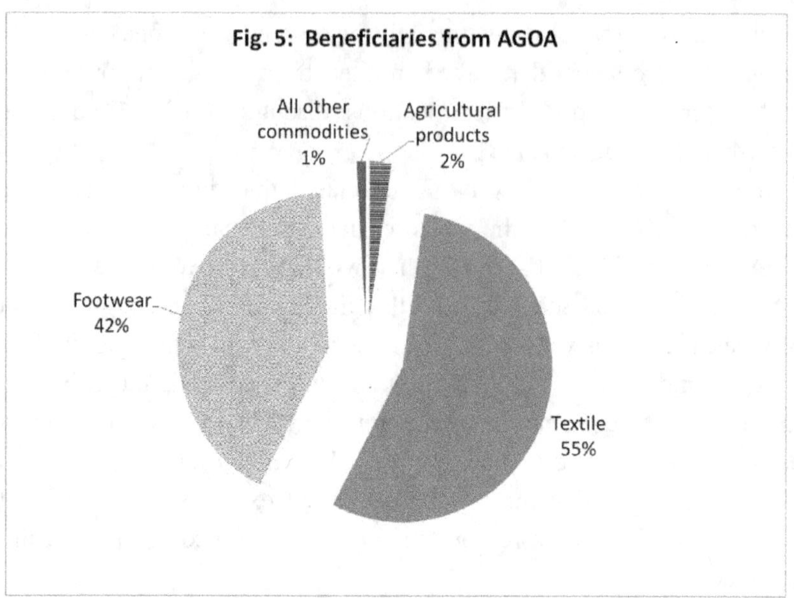

With such low wage rate, and perhaps similarly appalling monopoly prices for domestic raw material suppliers, then it follows that the largest proportion of the selling price of each item goes to operating surplus of the Huajian group. Additionally, the *Bloomberg* reporter witnessed a highly regimented military style punishment of Ethiopian workers on factory floors, adding insult to injury.

Listed in AGOA eligibility criteria I found the following – rule of law; political pluralism; right to due process; economic policies to reduce poverty; a system to combat bribery and corruption; and respect for internationally recognized human rights. It is an open secret that the situation in Ethiopia does not meet any one of these criteria. Why then is the US government turning a blind eye to the appalling situation in Ethiopia is a question I would leave to the conscious of law makers in that country.

Summary

In present day Ethiopia, there are two economies: (a) *the enclave economy*, extremely sophisticated and highly interconnected domestic and foreign firms that jointly control the commanding heights of the Ethiopian economy, (b) *the rest of the economy*, traditional as well as modern sectors where ordinary Ethiopians try to desperately make a living against all odds.

The two components coexist in a parasite and host like relationship. Economic policies such as devaluation are essentially designed to benefit the enclave economy, with no regard whatsoever to the effects of such policies on the rest of the Ethiopian economy, which is being increasingly marginalized. The facts presented in this piece revealed only the tip of the iceberg.

The focus in this piece has been on identifying which group of export producers would gain and which ones would lose. I did not make any attempt to explain wider issues such as the devastation happening to other domestic producers, like Ethiopia's traditional leather manufacturers, who are exposed to the Chinese giants, which are reaping the benefits that donors designed for them. Moreover, it does not require much analysis to establish that Ethiopian households as consumers would experience substantial welfare losses. Inflationary pressures from the latest devaluation would have at least as much effect as the previous one.

As noted earlier, the consumer price index had increased by 2.24 in just six years after 2010, that is to say, the welfare of an average Ethiopian family dropped at least by 50% in such a short span of time. This may sound an alarming figure, but this is only an average, which actually underestimates the cataclysmic welfare falls for fixed income groups, those who live on salaries and wages, such as civil servants.

This piece sets out to inquire the apparent insanity with with the decision to devalue the birr over and over again is made. Upon closer scrutiny, it becomes clear that the authorities are not that oblivious to the adverse consequences of devaluation; it is just that they have a set of priorities, which is at odds with what one would normally expect from a responsible government. The cunning element, the coupling of devaluation with interest rate hike, indicates that the authorities were aware of the looming inflationary pressure, which would adversely affect the welfare of the Ethiopian households as well as hurting domestic investment, but bizarrely the country's government does not seem to be concerned with neither protecting household welfare nor the survival of domestic small businesses.

References

[1] Ethiopia central bank announces 15% devaluation of Birr. All East Africa. Oct 11, 2017. https://www.alleastafrica.com/2017/10/11/ethiopia-central-bank-announces-15-devaluation-birr/

[2] Ethiopia Devalues Currency, Raises Interest Rates. Addis Fortune. Oct 10,2017. https://addisfortune.net/articles/ethiopia-devalues-currency-raises-interest-rates/

[3] ason McLure. Ethiopia Devalues Its Currency 17% Against Dollar. Bloomberg. September 1, 2010. https://www.bloomberg.com/news/articles/2010-09-01/ethiopia-devalues-its-birr-currency-17-against-dollar-central-bank-says

[4] World Bank. Ethiopia. https://data.worldbank.org/country/ethiopia?view=chart

[5] UN Comtrade Database. https://comtrade.un.org/data

[6] US Census Burea. Foreign Trade. Country and Product Trade Data.https://www.census.gov/foreign-trade/statistics/country/index.html

[7] US policy in Africa under a Trump presidency. MSNBC News (Panel discussion, video archive). http://www.msnbc.com/am-joy/watch/u-s-policy-in-africa-under-a-trump-presidency-830330947507

[8] The African Growth and Opportunity Act (AGOA). Country Info: Ethiopia. https://agoa.info/profiles/ethiopia.html

[9] The African Growth and Opportunity Act (AGOA). . The Four Pillars of U.S. Policy in Africa. https://bw.usembassy.gov/wp-content/uploads/sites/125/2016/09/AGOA-Workshop-March-2016.pdf

[10] Kevin Hamlin, Ilya Gridneff and William Davison. Ethiopia Becomes China's China in Search for Cheap Labor. Bloomberg. July

23, 2014. https://www.bloomberg.com/news/articles/2014-07-22/ethiopia-becomes-china-s-china-in-search-for-cheap-labor.

20. IMF Chief Christine Lagarde's Venture to Wonderland Ethiopia: Why Now?

December 28, 2017(OP)

On December 14, Christine Lagarde, the managing Director of the International Monetary Fund (IMF) arrived in Addis Ababa on a rare official visit to Ethiopia. The trip was significant for many reasons but most importantly for how and *when* it took place.

The IMF Director's Ethiopia visit calls to mind the classic novel – Alice in Wonderland! Alice's adventure began when she curiously followed *a white rabbit* and plunged through a rabbit hole to a fantasy world populated with peculiar anthropomorphic creatures.

Madam Lagarde may not be as inquisitive as Alice, but she did parachute into wonderland Ethiopia to talk with the authorities there, whose behaviors and actions are no less strange than those of the creatures in Alice Wonderland.

There are other parallels. Alice was the first real human to visit that utopia; similarly, Lagarde was the first IMF chief to visit Ethiopia in the organization's 72 years history. Understandably, Lagarde's visit to Ethiopia raised many eyebrows. What was the rationale for her visit? More importantly, what explains its timing?

The White Rabbit

To continue with Alice's analogy, it is useful to know if there was a white rabbit that Lagarde was pursuing. In other words, who was the likely agent responsible for facilitating her Ethiopia visit?

I was surprised to learn that IMF does not have a resident representative in Ethiopia. It is unclear whether it ever had one in the country. On the contrary, neighboring countries – Kenya, Sudan, Uganda, Tanzania, even the tiny Rwanda – each have a resident IMF representative.

That Ethiopia — Africa's second most populous country and one of its largest economies — does not have an IMF resident representative may sound extraordinary at first glance. However, a closer scrutiny underscores why IMF did not find it necessary to have a resident representative in the country.

Interestingly, Ethiopia seems to have a unique and somewhat informal arrangement to install its own "resident representative" inside IMF.

The seed of this cozy arrangement was sown in the early 1990s, when the late Meles Zenawi, who served as Ethiopia's prime minister for 22 years until his death in 2012. A master of political intrigues, in 1994, Zenawi implanted his own agent in IMF, a certain young economist named, Abebe Aemro Selassie.

Abebe was a principal economist in the Presidential Office – an Economic Advisor to Zenawi, when the latter was still President of Ethiopia during the transitional period after the demise of the communist Derg regime in 1991.

Zenawi's man at the IMF quickly rose through the ranks at the same time Ethiopia emerged as a donor darling. In September 2016, Lagarde promoted Abebe to the position of Director of African Department at IMF. While announcing his promotion, "Abe," said Lagarde, using a shorter, informal and affectionate nickname for Abebe, "brings a profound understanding of the challenges facing Africa, having worked closely with policymakers from across the region for much of his career." [1]

It is no coincidence that, only a year after promoting Zenawi's man at the IMF as the Director of the Africa region, Lagarde ventured to Ethiopia, a country that no other IMF leader visited before and one that doesn't even have a resident representative.

The minority regime in Addis Ababa has always found it profitable to invest the country's scarce resources on expensive lobbying firms to seek legitimacy from external sources, notably governments, multilateral institutions, and other bilateral agencies operating in various fields.

Ethiopia's current rulers have relentlessly pursued this strategy since coming to power in the early 1990s. Abebe was perhaps among the first batch of loyalist cronies dispatched around the world on similar missions — to secure support for the minority regime and ensure the latter's indefinite grip on power. Tedros Adhanom, who last year became Africa's first WHO's Director General, is among the latest such surrogates to ascend to global leadership. There are a number of ethnic Tigrayan "experts" who ascended to senior leadership positions over the last two decades at multinational institutions, including UNDP and the World Bank.

Why December 2017? Now that we have attempted to answer the question of *who* might be behind Lagarde's Ethiopia visit, let's turn to the more important question: *why now*?

For the uninitiated, Lagarde's mission was about economic policy or Ethiopia's IMF-backed double-digit growth myth. However, for serious Ethiopia watchers, the IMF Director's visit has more to do with internal politics than economics. No doubt that Ethiopia's foreign exchange reserve has plummeted in recent months; the country is left with enough to pay for only a few weeks of import bills.

However, to address this crisis, Ethiopia has already done what it was told to do by IMF – devalue the currency. The birr was devalued by 15 percent three weeks before Lagarde arrived. The birr has been devalued umpteen times in recent years without achieving the desired outcome. This tells us that the country's economic malaise had to be found elsewhere – in the domain of politics and governance.

When Lagarde landed in the capital, Ethiopia's political crisis was at its peak. First, the federal government was falling apart. The executive committee of the ruling Ethiopian People's Revolutionary Democratic Front (EPRDF) has been in a tense meeting for a few days in search of a consensus that remains elusive. The EPRDF meeting was preceded by a 35-day marathon session in Mekelle, the capital of Tigray State, to fix differences among members of the Tigrayan People's Liberation Front (TPLF), the dominant member of the four-party EPRDF coalition.

EPRDF's perennial problem and schism have reached a turning point, with TPLF refusing to share power in key federal government positions, its total control of commanding positions in the armed forces, as well as full monopoly of the country's intelligence services.

Second, a devastating war has intensified along Oromia and Somalia states border, a proxy war deliberately set up by TPLF through its divide and rule policy; deploying Ethiopia's defense forces and the federal police alongside the notorious and murderous militia of Somali Regional State, better known as the Liyu Police; itself funded and trained by TPLF to foment inter-ethnic clashes as a means of clinging to power.

Third, the Oromia-Somali fighting has already caused the internal displacement of over 700,000 Oromos — more than the number of Rohingya's displaced in Myanmar. The TPLF-controlled federal government and its international backers and the media have turned a blind eye to the unfolding humanitarian crisis in Oromia.

Consequently, the IDPs are now staying in makeshift camps set up single-handedly by the Oromia Regional Government and supported by resources mobilized from the Oromo people.

Fourth, scores of students have been killed at multiple universities across the country in inter-ethnic clashes instigated by TPLF-dominated dark forces in the security and intelligence forces.

It's in the thick of these political, economic, and humanitarian crises that Lagarde visited Ethiopia and then left without saying a word about the unfolding *crisis*. It appears that her visit was carefully arranged for the sole purpose of creating a semblance of normalcy, as if Ethiopia's current crisis is only the depletion of foreign exchange reserve. It was a last-ditch attempt by the Ethiopian authorities who leveraged their deep connection at the IMF to persuade Lagarde to fly in and offer some tacit approval to the crumpling TPLF machinery.

IMF's Credibility

Zenawi was farsighted enough to predict the high return on implanting surrogates in positions of power within key global institutions. The returns have been accruing to the EPRDF regime from the work of their man at IMF. Facilitating Lagarde's visit to Ethiopia at a time when the authorities needed a boost was only the tip of the iceberg. Abebe has done monumental deeds for the regime in his earlier position as a deputy director of IMF's Africa Division.

As a deputy, he led the team that works on economic forecasts and production of *Regional Economic Outlook for sub-Saharan Africa [2]*. This publication is a part of the *World Economic Outlook*, IMF's flagship publication, which is by far the single most important and highly influential document. It is widely read by policymakers, the media, academics, and practitioners all over the world.

As I explained last year, there are serious and inherent flaws with Ethiopia's accounting practices. It has puzzled many who have tried to make sense of the origin of Ethiopia's double-digit economic growth bonanza.

But How Badly Has Ethiopia's Economic Data Been Cooked at IMF?

I have explained at length the problems with Ethiopia's economic data in a piece entitled *Ethiopia's economic growth borrows from ENRON's accounting* (in this series). I won't repeat the evidences provided in that piece here. Instead, let's look at additional pieces of evidence related to IMF's role in skewing a vital component in economic growth forecasting: population.

As shown in Figure 1, IMF claims that Ethiopia's current population estimated at 92.7 million[3]. However, many internal and external sources, including the widely cited CIA Factbook, show that Ethiopia's population passed the 100 million mark a few years ago.

For example, the United Nations Population Fund (UNFPA), which records global vital population statistics, projects Ethiopia's population at 105 million. The July 2017 estimate by the CIA Factbook puts the number at 105.3 million [4]. This means that IMF is underestimating Ethiopia's population at least by a whopping 12.3 million.

That is roughly equal to the current population of Chad or Guinea; and greater than those of 23 Sub-Saharan African countries, including Rwanda, Burundi, Togo, Eritrea, and Sierra Leone.

This isn't a new practice at the IMF. The organization has underestimated Ethiopia's population for years. The gap between IMF and other population forecasts became increasingly wide over the last decade, particularly since early 2000s. It was around this time that Addis Ababa began to aggressively push the rapid economic growth narrative.

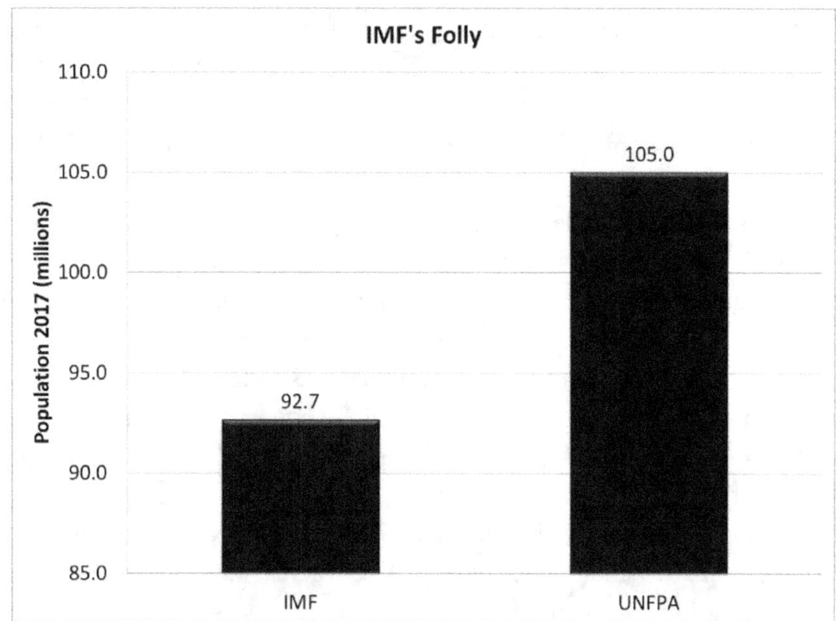

The reader may wonder how underestimating a country's total population helps Ethiopia. First, per capita GDP (GDP/Population) is by far the most important and commonly used economic indicator to assess a country's levels of prosperity. Critically, the authorities in Addis Ababa are vying to propel Ethiopia into joining the ranks of middle-income countries by 2025. They seem to think that they could meet that target by simply cooking economic data and doing little else.

Second, in addition to looking better relative to other nations, prosperity of nations is measured by looking at how per capita income — a proxy for standard of living —grows over time. Irresponsible regimes can show progress or prosperity by simply fudging the numbers. This can be done by overestimating the numerator (GDP) or underestimating the denominator (population) or a combination of the two figures.

IMF's Flagship as a Weapon of Enemy Destruction

IMF economic reports seem to have become another battlefield for Ethio-Eritrean war. While generating unrealistically high economic growth figures for Ethiopia, the organization was doing the exact opposite in Eritrea. Eritreans [5] have long alleged that it was Zenawi's man who was cooking data and bending facts at IMF, benefiting the regime in Addis Ababa and hurting Asmara, Ethiopia's archenemy.

Eritrean authorities have formally complained to IMF about the unethical standards — something the IMF had apparently admitted [6] and then claimed to have adjusted some figures. But, as shown below, no such adjustments seem to have taken place, at least in the 2017 *World Economic Outlook.*

There are credible evidences to suggest that Eritrea's economic growth performance was never as bad as it has been presented in IMF publications. For instance, the Economist Intelligence Unit (EIU)[6], Abebe Selassie's own former employer, estimated Eritrea's economic growth rate at 7 percent and 8 percent in 2013 and 2014 respectively.

However, according to Eritrea's GDP series reported in IMF's 2017 *World Economic Outlook,* Eritrea's real GDP growth was negative (-0.24 percent) in 2013 and 1.6 percent in 2014. Similarly, the African Development Bank [7] reported that Eritrea's Real GDP growth was 4.8 percent in 2015 and 3.8 percent in 2016, whereas IMF projected Eritrea's GDP at 1.43 percent and 0.36 percent respectively.

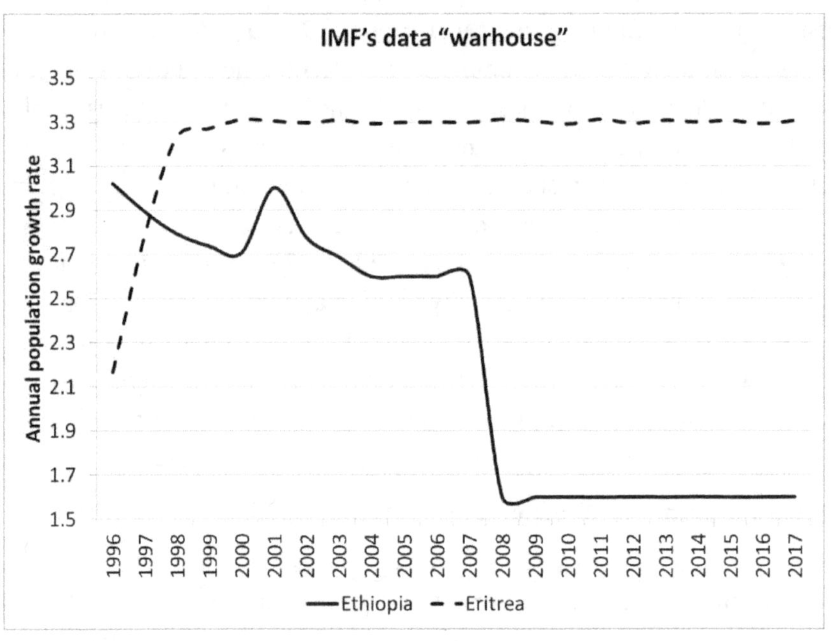

Nothing more clearly indicates the double standard, as well as the extremely low ethical standards, at IMF than the way Ethiopian and Eritrean population data are manipulated. Fig. 2 explains how IMF managed to grossly underestimate Ethiopia's population. The chart is generated using data from the 2017 World Economic Outlook, juxtaposing the two country's population growth rates for the last two decades.

In 1996, Ethiopia's population growth rate was around 3.0 percent while Eritrea's was 2.2 percent. This was much more realistic. Population growth rate comes from two sources – net in-migration (in migration minus out-migration) plus natural population growth rate (births minus deaths). Given that Eritrea has a very high out-migration and given that there is no miraculous way Ethiopia's natural growth could be lower than that of Eritrea, then we expect Ethiopia's population growth rate to be higher or at the very least about the same with that of Eritrea.

In that context, the IMF data in Fig. 2 does not make sense whatsoever. Eritrea's population growth rate was pushed up until it hit the 3.3 percent mark in about three years (1996 to 1999), and then it was frozen at that position. On the other hand, Ethiopia's population growth rate was being pulled down progressively over the years and finally made to plummet to a 1.6 percent in 2008. It has stayed there ever since, leaving a 1.7 percent gap between the two countries' population growth rates. Ironically, the same authorities who use the clout of their agent at IMF to inflate Eritrea's population growth rate, also undertake a huge propaganda campaign about excessive youth out-migration from Eritrea. They want to have it both ways.

White Elephants

In Alice Wonderland, "where is the garden?" Alice kept enquiring, after hearing from one of the creatures about a beautiful garden in that utopia. When she finally arrived, the young Alice saw some strange gardeners doing something rather silly. She was honest enough to tell them the truth: *why on earth are you painting a white rose with a red color?*

By contrast, during her Ethiopia visit, the French diplomat was extremely economical with the truth. Lagarde chose to visit one of Ethiopia's white elephants — a Chinese built industrial park — the latest obsession of Ethiopia's autocrats, who keep lurching from one mega project to another.

There are many reasons for their steadfast commitment to build one white elephant after another. First, it is all about land grab, "legally" confiscating public or private assets and transferring to themselves, their associates, and foreign firms. Second, mega projects are used as a vehicle for creating opportunities for highly interconnected crony businesses. Third, in the case of industrial parks, their presence gives a semblance of business friendly environment and a manufacturing boom to entice foreign investors and attract FDI.

The likes of Lagarde are quick to run away with only the third factor. I have struggled to find anything of substance to pick from her not so eventful visit to Ethiopia. Of course, she kept throwing around her ideological mantra at every occasion. She remarked [8], "I am really pleased to have seen some international companies from China and the Netherlands, manufacturing to international standards for export purposes," saying nothing about adverse consequences of the foreign direct investment in Ethiopia. Flexible monetary policy and privatization [9] were running themes of her discussions at gathering of experts from local and international organizations.

Perhaps Lagarde's visit to Ethiopia will be remembered for her cautious but lousy banter that "Ethiopia is doing well in terms of economic growth."[10] As discussed, her organization is responsible for cooking the numbers that generated the high economic growth rate she was talking about. The people of Ethiopia have not felt the effect of that growth; so they find irritating any mention of their country's nonexistent double-digit growth. In that respect, Lagarde, while polite to the Ethiopian elites who hosted her, she was largely tactless and even rude to the ordinary people in Ethiopia.

References

[1] IMF. IMF Managing Director Christine Lagarde Appoints Abebe Aemro Selassie as Director of the IMF's African Department. Press release September 15, 2016.
https://www.imf.org/en/News/Articles/2016/09/15/PR16409-IMF-Lagarde-Appoints-Selassie-as-Director-of-African-Department

[2] IMFBlog. Abebe Aemro Selassie.
https://blogs.imf.org/bloggers/abebe-aemro-selassie/

[3] IMF. The Federal Democratic Republic of Ethiopia. At a Glance. http://www.imf.org/en/Countries/ETH

[4] UNFPA, World Population Dashboard: Ethiopia. http://www.unfpa.org/data/world-population/ET

[5] The unethical TPLF mole inside IMF exposed. http://www.ethionation.com/sites/amharic_news/52262-oops-news-the-unethical-tplf-mole-inside-imf-exposed-imf-revised-eritrea-economic-growth-back-several-years.html

[6] The IMF admits Eritrea's economy was more robust than previously estimated. The Mandote. http://www.madote.com/2016/04/imf-admits-eritrea-economys-was-more.html

[7] AFDB. Eritrea Economic Outlook. https://www.afdb.org/en/countries/east-africa/eritrea/

[8] Christine Lagarde , IMF Managing Director, visited Ethiopia. Borkena News, December 15,2017. https://www.borkena.com/2017/12/15/ethiopia-christine-lagarde-imf-managing-director-visited-the-country/

[9] Birhanu Fikade. IMF chief calls for opening up of economy. The Ethiopian Reporter December 2017 . https://www.thereporterethiopia.com/article/imf-chief-calls-opening-economy

[10] IMF Chief Says Ethiopia Doing Well in Terms of Economic Growth. http://allafrica.com/stories/201712190521.html (Original article by Ethiopian Herald)

21. Ethiopia's Low Wage is a Curse, Not a Blessing!

April 25, 2018 (AS)

The EPRDF government has succeeded in attracting a good number of foreign firms by advertising Ethiopia as a low wage country. Ethiopia's investment authority publicity materials graphically display Ethiopia's extremely low wage, also stating that the country does not have a minimum wage applicable to the private sector [1].

Hailemariam Desalegn, ex-prime minister of Ethiopia, claimed that Ethiopia out smarted the rest of Africa in attracting foreign firms: in order "to achieve our advantage in light manufacturing, we have kept such costs [wage] low" [2]. Abdulfetah Abdulah, Ethiopia's minister of labor and social affairs also said: "We need to be competitive to attract foreign direct investment and we need to create employment." said Minister of Labor Social Affairs [3]. The local English weekly, *Addis Fortune,* also once came up with a headline: "Wages Too Soon To Ponder", essentially to dismiss any consideration of labor law to protect workers [4].

Clearly, the Ethiopian government has seen low wage as a blessing, a comparative advantage to cure the country's economic malaise. The IFPRI once quoted an Ethiopian Investment Commission report [5] that "the average wage of workers in the leather factories is US\$ 45 per month, while the minimum wage in Guangdong is about US\$300". On the other hand, it is reported [6] that "entry-level salaries in Ethiopia range from \$35 to \$40 per month, significantly below average Chinese manufacturing wages of $629 per month [7], a figure reported to have tripled between 2000 and 2010." This means that the wage rate Chinese firms pay in Ethiopia would range between 6% to 14% the prevailing factory wages in China.

In this piece, I will investigate whether there is any empirical evidence to substantiate Ethiopia's overzealous commitment to industrialize by capitalizing on low wage. By doing so, I will attempt to seek answers to these and related questions such as how low is Ethiopia's wage rate? How does Ethiopia's wage and cost of living compare with corresponding figures from the neighboring countries? I will not only confine my analysis to wages paid by foreign firms but also discuss Ethiopia's wage policy and pay structure more broadly.

An Anecdote

Policy makers, researchers, and donors alike have taken it for granted that Ethiopia's wage is low just like any other developing economy. That Ethiopia is an outlier has largely remained unrecognized. In spite of researching on the Ethiopian economy for many years, I have come to realize that I was not paying enough attention to the abnormality of Ethiopia's pay structure.

That was until a random day when I came across with a specific job advert in Kenya. That job was for a research assistant, a fresh MA graduate in agricultural economics. I learnt that monthly salary for that job was in the range of Ksh90,000 to 120,000 depending on experience. At the time, the prevailing exchange rate was 1 birr for 5 Ksh. So I learnt that a young fresh graduate in Kenya was expected to earn about Ksh 105,000 (21,000 birr) per month.

At the time, I knew the most experienced Professor at Addis Abeba University earned a gross salary of around 6,000 birr per month. It meant that a young graduate, perhaps entering the labor market in Kenya for the first time, earned about four times the salary of a distinguished Ethiopian Professor with 30 or more years teaching and research experience.

I found it mind-boggling – I wondered how Ethiopia got itself into this odd situation. I am still searching an answer for that question but one thing is clear – that anecdote was a revelation for me, I never thought about Ethiopia's wage the same way I did before. It was a powerful anecdote that inspired me to do more in gathering data and examining the patterns. In the subsequent sections, I will present and discuss some of the data I have collected and analyzed.

Teacher's Salaries

I was hanging onto some hope that perhaps the overall the situation was not as disastrous as implied my anecdote. To begin with, I continued to compare Ethiopia with Kenya. The WageIndicator [8] database provides a comprehensive and very detailed data for many countries in the world.

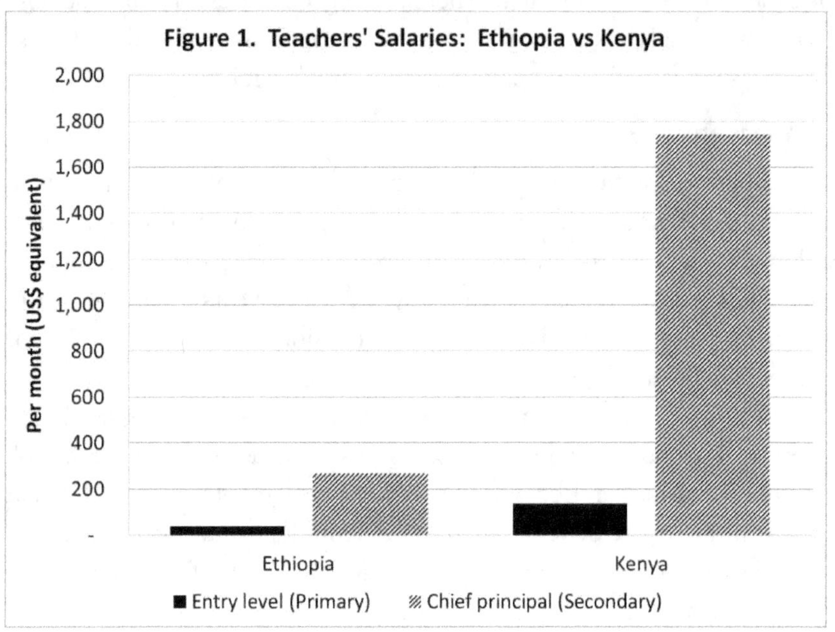

Detailed data on public sector salaries in Kenya and Ethiopia are available in that database, with all sub-sectors and most salary scales. For the sake of brevity, I selected teacher's salary for comparison. Teacher's salary scales in both countries followed a ten level structure, from scale 1 to 10 but it would suffice to compare typical salary at entry level (at early elementary school) and the top grade, principal of a high school.

An elementary school teacher, say at kindergarten in Nairobi, earns about the equivalent of $267, while an Ethiopian teacher in the same position earns $38. This means at entry level Kenyan elementary teacher salary is seven times (or about 600% more than) that of Ethiopia's. At the opposite scale, an experienced secondary school principal earns $1,743 per month in Kenya. The corresponding figure in Ethiopia's scale is $136. It follows that at top grade a Kenyan secondary school principal earns about 13 times (or about 1200% more than) her/his counterpart in Ethiopia.

These indicate the anecdote I reported earlier did not represent an isolated incidence at all, it just revealed the tip of the iceberg, a shockingly contrasting patterns of salary structures between the two neighboring countries.

Minimum Wage

Ethiopia does not seem to have a universal minimum wage applicable to all sectors and employees. What it has instead is a loosely applicable minimum wage of 420 birr/month ($15.5 at current exchange rate), which is applicable to civil service employment.

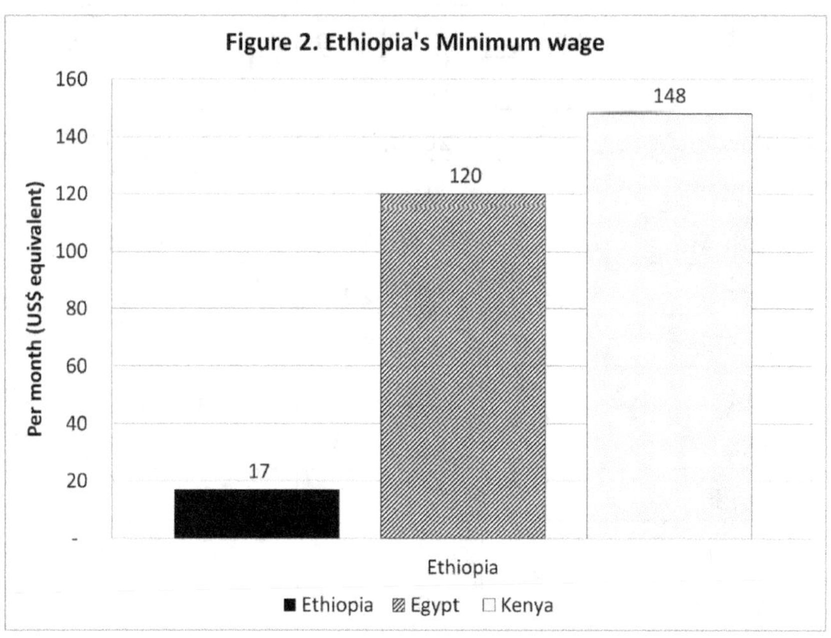

This is not binding in the rest of the economy, particularly the private sector. In the International Labor Organization (ILO) statistical database [9], Ethiopia's minimum wage is reported alongside with figures for other countries in the world. The year 2012 was the last year Ethiopia's data was reported in that database. I selected two neighboring countries, Kenya and Egypt, who had figures for that year and plotted them in the Figure 2.

Ethiopia's minimum wage was so low that it is less than a tenth of the two neighboring countries (11% and 14%, respectively of minimum wages in Kenya and Egypt).

Average Earnings

I have so far benchmarked Ethiopia's wage in a selected sector (education) and the indicative wage floor, the minimum wage. Now it is appropriate to pull these together and get a sense of magnitude at economy-wide level. For this, I turn to ILO average monthly earnings database [9]. Data for ten African countries for whom ILO reported data on this indicator is presented in the table below.

Economy-wide average monthly earnings		
Country	Years	USD
Botswana	2010, 2011	687
Namibia	2013-2016	619
South Africa	2013, 2015	546
Niger	2011-2014	244
Tanzania	2011-2014	216
Egypt	2011-2016	174
Mali	2014-1016	131
Uganda	2,012	106
Ruwanda	2,014	98
Ethiopia	2010-2012	65

The countries are ranked in descending order of the level of their monthly earnings (source: created by the author from ILO 2018 Monthly earnings) [10]. In order to smooth out data and avoid relying on data reported on a single year, averages of available years after 2010 was used.

Even at economy-wide level, Ethiopia still compared so miserably with the selected countries. Ethiopia is stuck at the bottom of the pile. Ethiopia's monthly average earning ranged from roughly a tenth of Namibia's and two-third of Rwanda's.

Cost of Living Index

The extent to which low wage would adversely affect the standard of living of wage earners critically depend on the country's cost of living. Ethiopia's low wage could be justified if cost of living in Ethiopia is lower than those in other countries. Unfortunately, however, available evidences indicate cost of living in Ethiopia is not low at all.

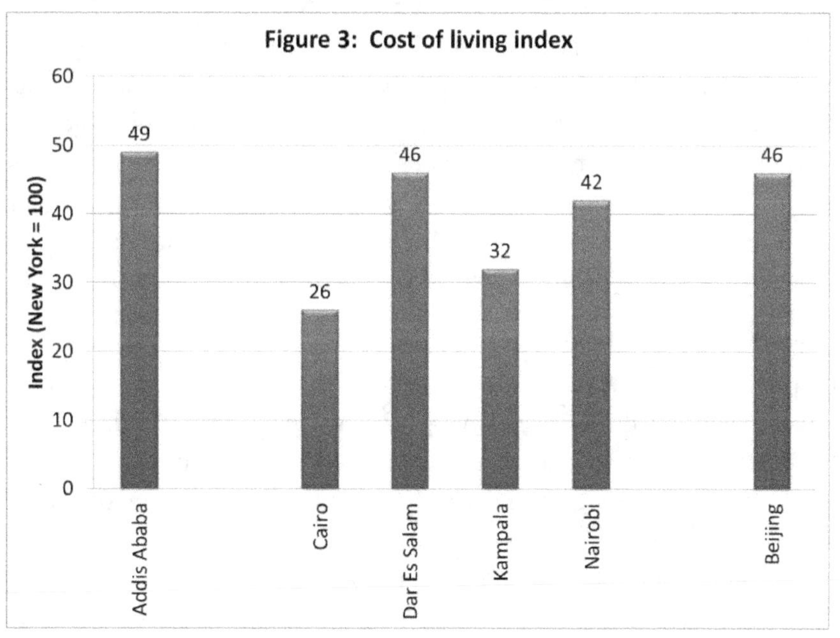

The cost of living indicators database [11] provides comprehensive and consistent indicators for most cities in the world. Figure 3 compares Addis Ababa's cost of living with four other countries in East Africa, alongside with Beijing. The cost of living indices were constructed by using New York as a yardstick (New York = 100). For instance, Beijing (46%) means, Beijing's cost of living index is about 46% of that of the cost of living index for New York.

Addis Abeba's cost of living is about 50% of that of New York, the highest cost of living index plotted in Figure 3. For instance, Ethiopia's average economy-wide monthly earning is about a third of that of Egypt but cost of living index in Addis Abeba is roughly twice the corresponding figure for Cairo. Teachers in Nairobi earn at least seven times more than their counterparts in Addis Abeba but Nairobi's cost of living is 7% lower than that of Addis Abeba.

According to detailed information in the cost of living index database, the cost a loaf of fresh white Bread (500g) in Addis Abeba is 57% more expensive than its cost in Nairobi. The rent of a three-bedroom apartment in Addis Abeba is at least 150% more than in Nairobi. The cost of a Toyota Corolla 1.6l 97kW Comfort (Or Equivalent New Car) is about 200% more expensive in Addis Abeba than in Nairobi.

Ironically, Addis Abeba's cost of living index is higher than that of Beijing. Chinese manufacturers have been enticed to relocate to Addis Abeba on the ground that Ethiopia has an exceptionally low wage, the wage rate in Addis being advertised as a seventh of the prevailing wage rate in China! However, Ethiopian factory workers who are paid less than a seventh of the Chinese wage rate are obliged to survive in a city whose cost of living index is higher than that of Beijing.

Living Wage

Another piece of evidence on Ethiopia's cost of living comes from a recently completed study on living wages, sponsored by the Global Wage Coalition [12], and conducted through a structured survey of flower farms clustered around Ziway (about 164 km South of Addis Abeba).

The study collected data on the *prevailing wages* on the flower farms. The study also thoroughly estimated a *living wage*, that is to say, how much the workers needed to spend to satisfy their basic needs. The study revealed interesting facts that the living wage in the area was around birr 3,367 but the prevailing wage paid to workers was on average about birr 1,058. It should be noted that Ziway is a non-metropolitan area, whose cost of living is expected to me much lower than that of Addis Abeba.

The salary the workers were paid covered only a third of their cost of living! It is anybody's guess as to how the workers would survive in such dire circumstances. A familiar coping mechanism is just to cut deep into to their living standards, e.g. eating only once or twice at best per day to try to make ends meet.

A Curse Indeed!

Evidences adduced in the preceding sections indicate that Ethiopia's wage policy has been thoroughly misguided in considering the country's prevailing low wage as a blessing. Ethiopia's low wage has been a crippling malaise in the country's economy, like an elusive illness that remained un-diagnosed for a long period.

A debate over whether or not Ethiopia's low wage is a curse or a blessing would make sense only if Ethiopia has just a "normally" low wage. For instance, if Ethiopian teacher's salary were about 25% or 75% of that of Kenya provided that Ethiopia's cost of living is not hugely higher than in Kenya, then it would all be fine.

However, here we are talking about Ethiopia's low wage falling below its neighbor's by a factor of five to fifteen. In other words, Ethiopia's wage is not just low, but it is "abnormally" low. The authorities try to consider this as a comparative economic advantage simply because either they have never bothered to find out how deeply flawed Ethiopia's wage is or else the authorities were ill-informed about the implication of running an economy based on such a shockingly low wage. There are far reaching adverse consequences emanating from such an abnormally low wage.

First, the standard of living of citizens is deeply connected to earnings they get from their livelihood activities. As noted earlier, Ethiopia's working class are currently getting a living wage that is a fraction of their living wage. Wages, efficiency wages in the jargon, are mechanisms through which workforces are encouraged to exert efforts in in the process of creating wealth. It is to the best interest of employers to pay reasonable amounts to employees. Efficiency wages serve as incentives to work, a lubricant that smoothens out rough edges in economic relationships. In a very low wage economy, this inbuilt mechanism is eroded. The incentive to work fades away.

Second, the implication of low pay for corruption can by no means be exaggerated. Pathetically small wage in civil services, for instance, does not only mean lack of incentive to work but also nudging employees to resort to getting what they deserve by some other means, such as bribes.

Third, the livelihood of those who do not depend on wages firmly hinges on the purchasing power of wage earners. For instance, Ethiopia's farmers are sandwiched between adverse global market conditions and weak domestic market. They are compelled to produce at subsistence level, refraining from producing surpluses for domestic markets. There were times when Ethiopia's farmers were enticed to producing surpluses. They went ahead and produced surpluses, way beyond the economy could absorb. They had to dump their produce at a fraction of their cost of production, selling their assets, such as oxen to pay debts they incurred in buying improved seeds and fertilizers.

But How Come?

It is clear from the foregoing discussion that Ethiopia is an odd one out in the world as far as its wage and salary structure is concerned. But how on earth this peculiar pay structure came into existence in the first place? Why is Ethiopia so different from the rest of the world?

Seeking answers to such a complex question falls beyond the scope of this piece. I limit my commentary to making general remarks on the possibility of historical factors being responsible for such an anomaly: It is possible to speculate that a responsible explanation may lie in the fact that Ethiopia has never been colonized!

Most other countries in the world have inherited a pay structure rooted in some European colonial legacy. For that reason, pay structures of most developing economies are reasonably comparable. Each country evolved from a common base during the postcolonial era, with some degree of divergence over time.

On the other hand, Ethiopia's civil service pay, which have set the standards for the rest of the economy, evolved from medieval feudal system, perhaps from zero base in that there were times when citizens performed civil service duties to the government for free, still worse incurring costs themselves, and hence a perverse case of negative wage. It is from such base that the current structure have evolved at frustratingly slow pace. That way, Ethiopia's pay structure remained misaligned with pay structures in rest of the world. The misalignment has remained in place. Critically, it has never been recognized as an explanatory factor for the country's socio-economic ailment.

Misdiagnosed, Already

The challenges associated with the appallingly low wage in Ethiopia is beginning to attract the attention of the international community. Perhaps in consultation with the Ethiopian government, the ILO has recently sponsored an exploratory study for a minimum wage system in Ethiopia [13].

The title of the study being commissioned indicates that the ILO has already misdiagnosed Ethiopia's low wage illness, already deciding minimum wage as a solution. It is just a matter of finding out at which level to set Ethiopia future minimum wage. As noted earlier, the existing non-binding minimum wage applies only to civil service employees, but inevitably this will be made binding and then extended to cover the rest of the economy, both private and public sectors.

I would argue that the ILO approach to tackle Ethiopia's low wage amounts to trying to heal a chronic illness by offering a painkiller. Critically, it should be recognized that minimum wage laws are meant to address anomalies in wage distributions *in contexts where there are no problems with the average wage as such*, but *only that some are paid extremely low wages*. In such cases, minimum wage laws introduce a binding minimum wage, a wage floor, below which it would be illegal for employers to pay, but the law leaves the distribution around the average intact. This way, members of the society who were left behind because of low wages would be pulled up, allowing them to get a living wage, a level of wage that would enable them to achieve a standard of living deemed acceptable by the society.

However, *every wage earner in Ethiopia is paid a level of wage that does not offer a decent living standard.* In other words, *every wage earner in that country is essentially left behind in two ways* – relative to the cost of living (e.g. prevailing wage being a third of the living wage) as well as relative wage rates in the rest of the world.

Ethiopia needs a complete revamping of the wage structure in such a way that the entire wage structure moves to the right, so that Ethiopia would be aligned for the first time with other countries, by removing the embarrassing situation so that Ethiopian teachers would be paid a level of salary comparable to the rest of the developing economies.

Side Effects?

Revamping the entire wage system of a nation is bound to be a complicated business. It requires a thoroughly drawn out and daring policy move to undertake such a paramount task. Inevitably, there will be some side effects. However, it should be noted that this is going to be a one-off policy move and that there is nothing beyond creative human endeavor. As always, if there is a political will, certainly there will be a way.

First, possible adverse effect on Foreign Direct Investment immediately comes to mind. However, there is a strong evidence to suggest that, bizarrely, the abnormally low wage in the country is adversely affecting foreign investors primarily in recruitment and retention of workers. A study sponsored by Innovations for Poverty Action [14] and completed in 2017 found out that at least 77% of workers employed in Ethiopia's mushrooming factories quit their jobs within a year of their recruitment on the ground that the factory wages proved to be inferior to their previous earnings in the informal sector, including farming. Importantly, those who left have never considered looking for jobs with other factories.

The other possible adverse effect would be some inflationary pressure. A carefully coordinated policy package can dampen adverse inflationary effects emanating from adjustments to wages, particularly given that the country has so much underutilized resources, including unemployed or underemployed work force. In any event, it would not be wise to live with a chronic illness for fear of side effects that may result from a surgical procedure.

References

[1] Ethiopian Investment Agency. Overview of Ethiopian Investment Opportunities and Policies. APRIL 2014.
https://www.flandersinvestmentandtrade.com/export/sites/.../1271405 08115349_2.pdf

[2] Greg Mills. Ethiopia's Hailemariam Desalegn: Growth has to be shared to be sustainable. The Dailymaverick, June 7, 2016. https://www.dailymaverick.co.za/article/2016-06-07-ethiopias-hailemariam-desalegn-growth-has-to-be-shared-to-be-sustainable/#.WuAtPExuIja

[3] Eskedar Kifle. Minimum wage needed to stop worker exploitation, says International Trade Union Confederation. Capital Ethiopia, January 22, 2018. http://capitalethiopia.com/2018/01/22/minimum-wage-needed-stop-worker-exploitation-says-international-trade-union-confederation/?pr=55634&lang=pt

[4] Wages Too Soon to Ponder. Addis Fortune (Editorial). Jan 27,2018. https://addisfortune.net/columns/wages-too-soon-to-ponder/

[5] Françoise NICOLAS. Chinese Investors in Ethiopia: The Perfect Match? IFRI (Centre for Asian Studies). March 2017. https://www.ifri.org/sites/default/files/atoms/files/nicolas_chinese_investors_ethiopia_2017.pdf

[6] Simona Foltyn. Ethiopia: Booming business, underpaid workers. Low wages have attracted foreign players to the poor African country, but labourers are hoping for better salaries. Bloomberg. 29 Dec 2014. http://www.aljazeera.com/indepth/features/2014/12/ethiopia-booming-business-underpaid-workers-20141228732485264.html

[7] ILO. Monthly earnings database. http://www.ilo.org/ilostat/faces/oracle/webcenter/portalapp/pagehierarchy/Page3.jspx?MBI_ID=435

[8] Wage Indicator Foundation. WageIndicator databases . https://wageindicator.org/main

[9] Trading Economics. China Average Yearly Wages in Manufacturing 1978-2018. http://www.tradingeconomics.com/china/wages-in-manufacturing

[10] NWM (National Minimum Wages Database). Tanzania - Minimum wages. https://countryeconomy.com/national-minimum-wage/tanzania

[11] Gigsa Tesso. Commentary on the current status of Afan Oromo in Gimbi town, West Oromia. August 21, 2013. http://ethiofreespeech.blogspot.com/2013/08/commentary-on-current-status-of-afan.html

 [12] Melese, A. T. (2017). Living Wage Report Non-Metropolitan Urban Ethiopia Ziway Region: Context Provided in the Horticulture Sector. The Global Living Wage Coalition. https://rucforsk.ruc.dk/ws/portalfiles/portal/60982905

[13] ILO. An exploratory study for a minimum wage system in Ethiopia . Call for consultancy service, Terms of Reference (TOR). http://www.ilo.org/addisababa/about-us/offices/addis-ababa/WCMS_573550/lang--en/index.htm

[14] Chris Blattman and Stefan Dercon. Comparing the Impacts of Industrial Jobs and Self-Employment in Ethiopia. Innovations for Poverty Action (IPA). https://www.povertyactionlab.org/evaluation/comparing-impacts-industrial-jobs-and-self-employment-ethiopia

22. Addis Ababa: An Enigmatic City

May 10, 2018(AS)

At its birth, Ethiopia's capital city was given a romantic and beautiful name – *Addis Ababa* meaning *New Flower*. As time went by, however, Addis Ababa grew into an enigmatic city. To a foreigner, the city is a mysterious and exotic place, a vibrant cosmopolitan city that offers a unique blend of culture and cuisine, a good value for money with tourist spending. Ethiopians would find Addis Ababa a joyful place too but they have increasingly begun to recognize the charm they see in it is that of a prodigal daughter type. To begin with, Addis Ababa is rapidly becoming a place in which the majority of Ethiopians cannot afford to live.

Since the tragic and disastrous events surrounding the botched Addis master plan, infamously referred to by protesters as "master killer", Addis Ababa has become more of a beast than a beauty in the minds of millions of Ethiopians [1]. It may have sounded as if the city's beautiful name was coined to mask its ugly functions in the country's social and economic history in its later years.

But what has gone wrong with Addis Ababa's functions in Ethiopia's economy? In this piece I will attempt to answer these and related questions. I will confine my analysis mainly to the role of the city in Ethiopia's economic development; specifically using urban economics as an analytical frame. I will then briefly touch on issues related to social and community cohesion as well as sustainable city development.

The Setting

In order to explain Addis Ababa's functions in Ethiopia's economy, it is appropriate to briefly discuss the setting, the extent of Ethiopia's urbanization. The rate of urbanization is often measured by expressing *total urban population* as a ratio of *total population* of that country. By this criterion, Ethiopia is one of the least urbanized countries in the world.

According to the Word Bank's flagship publication [2], the World Development Indicator, about 20% of Ethiopia's population lived in urban areas in 2016, ranking 248th out of 260 countries surveyed, according to that report. From Africa, only five countries fell below Ethiopia: South Sudan and Niger (19% each), Uganda and Malawi (16% each), and Burundi with 12%.

The health of overall *urbanization* or *modernization* of a *developing economy* is measured by the extent of *structural transformation* – a change in the structure and composition of the economy from predominantly rural and agricultural to urban and industrial. Only 9% of Ethiopia's work force was employed in the industrial sector in 2016. Even this might be an overestimation in that Ethiopia's industrial employment have been hugely inflated by the construction boom, due largely to the mushrooming mega public projects in recent decades.

In that case, it is appropriate to focus on manufacturing, which indicates the extent of *substantive or real structural transformation*. Between 2010 and 2016, the share of manufacturing in Ethiopia's GDP was 4.2% on average [2]. The corresponding average contribution during the six years preceding 1990 was 5%, that is to say a decline by 0.8% in the relative position of manufacturing in Ethiopia's economy over the last three decades. This means the hype about Ethiopia's economic growth miracles and transformations seems to have come to naught.

The rate of urbanization discussed above simply indicates the extent to which the structure of the economy and society is being transformed from traditional to modern, both in terms of residential places of the population (rural to urban) and structure of the economy (agricultural to industrial). With change in structure in the sectoral composition of the economy, the relative sizes of the two spatial dimensions (urban and rural) are expected to change over time – the former expanding the latter contracting.

Critically, the two components – the modern/urban/industrial and traditional/rural/agricultural – economies do not simply coexist but also they do interact in different markets, exchanging goods and services, also in labor markets through rural-urban migration. The latter becomes possible through improvements in agricultural productivity, which makes it possible to release labor for the modern industrial sector.

Lopsided

The role of Addis Ababa should be discussed in the context of the shallow structural transformation of the country – even the extremely low rate of urbanization is not accompanied with industrialization or manufacturing development to any real extent.

Largest city to second largest city population ratios (2015)	
Country/Cities	Ratio
Africa:	
Ethiopia - Addis Ababa : Adama	**10.1**
Rwanda - Kigali : Gosenyi	6.8
Tanzania - Dar es Salam : Mwanza	6.2
Uganda - Kampala : Nansana	4.1
Kenya - Nairobi : Mombasa	3.4
Nigeria-Labos:Kano	3.3
South Africa-Johannesburg:Cape Town	2.3
Egypt - Cairo : Alexandaria	1.9
Congo - Brazzaville : Pointe-Noire	1.9
Ghana - Acra : Kumasi	1.0
Rest of the world:	
UK - London:Birmingham	7.8
France -Paris:Marseille	2.6
Russia -Moscow:St Petersberg	2.3
USA -New York:Los Angeles	2.1
Germany - Berlin:Hamburg	2.0

Now it is appropriate to focus the discussion on Addis Abeba itself;

specifically, the city's *relative size* and *its functions*. The functions of urban areas in energizing the national economy, specifically enhancing productivity in the rural and peripheral locations, would critically depend on the *size* and *structure* of the urban systems.

In a modernizing and urbanizing economy, urban systems are expected to follow a pyramid like cascading structure with the largest city in the center and the *size and distribution* of the rest of cities in the urban hierarchical system following a certain pattern. This is governed by what urban economists and geographers call *Zipf's law* [3]. According to this law, the population of the city on top, the mega city, is expected to be: about *two* times the population of the *second* largest city, and *three* times that of the *third* largest city, *four* times that of the *fourth* largest city, and so on. City rank size distributions in most countries may not exactly fit to this analytical frame but they do closely follow this pattern of distribution

However, the rank and size structure of Ethiopia's cities seem to defy Zipf's Law. Ethiopia is a rare and special case. Addis Abeba dwarfs the rest of cities in Ethiopia to a baffling extent. The table here shows the extent of abnormality of Addis Abeba. In order to facilitate comparability, population data for all countries and cities presented in the table are obtained from the same source [4].

Ten African countries and five from the rest of the world are selected and then ranked according to the ratio of the largest to the second largest cities in each country. Ethiopia comes on top, with the ratio of the population of Addis Abeba to Adama, Ethiopia's second largest city, standing at a whopping 10.1 ratio. As noted earlier, this ratio is expected to be close to 2. Kigali and Dar Es Salam are the other two African countries that show a degree of abnormality but theirs come nowhere near that of Addis Abeba.

The Zipf ratios of most mega cities of the rest of African fall in the normal range. Similarly, ratios computed for other countries in the rest of the world even more so, except for London, whose population is about eight times that of Birmingham, UK's second largest city. Even London's ratio falls way below that of Addis Ababa.

Addis Abeba is an extreme example of lopsided structure in urban systems. Urban functions in economic development of a country are greatly influenced by the extent to which the urban system follows a balanced growth. Urban hierarchy are channels through which innovations and new ideas are diffused through the national economy in a top-down fashion, from mega cities, secondary cities, medium sized cities and all the way down to agropolitan centers or small towns in rural areas.

Forces of agglomeration work the other way, resources moving up the hierarchy to larger and larger centers. Balanced urban development means a symbiotic relationship between the center and the periphery, with equilibrating forces of agglomerations and dispersion.

Addis Abeba seems to have grown at the expense of lower level cities, the power of agglomeration dominating the forces of spread. Addis literally sucks resources from the periphery to itself, with little or nothing flowing in the opposite direction down the urban hierarchy. The relationship between Addis and its periphery have become parasitic rather than symbiotic.

Power to the Powerful

It is beyond the scope of this piece to discuss the extent to which Addis Abeba has been sucking disproportionately enormous share of the country's resources to itself. It may suffice to briefly discuss Addis Abeba's share in total electricity generated and distributed in Ethiopia.

The Ethiopian Electric Power Office, (EEPO), has about fifteen regions of its own, four of them being different sub-districts of Addis Abeba. A report entitled Powering Africa 2014[5] provides allocation of power to the fifteen EEPO, previously known as EEPCO, regions in 2012. The electricity allocation data obtained from this source and population data obtained from the World Bank [2] were jointly used to create the figure presented here.

Addis Abeba has about 4% share in total population of Ethiopia, yet it amasses a 59% share in total electricity produced and distributed in Ethiopia. In other words, while 4% of Ethiopia's population consumes 59% of total electricity, 96% of Ethiopia's population gets the remaining 41%.

Perhaps it is appropriate to compare Addis Abeba's share in total urban population, on the ground that most rural areas are not connected to the electricity grid. Addis Abeba, with 19% share in total urban population, gets 59% share in power allocation, while the rest of urban centers, whose share in total urban population is 81%, survive on 41% of the total electricity produced and distributed by EEPO (then EEPCO) in 2012.

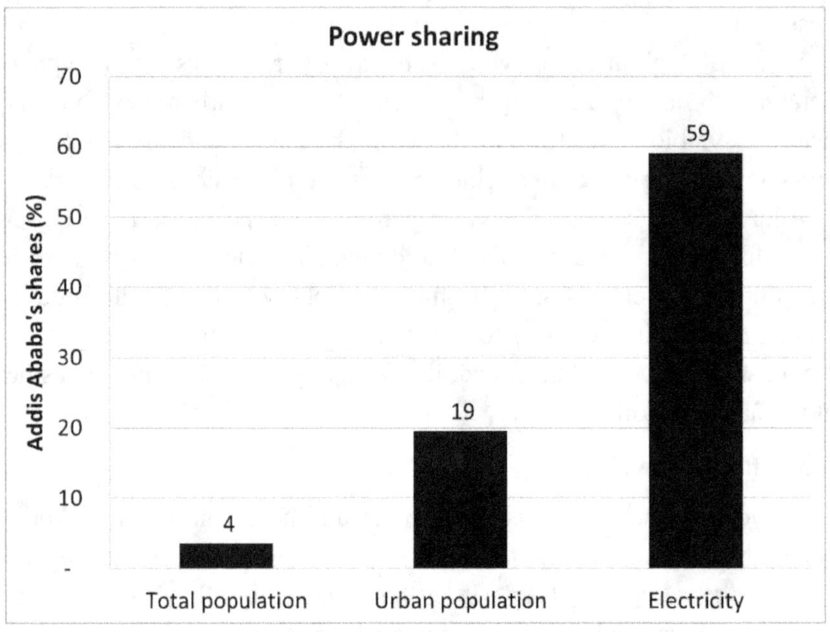

The population based comparison is deliberate regardless of whether power allocated to Addis Abeba was not entirely used at household's residential homes. The disproportionately large share of Addis Abeba has to be judged not just based on final consumption by households but also existence of comparably larger and larger shares of investment opportunities and hence businesses, which have increasingly favored to locate themselves in Addis Abeba.

Fuel to the Flame

The purpose of urban public policy is to mitigate against forces of agglomeration. This is done by tilting the balance in favor of forces of dispersion in such a way that urban systems would be nudged toward a balanced growth path. Forces of agglomerations work through invisible market force, known to regional scientists as *circular cumulative causation.*

Businesses tend to locate where people live. People choose to live where businesses are located. People follow jobs, jobs follow people. These circular causations reinforce each other and then lead to something like Addis Abeba. Left to market devices, the forces of agglomeration would always win, progressively weakening the forces of diffusion down the urban hierarchy. That is why sound urban policy would play a critical role in creating a healthy and balanced urban system.

Ethiopia's city planners seem to have an uncontrollable urge to add fuel to the flame, encouraging and reinforcing the forces of agglomeration already at play. It sounds as if urban development planners in Ethiopia have been actively cooperating with the market forces in earnest, literally saying to forces of agglomeration – anything you do we can do better!

In that regard, the debacle with the failed Addis Abeba Master Plan [6] in particular cannot be expressed merely as a misguided urban policy. It is way more than that. The scale of chaos that accompanied that Master Plan can be illustrated by the geographic expansion contemplated in that master plan – a 21 fold increment of the size of Addis Abeba; the so-called planners simply hallucinated to increase the current 52 thousand hectares to 1.1 million hectares!

Even without expanding it 21 times its current size, Addis Abeba has already become such an amorphously shaped mega city in its size as compared to the country's urban hierarchy. To begin with, even if Addis Abeba has had a normal relative size in the urban system, a city planners' vision to expand the size to such proportion is certainly unheard of in urban planning history of any country in the world.

In most metropolitan region of the world, a small fractional encroachment into prime farm lands would be scandalous and raises uproars among citizens who would be rightly concerned with adverse consequences of sub-urbanization on the livelihoods of farming communities and the natural environment.

Self-degradation

The analysis so far has focused on the *economic* relationship between Addis Abeba, the center, and the rest of Ethiopia, the periphery. Now it is appropriate to briefly discuss *social* and *community cohesion* within the boundary of Addis Abeba as well as its relationship with communities living in its neighboring districts, the so-called "Special

Zone of the Oromia Regional State".

A city is analogous to a living organism: consumes materials, metalizes, grows old, regenerates or renews itself. Cities are made up of units of places, neighborhoods, and units of communities, households. Any harm a city development plan inflicts on its people and the physical environment can be legitimately referred to as self-destruction.

In that regard, Ethiopia's capital city seems to have portrayed persistently a self-cannibalistic behavior over the years. Its regeneration and renewal is often accompanied with self-destruction – annihilating communities and destroying their livelihoods. One does not need to go far back in Addis Abeba's history to substantiate this claim. I can adduce two extraordinary and tragic episodes, extreme cruelties currently being perpetrated against the very people Addis Abeba's growth is meant to serve.

The scene of the first episode is the center of old Addis Abeba, where callous destruction of the city's established communities have taken place at a massive scale [7]. Communities were evicted to give way to regeneration. In the minds of Addis City planners, regeneration means construction of high rise commercial and residential building, with no regard whatsoever for the human dimension.

Regeneration and renewal are essential and inescapable facts in the history of any city in the world. However, community participation ensures humane ways of undertaking such disruption, for instance, by sufficiently compensating households evicted from family homes they have occupied for generations.

However, Addis' recklessly adventurous regeneration plan obliterated the economic livelihoods as well as the social fabrics of hundreds of thousands of extremely poor households. Those whose homes were demolished might have been given "social housing" at the fringes of Addis Abeba, but it was abundantly clear that their new homes would never suit their lifestyles.

Still worse, the rent of those "social houses" were set so high that they were way beyond what the ordinary poor households could afford. In the circumstances, most poor households were forced to let out their new houses to those who could afford; rent income being channeled to pay mortgages. It is anybody's guess as to what happened to those unfortunate victims of Addis Abeba's regeneration.

The physical demolition of buildings and livelihoods in the center was accompanied by yet another destruction of lives and livelihoods of farming communities just across the boundary of Addis Abeba and within the Oromia special zone. We often mistakenly conclude that the master plan was stopped in good time. The fact is, by the time the master plan was stopped, hundreds of thousands of farming households were already evicted from their ancestral lands without proper compensations. Acreages of prime agricultural lands were amassed by property developers, partly to develop luxury homes for the rich and partly for social housing to resettle those evicted in the first episode. The cruel treatment of Oromo farmers simply defies belief [8].

No wonder then that the thoughtless actions of Addis Abeba's city planners have eventually triggered the widespread popular protest that has shaken the country to its foundation during the last four years. It should be underlined that what is lost to communities at both ends, the center and suburb of Addis Abeba, was gained by corrupt land grabbing officials and property [9]. developers. In a way, Addis Abeba's growth model seems to have been obeying a zero-sum-game rule.

The two tragic episodes that have concurrently unfolded at the center and fringe of Addis Abeba were just tips of the iceberg. So far I have only touched on economic and social ills traceable to Addis Abeba's malfunctions as a capital city. As any Ethiopian with a hint of environmental concern would tell, 'Green space' has not yet entered the vocabulary of Addis' city planners – city planning seems to be understood as covering every inch of the city space with concrete slabs.

In a nutshell Ethiopia's urban planners would need to very seriously rethink and reformulate its approach to sustainable city development, firmly embracing the three pillars of sustainability – social, economic and environmental. These would need to be set in the context of broader urban public policy of the country

References

[1] http://addisstandard.com/analysis-addis-abeba-city-struggling-weight-failures-triggers-fresh-minefield/

[2] United Nations Population Division. World Urbanization

Prospects: 2014 Revision.
https://data.worldbank.org/indicator/SP.URB.TOTL.IN.ZS

[3] Zipf's Law for Cities – A Simple Explanation for Urban
Populations Networks: Course blog for INFO 2040/CS 2850/Econ
2040/SOC 2090. http://blogs.cornell.edu/info2040/2016/11/13/zipfs-
law-for-cities-a-simple-explanation-for-urban-populations/

[4] City Population. Population Statistics for Countries,
Administrative Areas, Cities and Agglomerations – Interactive Maps
and Charts. https://www.citypopulation.de/

[5] Ethiopian Electric Power. http://pubs.naruc.org/pub/537C14D4-
2354-D714-511E-CB19B0D7EBD9.

[6] Ezana Haddis. How not to make a master plan. Addis Standard.
June 27, 2014 http://addisstandard.com/how-not-to-make-a-master-
plan/

[7] Samuel Bogale. Addis Abeba may never house its dispossessed,
unsheltered inner-city dwellers. Aaddis Standard. September 4, 2017.
http://addisstandard.com/analysis-addis-abeba-may-never-house-
dispossessed-unsheltered-inner-city-dwellers/

[8] Addis Standard, Selected video archives on Oromo Protests.
https://twitter.com/addisstandard/status/988800704868478976

[9] Addis Standard, More images and archives on Oromo Protests.
http://www.ena.gov.et/index.php/social/item/2504-2018-04-24-22-
28-46

23. How Can Ethiopia Boost Remittance Inflows?

July 24, 2018(AS)

Ethiopia has been in a dire state of foreign exchange crisis for the last few years. PM Abiy has made a plea to the Ethiopian diaspora to come to the rescue of their country by sending hard currencies back home [1]. In this piece I will assess gaps between actual and potential inflows and then explore options to boost remittances.

Figures

The data plotted in the Figure 1 was obtained from the World Bank migration and remittances database, It shows the dynamics of remittances during 2010 to 2017 [2]. Remittance inflow was only US$345 million in 2010 but it sharply rose to US$1,796 million in 2014, and then plummeted to US$816 million in 2017, about 45% of the peak reached in 2014.

2014 was the year Oromo Protests was ignited in Ambo, spread to the rest of Oromia like a forest fire, and finally engulfed the whole nation, when Amhara Resistance followed suit. A relentless campaign ended up with a remittance boycott to punish the regime that desperately needed hard currency to sustain itself and stay on power.

In Figure 1, the solid line shows a plot of actual remittance inflows, but the dotted line projects the 2010 to 2014 trend up to 2017, that is to say what would have happened if the remittance boycott did not take place. The gaps between the solid and dotted lines indicate the amount remittance inflow that remained unrealized due to the remittance boycott.

Remittance inflow would have reached US$2,496 million by 2017 if the situation stayed normal. Ethiopia lost remittance inflows amounting to US$765 million in 2015, US$1,402 million in 2016, and US$1,681 in 2017. The losses over the three years period amounted to US$3,847 that is to day Ethiopia lost nearly US$4 billion of remittance inflows during that period.

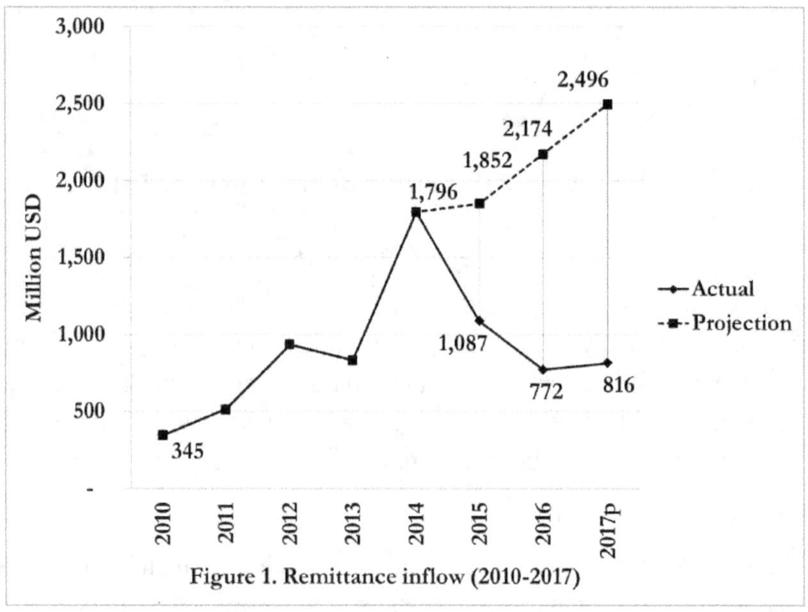

Figure 1. Remittance inflow (2010-2017)

Facts

There are gaps between figures and facts as far as remittance inflow to Ethiopia is concerned. The World Bank estimates seem to grossly underestimate the facts on the ground. I would adduce two pieces of evidences.

Firstly, in the World Bank database, remittance figures are very closely related to stock of migrants, that is the total number of migrant outflows from that country over several years. The number of Ethiopian migrants living in most countries tends to be under reported. It follows that remittances to Ethiopia from most country is underestimated.

Let's take the case of Kuwait, a country whose situation I know closely. In the World Bank database, the number of Ethiopian migrants living and working in Kuwait and the amount of remittance in 2017 were given as 3,917 and US$5 million respectively. However, official statistics in Kuwait indicates that there are at least 74,000 <u>Ethiopians living and working in Kuwait</u> [3]. If we apply remittance per migrant in the World Bank estimates to the latter figure then the amount of remittance from Kuwait would rise from US$5 million to US$94 million. The case of Kuwait could be rather extreme but certainly unlikely to be an isolated one.

Secondly, as I have reported in *rush for the exits: why is Ethiopia's capital flight accelerating?* (in this series), remittances to Ethiopia tend to get underestimated for many other reasons. Sizeable gaps have always existed between Ethiopia's the official and the parallel currency exchange markets. For this reason, substantial sum of remittance transfers have taken place through informal channels [4]. In order to get better rates and also avoid transfer fees, Ethiopians in diaspora choose to carry hard currencies with them and then directly exchange it to birr in local underground markets.

Alternatively, they commonly send hard currencies via friends or any traveller they would trust. The World Bank estimated that 14% of Ethiopians to whom money was transferred from abroad in 2010 got it through travelers [5]. The other dimension of informal transfer is the case of hard currency remaining abroad because of a more sophisticated black market operators who act pretty much like the way foreign money transfer services.

Stocktaking

The figures and facts discussed in the preceding sections can serve as a stocktaking exercise. The remittance boycott might have had unfortunate consequences on the economy but it also provided the authorities with excellent insights that the diaspora communities have extraordinarily capacity to quickly adjust remittance inflows depending on circumstances.

The boycott campaign was a call not to send money through official channels. It was a negative shock, deliberately so to hurt the regime at the time. PM Abiy's recent plea can be seen as a positive stimulus to inspire the diaspora community to come to the rescue of their motherland, alleviating the nation from the ongoing foreign exchange crisis. Given PM Abiy's goodwill and positive image among all sections of Ethiopians, both at home and abroad, I have no doubt the setback in the remittance inflow would be very quickly reversed and the hard currency inflow would buck up to its previoustrend in the near future.

How soon this can happen will depend on how proactively the monetary authorities would put the right incentives in place. The authorities can learn at least two things from the remittance boycott. First, there is a lesson on the behavior of the Ethiopian diaspora. If the diaspora have responded to a disincentive, then it follows that they can also respond to incentives as quickly and as decisively.

Second, the authorities now have a sense of magnitude, quantifiable figures with which to start planning remittance inflow targets. In response to the remittance boycott, remittance inflow deviated from the trend, causing a cumulative shortfall of about US$4 billion. It is expected a positive stimulus to remittance inflow would generate additional US$4 billion over the coming three years, one billion USD additional inflow per year. I stress that these figures would considerably underestimate the underlying facts, as stated earlier.

In a <u>World Bank survey of 2010 [5]</u>, remittance recipients utilized the money they received in the following proportions: 57% daily expenses, 29% university education, 9% small businesses, 4% savings and 1% housing. It seems this survey focused on money transferred exclusively for use by recipients' relatives. However, individuals in the diaspora community do transfer sizeable funds for their own savings (e.g. domestic workers in the Middle East) as well as investments (e.g. buying or building houses). The monetary authorities would need to undertake a more thorough and comprehensive study as part of a baseline assessment to inform remittance policy design.

Anomalies

Little do the top level authorities like PM Abiy know that there are obstacles deliberately put in place to obstruct normal inflow of remittances. Who created such strange obstacles and why remains unclear. It is paramount that the authorities are aware about the existence of anomalies in Ethiopia's remittance inflow system and undertake a thorough diagnosis with a view of removing them.

I would illustrate this using data presented in Table 1. A while back I walked into a branch of money transfer operator known as Bahrain Exchange in Kuwait. As usual, popular currencies and their daily exchange rates were listed on the board in two columns, as shown in Table 1: one rate for crediting to a bank account and another rate for cash pick-up. As it happened the Ethiopian birr was one of the popular currencies listed.

I was shocked to learn that the rate for the Ethiopian birr was the odd one out on that board. In order to make this clearer in Table 1, I have created a third column, "bank to cash (%)" by expressing the 'credit to bank account' as a percentage of 'cash pick-up'. For most countries this ratio is close to 100% but for Ethiopia it is 74%.

Table 1. Ethiopia's remittance anomaly!

Currency	Credit to a Bank	Cash Pick-Up	Bank to cash
Eritrean Nakfa	48.35	48.20	100.32
Ethiopian Birr	66.72	89.87	74.25
Egyptian Pound	58.57	58.49	100.14
Indian Rupee	225.01	224.52	100.21
Bangladesh Takka	275.64	276.91	99.54
Sri Lankan Rupee	526.76	527.18	99.92
Philippine Peso	175.79	176.31	99.71
Nepalese Rupee	359.71	360.79	99.70
Pakistani Rupee	400.51	419.62	95.45
US Dollar	3.30	3.29	100.12
British Pound	2.50	2.52	99.33

Source: Bahrain Exchange Kuwait (*https://www.bec.com.kw/currency-exchange-rates?atype=money&continent=popular*) Money Transfer Rates per Kuwaiti Dinar (KWD) @ 10:43pm 17th Jul 2018

This implies that Ethiopian authorities have created a system that actively discriminates against transferring to bank accounts, the most convenient money transfer mechanism! Currently, if one Kuwaiti Dinar (KWD) is transferred to a bank account, only 68 birr arrives but if it is a cash pick-up, then the beneficiary would receive 90 birr, a difference of 22 birr per KWD, I found this mind-boggling, it defies logic!

I was so baffled with my encounter that I had to seek for explanation from the staff. However, they could not offer any help except to acknowledge that it was a weird stuff indeed, adding that if I insisted to send to a bank account then I could do so only if I have an account with the Commercial Bank of Ethiopia. However, cash pick-up services are available at any branch of many banks in Ethiopian including private banks. The disincentive created against transferring to a bank account must have had incalculable damages at many levels.

First, ruling out the most convenient currency transfer through official channels thereby worsening Ethiopia's foreign exchange crisis. At least 95% of those who live in Kuwait are domestic workers, earning extremely low wages in the households sector. Their monthly earning would range somewhere between KWD 80 to 150 per month (US$260 to 490). The size of their income could be low but their saving rate is extremely high, at least around 75% of their monthly earnings! A simple calculation would establish that at the very least US$300 million would have been remitted from Kuwait annually if the situation were right. That potential remains unrealized, at least not visible in official flows.

At this juncture I would hasten to add that Ethiopian Embassies in the Middle East, who closely know the situation, have often turned a blind eye to the appalling situation. Instead of helping the hundreds of thousands domestic workers with secure way of transferring their savings through formal channels, they often add another layer of red tape, by encouraging them to come to embassies to open a bank account back home, and making initial transfer money through them.

The foreign exchange revenue lost to the Ethiopian economy is nothing compared to the incalculable damages that occurred to the lives and livelihoods of those domestic workers. The system literally forced them to use only one transfer option – cash pick-up by a family member, a relative, or a friend! More often than not, they end up losing their hard earned incomes because those entrusted with the money would end up spending it either partly or entirely.

Incentives

The authorities should aim to realize the full potential of the remittance inflows. This requires more ambitious and far reaching measures than inducing remittances to relatives back home. The most radical measure would be to encourage diaspora saving accounts in foreign currencies in the Ethiopian banking system.

(a) Saving Accounts in Foreign Currencies. As a matter of fact, there is already a policy of diaspora saving accounts in the Ethiopia. However, it seems this was never taken seriously neither by the authorities nor by the diaspora community. To be honest, the banking practice used to served it proved to be exceptionally substandard.

Here is my anecdote. I opened an dollar account and deposited a certain amount, hoping I would start a regular saving into that account. At the end of the transaction, I expected a standard document to prove that I opened and own an account. However, I was told they had not started issuing a saving book for a dollar account. I asked what evidence would I have for my deposit then.

I was told I could use the receipt I was given for the deposit. It all sounded an archaic banking practice. I asked if I could talk to the manager. The manager kindly agreed to discuss the matter with me, but at the end of the day he could not offer any sound explanation. I was taken aback by the whole affair. I never bothered to top up that deposit account. Whatever I deposited I had to use as quickly as I could. The moral of this story is that a solid incentive system to attract hard currency would start with confidence building measures which would include modernizing the banking practices.

(b) Competitive and attractive interest rates for hard currency saving accounts. This measure would induce the diaspora community to choose saving more with Ethiopian domestic banks than anywhere else in the world. Fortunately, given the extremely low interest rates in most countries, only a marginal increment on top of interest rates elsewhere would induce substantial hard currency inflows.

(c) Structure interest rates based on access to the funds. It is standard banking practice that saving interest rates would depend on frequency of fund withdrawals. An instant access saving account would attract relatively smaller interest rates, although in the case of Ethiopia's diaspora account, even this has to be reasonably high to entice more potential savers. However, saving accounts with fixed term notice periods (e.g. three months, six months, or 12 months or more) should be made available at higher rates. The existence of such longer term options would create considerable amount of hard currency pool in the Ethiopian banking system.

For instance, in the worst case scenario, Ethiopia's diaspora community has transferred around one billion USD in 2017, mostly to support relatives. If they can transfer that much to support family then they can save at least as much amount for themselves. It is the potential of attracting what is left in their foreign bank accounts, at least one billion USD being deposited in Ethiopia's banking system every year. The cumulative stock of hard currency in Ethiopia can rise very quickly in a few years.

(d) Encouraging investment. There have often been relentless campaigns to entice the diaspora community to consider investment opportunities but, like everything else, the calls remained empty words and meaningless gestures which have never been taken seriously by everyone involved. This was so partly because of mutual distrust between the Ethiopian diaspora and the authorities. The campaign itself was more political than economic motive.

Now the situation is different, the fog of mutual distrust seem to have faded away and it is high time that the authorities engage in earnest with the diaspora community and invite them to invest in their homeland. Perhaps this requires at least two sets of accompanying measures. Removing existing restrictions and exceptions with where Ethiopia's diaspora can invest. For instance, currently the financial sector is not open to the Ethiopian diaspora community. Lifting the ban on dual citizenship is required, this is simply to acknowledge the sense of belongingness which is already in place.

(e) Recognition and prizes. These are part of the incentive mechanism. For instance, Bangladesh experienced a similar downward trend in remittance inflows a few years back. They immediately put in place measures to reverse the trend and with considerable success. Remittance inflows increased by more than 35% by October 2017 [7]. Also, they introduced a range of prizes for individual remitters in different categories, as well as banks that implemented the policies, depending on the amount of remittances they have attracted.

Challenges

Two challenges would remain. First, the incentive to open dollar saving accounts would to a certain extent divert remittances from informal to formal channels. The reason is that the hard currency would stay deposited in Ethiopia and the depositor will have the opportunity to exchange it to local currency in the future at a better official rate.

The assurance of this accrued benefits as well as the attractive interest rates are expected to reduce the gap between what the remitter would get through the formal and informal channels. However, it is highly unlikely that such expected benefits would make Ethiopia's black market in hard currencies to disappear. This is particularly the case given Ethiopia's extremely high propensity to import goods and services from the rest of the world.

Second, paradoxically, successes in inducing remittance inflows would inevitably make the birr appreciate and hence hurt exports of goods and services, the gain through remittances would induce losses in goods markets. Incidentally, although this has not been discussed much in the past, it is this inbuilt conflict which must have been the underlying causes of Ethiopia's recurring devaluations during the last decade.

The combined effects of persistence in parallel currency market and adverse effects of success in attracting remittance inflows would inevitably pose a policy dilemma. However, there is nothing beyond human endeavor. Extraordinary situations require extraordinary measures. For instance, it is a common practice for a country under substantial balance of payments difficulty to resort to a dual exchange rate mechanism for a certain period of time.

This would involve adopting a floating or market determined exchange rate in one market (e.g. remittances and capital inflows) and fixed or pegged exchange regime in another market (e.g. in import and export markets). This requires innovative policy-making on part of Ethiopia's monetary authorities.

Awareness

In the past, there were awareness cum propaganda campaigns to engage with the diaspora community but accompanied with little else. Now it would prove useful to change the sequence – putting in place the right incentive structures and then engage in an extensive publicity campaign to raise awareness among the diaspora community about the opportunities created. There is no need to approach the diaspora with a plea. What needs to be done is to create conditions whereby the actions of the diaspora would amount to simultaneously helping their motherland and helping themselves.

Incidentally, PM Abiy can bring in more billions of dollars into National Bank of Ethiopia by instructing Ethiopian Embassies in the Middle East to properly do their job of facilitating remittance transfers in the simplest ways possible than by lobbying leaders of those countries to extend their helping hands.

References

[1] ETV. PM Abiy About Foreign Exchange.
https://youtu.be/ClSNT-by9SQ

[2] World Bank. Migration and Remittances Data.
http://www.worldbank.org/en/topic/migrationremittancesdiasporaissu
es/brief/migration-remittances-data

[3] Kuwait Population 2018.
http://worldpopulationreview.com/countries/kuwait-population/

[4] Dawit Endeshaw. Ethiopia: Remittance Dilemma. Wardeer
News, January 5, 2015 http://www.wardheernews.com/ethiopia-
remittance-dilemma/

[5] Edward Al-Hussainy.. Ethiopia - Future of African Remittances:
National Surveys 2010. The World Bank.
http://microdata.worldbank.org/index.php/catalog/595/related_materi
als

[6] Bahrain Exchange (BEC). Currency Exchange Rates Today.
https://www.bec.com.kw/currency-exchange-
rates?atype=money&continent=popular

[7] BB to give award to encourage inflow of remittances,

TheIndependent, 13 September, 2017.
http://www.theindependentbd.com/printversion/details/113735

24. Punitive Import Tax on Cars Deprive Ethiopians a Driving Seat, Undeservedly, and Hurt the Country

August 09, 2018 (AS)

A provocative question was posed to PM Abiy Ahmed at one of the public meetings during his recent visit to the USA. From the way PM Abiy replied, I guess the question was related to possibility of granting car import duty exemptions to diaspora who might consider returning and settling back home in Ethiopia. The context to the question was Ethiopia's extremely punitive car import tax, a major source of frustration among Ethiopians back home as well as in diaspora who contemplate to return home.

In his response to the question, PM Abiy justified Ethiopia's extremely high car ownership taxes by citing the country's capacity to build roads and import fuels. No doubt, capacity to build and maintain roads have to be taken into account while determining quantities of cars to be imported. However, I would argue the issue is a great deal more complex than simple connections of issues within the transport domain. In this piece, I would attempt to shed some light on broader issues related to Ethiopia's existing car ownership policy and then bring out some hidden conflicts and contradictions.

Benchmarking

It would prove useful to begin by putting matters in some perspective. This is done by benchmarking car ownership in Ethiopia with other countries. Data presented in the table below compares Ethiopia with selected countries. Using 2014 data, 190 countries were ranked in descending order of number of cars per 1000 people [1].

The USA comes third in the list with 797 cars per 1000 people, surpassed only by (San Marino 1,263 and Monaco, 899). Ethiopia is found at the opposite end of the scale, coming 186th out of 190 countries, with only 3 cars per 1000 people. In other words, if Ethiopians would volunteer to take turns to drive available cars, each keeping a car for a day, then it would mean one would need to wait for nearly three years before one's turn would arrive.

Ethiopia is among the least motorized country on this planet. The country is situated literally at the very bottom of the list of nations in car ownership. This has not happened by accident.

Motor vehicles per 1000 people: Countries 2014		
Rank	Country	No of cars per 1000 people
3	USA	797
50	Hungary	345
100	Zimbabwe	114
150	Kenya	24
172	Tanzania	7
179	Rwanda	5
186	Ethiopia	3
190	Togo	2

Import Duty

Successive regimes in Ethiopia have made it their duty to deprive Ethiopians from owning a car. This was accomplished by imposing an exorbitantly high car import duties and related car ownership taxes. The combined effects of high import taxes and the unfavorable structure of vehicle import market has been that cost of vehicles has always been prohibitively high in Ethiopia.

Deloitte Africa Automotive Insights [2], a study completed in 2018, reported that effective tax rates were 329% and 289%, respectively, on a Toyota Vitz 2003 and Toyota Land Cruiser 2010. This confirmed what Ethiopians already know by heart, that various taxes associated with vehicle imports would quickly build up to reach over three times the purchase price at the country of origin. It is difficult to imagine that car import duty to this scale would ever exist anywhere else in the world.

Ethiopia's abnormally high cost of cars has often raised eyebrows of many observers. Noticing that the cost of a Toyota Vitz was $16,000 in Ethiopia (twice its price in the neighboring Kenya), a BBC reporter was so astonished to wonder: "Why are cars so expensive in Ethiopia?"[3].

Elderly Cars

Concerned with environmental impacts of aged cars in Africa, the United Nations Environmental Program (UNEP) has recently produced an Africa Used Vehicle Report (completed in March 2018) [4]. African countries were classified into different categories depending on their used car import regulations:

- 4 countries with total ban of used car imports (Egypt, Moroco, Sudan, and South Africa)
- 10 countries *strong* (banning imports of cars older than 5 years)
- 16 countries as *fair* (allowing 6-9 year olds and adopting incrementally higher taxes on those older than 10 years)
- 24 countries as *weak,* allowing over 10 old cars, some with regulations in place imposing higher taxes while others having no regulation at all.

Ethiopia was classified in the last group, allowing imports of cars with any age and no regulation in place! Ethiopia's regulation regarding used car imports seems to be even perverse in some cases. A BBC reporter interviewed an Ethiopian tax officer why Ethiopia's vehicle import duties are unreasonably high. The tariff officer at the Ethiopia's customs authority [3]defended the existing regulations stating that Ethiopia's taxation policy was fair in that it gives *discounts for buying second-hand cars!*

The remark made by this tax officer sums up the extent of utter lack of awareness among the authorities regarding wider economic, social and environmental implications of encouraging used car imports. As far as car ownership is concerned, successive regimes in Ethiopia seem to have always been concerned with a single-issue – government revenue maximization!

Even then, the tax officer was not being honest in that import duties do not actually fall proportionately with age of cars. Regardless of the age of the vehicle, a uniform 30% depreciation is applied to assess import duties, underlining the fact that the authorities are primarily interested in extracting as much tax revenue as possible, with no other consideration whatsoever!

It seems also that the bar on vehicle inspection standards have been gradually lowered over the years so much that vehicle age do not seem receive much weight when Ethiopian transport authority undertakes annual inspections for road-worthiness of vehicles.

An Anecdote

In order to illustrate how grave the situation is, I would like to share my anecdote. Some years ago I arrived back home after living abroad for several years. I was excited to observe that facilities at the Bole International Airport were modernized, but only to get depressed by what I observed looking down from the elevated place at the exit from the Airport.

I saw a sea of extremely old and rusty cars parked next to each other for as far as I could see ahead on the otherwise modernized tarmacs of the airport terminal car park spaces! The car park looked more like a scrapped car collection center, ready to be shipped to Korea for recycling, rather than cars waiting to pick passengers from an airport terminal.

A day or so latter I visited my cousin who lived at the outskirt of Addis Abeba. I left her home late evening and hired one of those elderly Lada taxis. The car was too old to be roadworthy but it did not matter, by then I was sufficiently sensitized to the situation. I was rather uncomfortable about something else – the taxi driver was busy talking over the phone! I overheard he was negotiating with another taxi driver. Noticing my curiosity, after finishing his conversation, he turned to me and politely said, "sir, I am hiring another taxi for you!" "But we have agreed you would take us up to the Stadium," retorted a friend who was accompanying me. I was not prepared for what he said next, "but sir, this taxi I am driving does not have any lights and I cannot afford to go all the way to the stadium. He told me that he was driving guided by streetlights! "No worries, sir, you will not be charged again, I will pay my friend who will take you up to your destination".

I was left speechless. Anyway, I agreed to his terms, I did not see any point in nagging him any further, in the circumstances he did what he could do. Instead I began to engage myself in a situation analysis – inspecting the visible parts inside the taxi! I noticed covers were cracked open and wires exposed and protruded at many places. A bunch of wires at the bottom of the steering wheel was hanging down between the legs of the driver. It was beyond me to comprehend how that driver managed to get that car moving on the road. The whole thing sounded comical and theatrical. It was a happy conclusion though, with the help of the Almighty and the driver, we safely arrived at our destination.

Road Fatalities

Like in most other cases in the Ethiopian economy, the cost of bad public policy has always been born by Ethiopians who often pay in-kind – with their lives! Ethiopia has a backlog of large road unworthy fleets stocked up over the years! It is not rocket science to know the consequences of deliberately releasing obsolete cars onto the roads. The latest available figures on road fatalities [5]were compiled for 2013 and published by the World Health Organization (WHO). Deaths due to traffic accidents on Ethiopian roads were presented with a wide margin, ranging from 18,528 to 29,146 in that year. This gives about 25 person per 100,000 people, Ethiopia ranked about 43rd in the world.

However, I hasten to add that this is a rather misleading indicator on at least two grounds. First, WHO compiles data using official sources – reports from the police and hospitals! However, an independent recent study [6] confirmed that Ethiopia's police sources captured only 57% to 61% of deaths while the hospital sources captured about 33% of deaths. This indicates that fatality rates reported by WHO is likely to grossly underestimate the road fatality rates in Ethiopia.

Second, the "death per 100,000 people" statistics WHO reports is actually a rather silly statistics, it is biased downwards for a country that has a large population. The alternative is to express road fatality rate in terms of deaths per 100,000 vehicles [7]. For Ethiopia, this gives 5,000 deaths per 100,000 vehicles on Ethiopia's roads in 2013. By this criteria Ethiopia's position suddenly changes, moving from 43rd to 5th in the world (after Guinea, Benin, DRC, and Sao Tome). This reflects the true picture of the reality on the ground, a few extremely old cars causing havoc on Ethiopia's roads.

Welfare

Ethiopian authorities still seem to hold a medieval mindset, oblivious to the fact that cars are no more luxuries but necessities to families who live in the modern world. Being confronted with relentlessly stubborn regimes, Ethiopian households have had to adjust and survive with a standard of living way below those who live beyond the country's borders. In other words, while some citizen pay in-kind through their lives, those who survived fatalities are condemned to incur a variant of in-kind cost, accepting a lower standard of living than they would not deserve in normal circumstances.

I have had the opportunity to live in Kenya, with my duties involving frequent shuttles to Ethiopia. It was a painful experience for me to observe, for instance, that secretaries at Nairobi University could afford to buy and drive fresh looking new cars, the kind Addis Ababa University Professor would not even contemplate to window shop, never mind buying an driving! This is partly explained by wage differences, and partly by car availability at affordable prices.

Economy and Environment

So far we have focused on in-kind costs, precious lives and lower living standards, that Ethiopian households have had to endure. Ethiopia's car ownership policy does not only have socially harmful effects but it is also economically damaging. There are explicit and quantifiable monetary costs to private households as well as to the government.

To start with private costs, the excessive import taxes do not only inflate prices of vehicles but also their spare parts. Needless to say that old cars require frequent maintenance, which have often eaten into the meager household budget.

In another piece entitled *Ethiopia's low wage curse_Ethiopia's low wage is a curse, not a blessing (in this series),* I have discussed that Ethiopia's dismal pay structure (e.g. Ethiopia's teachers on average earning about one-seventh to one-thirteenth of salaries paid to Kenyan teachers!) As a coping mechanism, Ethiopian households have tended to opt for non-genuine spare parts because of their lower price [2], which could partly explain high fatalities on the road, or even more frequent maintenance.

Now about costs to the government and the wider economy. The damaging economic impacts of old fleets on the wider economy cannot be overemphasized. Let's start with cost of spare parts which would need to be imported and in larger quantities than would be the case if the fleets have had lower average age. The extent to which spare part imports has been a drain on the country's scarce foreign exchange is yet to be studied. A comparative analysis with other countries would inevitably reveal some interesting results.

Fuel economy and CO_2 emissions			
	Year of production		Difference
Toyota Corolla*	1986	2003	(2003 less 1986)
Fuel economy (km/Litre)	12.2	15.3	3.1
GHG Emission (gCO2/km)	192.9	153.8	-39.1
Annual fuel cost (US$)	2033	1621	-411.9
All Fleet			
Total fleet (2015)**			587,400
Old cars (%)**			499,290
Savings on fuel cost (mUS$/year			-206
Reduc. in CO2 emission (tons/year)			-722,323

Sources: *Global Fuel Economy Initiative Study in Ethiopia 2012
**Deloitte Africa Automotive Insights

Importantly, fuel economy has been the main driving force shaping public policy on car ownership in the rest of the world. Fuel economy is a double-edged sword, it serves both economic and environmental goals. In order to illustrate this, relevant data was brought together from various sources and compiled in the table below. The upper part of the table compares two Toyota Corola models – one from 1986 and the other 2003 model, a relatively recent model by Ethiopian standard. The data was obtained from Global Fuel Economy Initiative Study in Ethiopia 2012 [8].

The 1986 and 2003 models would run with 12.2 and 15.3 km/litre respectively, that is a 3.1 km difference per liter! Similarly, there is a 39.1 grams CO_2 emissions difference per km between the old and the new models. The 2012 fuel economy report on Ethiopia stated average annual mileage of passenger cars was 24,000, trucks and buses were 50,000km each. If we apply the current US$0.67 (birr 18.77) per liter fuel cost in Ethiopia [9], then we establish there would be US$267.2 saving by changing to the relatively recent model.

The Deloitte Africa Automotive Insights [2] report cited earlier stated that there were about 600,000 vehicles in Ethiopia and the bulk of them (85%) were classified as old fleets. If we gross up the figures fuel economy data reported in the upper part of the table, then we get that total additional fuel cost saving would be about US$206 million and CO_2 emission would be reduced by about 722,323 tons per year, about 7% of Ethiopia's total CO_2 emission. The annual economic cost reported in the table above is likely to be a small fraction of total costs, which should include additional costs on spare part imports. Similarly, the CO_2 emission is likely to be the minimum expected.

Policy Inertia

Ethiopia's car ownership policy is one of those policies that have persisted over decades, being handed over from one regime to the next. The power of economic policy inertia in Ethiopia has been so much that they can elude even well intended, progressive and bright leaders like PM Abiy. That is what I learnt from his reply to the question regarding car import duty, which was posed to him from one of his audience at that public gathering in the USA.

I am certain his reaction would have been completely different if he was reminded that the existing policy, which allowed proliferation of road unworthy cars in the country, is responsible for the fatalities and carnage that regularly take place on Ethiopia's roads on daily basis. Similarly, perhaps PM Abiy is not informed that there are only two cars per 1000 Ethiopians, and the existing policy has condemned Ethiopians to lead a standard of living way below those of people in neighboring countries.

Clearly, there is no justification for Ethiopia to retain its current car ownership policy. It is economically inefficient, socially unacceptable and environmentally damaging. The sooner it is scarped the better. Above all, Ethiopians deserve to climb into a driving seat like everyone else.

References

[1] NationMaster. Transport > Road > Motor vehicles per 1000 people: Countries Compared: Motor vehicles per 1000 people. http://www.nationmaster.com/country-info/stats/Transport/Road/Motor-vehicles-per-1000-people

[2] Deloitte Africa Automotive Insights. Navigating the African Automotive Sector: Ethiopia, Kenya and Nigeria. https://www2.deloitte.com/za/en/pages/manufacturing/articles/naviga ting-the-african-automotive-sector--ethiopia--kenya-and-ni.html

[3] Emmanuel Igunza. Why are cars so expensive in Ethiopia? BBC Africa, Addis Ababa. 16 January 2017. https://www.bbc.com/news/world-africa-38607986

[4] Ariadne Baskin. Africa Used Vehicle Report (Prepared by United Nations Environment Programme) African Clean Mobility Week. March 13 2018. https://wedocs.unep.org/bitstream/handle/20.500.11822/25233/Africa UsedVehicleReport.pdf?sequence=1&isAllowed=y

[5] World Health Organization (WHO). Violence and Injury Prevention: Global status report on road safety 2015. http://www.who.int/violence_injury_prevention/road_safety_status/2 015/GSRRS2015_data/en/

[6] Teferi Abegaz, Yemane Berhane, Alemayehu Worku, Abebe

Assrat, and Abebayehu Assefa. 2014. Road Traffic Deaths and Injuries Are Under-Reported in Ethiopia: A Capture-Recapture Method. PLoS One. 2014; 9(7)
https://www.ncbi.nlm.nih.gov/pmc/articles/PMC4108419/

[7] List of countries by traffic-related death rate.
https://en.wikipedia.org/wiki/List_of_countries_by_traffic-related_death_rate#cite_note-datatables-5

[8] Addis Ababa Institute of Technology 2012. Pilot Report on Global Fuel Economy Initiative Study on Ethiopia.
https://www.globalfueleconomy.org/media/461026/africa_final-report-ethiopia.pdf

[9] Gasoline prices in Addis Ababa, Ethiopia
https://www.globalpetrolprices.com/Ethiopia/Addis_Ababa/gasoline_prices/

25. What is Happening to EPRDF's Developmental State?

October 29, 2018 (AS)

It would prove useful to re-iterate the fundamental reasons that caused popular uprisings in Ethiopia during the last few years, forcing the ruling party EPRDF to crack open and eventually begin to unleash the on-going reform. The slogans held during those protests may vary but their root causes could be summed up under two deceptive ideologies of the EPRDF: *democratic centralism* and *developmental state!*

For the on-going reform to succeed, the two problematic ideological basis of the EPRDF governance must be simultaneously transformed. It seems this has not been happening. By now, we know what has been happening to democratic centralism. However, it is unclear to me what PM Abiy's administration is intending to do with the developmental state model.

In this piece, I will begin by highlighting EPRDF's haphazard attempts to dovetail the two ideological pillars during the pre-reform era. I will then proceed to discussing the necessity of synchronizing the processes of political and economic reforms. All along, the focus will be on options in designing and implementing a far-reaching economic reform to transform the lives and livelihoods of millions of Ethiopians.

Stick and Carrot

EPRDF declared they have transformed Ethiopia into a federally constituted country. This essentially meant a decentralized and democratic system of governance. However, every right that came with federalism was snatched away through democratic centralism, which obviously was an antithesis of decentralized governance.

Even with good intentions, inevitably conflicts do arise in complex situations of governing a diverse and complex society like Ethiopia and these would lead to unintended and contradictory outcomes. However, one of the peculiarities of the EPRDF era was that the architects of democratic centralism were very well aware of the contradictions they were building into a federalist system.

It was precisely for this reason that the developmental state model was crafted and offered to the people of Ethiopian as a carrot to camouflage political control through democratic centralism. This was meant to divert attention away from the politics to the economy. Firm political control through democratic centralism as stick and dishonest promise of economic growth through developmental state.

The fact was the developmental state in economic strategy was no less dishonest and mischievous than the democratic centralism in political domain. Regardless, society was expected to tolerate the pain of democratic centralism in return for rewards that would come from developmental state's "rapid economic growth".

It should be noted that there was nothing inherently wrong with the developmental state. For anyone familiar with economic history, the developmental state has nothing to do with government using its long hands to own and run businesses in every sector. It has nothing to do with establishing complex network of domestic and international businesses to promote crony capitalism. Mega infrastructure projects have never been an exclusive feature of a developmental state. All governments do undertake large construction projects.

However, EPRDF applied it so irresponsibly that the developmental state model arrived in Ethiopia and lost its true meaning. Elsewhere, developmental state is essentially a feature of responsible economic governance. The state looking after and enabling economic functions of citizens, like parents nurturing and bringing up capabilities of family members to become independent and productive members in their family and ultimately their nation. It is all about supporting businesses, small or big, to create jobs and generate wealth. For instance, government protecting smallholder agriculture from exposure to the world market in input markets (e.g. offering fertilizer subsidy) and output markets (e.g. offering price supports, buying and storing, etc.) are supposed to be meaningful and appropriate features of the developmental state.

Democratic Centralism, Gone Forever

In terms of reforming the EPRDF, the political liberalization has registered monumental achievements in less than six months through smart and farsighted leadership skills of Team Lemma and PM Abiy's administration. For most Ethiopians it has been exciting to witness that the old EPRDF political ideology of democratic centralism has gone forever. Team Lemma and PM Abiy have obliterated that crippling ideology and opened the door for genuine federalist Ethiopia, sowing a seed of hope for democratic governance in Ethiopia.

In the political domain, the reform process has even gone beyond internal reform of the EPRDF itself. The sense of confidence and optimism that the architects of the reform have created have been so much so that they have even managed to persuade opposition parties from all corners of the world to return home to the extent that none left outside. Realignments of interest groups has been taking place, paving the way for the formation of strong opposition parties and healthy competitive political space.

Economic Reform – A Nonstarter?

In sharp contrast to my delights with PM Abiy's achievements in reforming the Ethiopia's politics, I have to admit I am frustrated with what has been happening with regard to reforms in the economic domain. It is appropriate to ask, "what happened to EPRDF's developmental state?"

It is possible that PM Abiy and Team Lemma have thought of sequencing the reform process: to deal with the political reform first and proceed to economic reform. I would go along that logic some distance but I think there is already a substantial delay in activating the process of economic reform. It would prove fatal to delay it any further. Let me explain why it is extremely important for PM Abiy to shift emphasis to economic reform without any further delay.

It is "the Economy, Stupid!"

The economy is too important to keep on hold. In the current Ethiopian context, economic reform is no less urgent than political reform. Here is some logic from across the Atlantic: "In the 1992 U.S. presidential campaign between incumbent President George H.W. Bush and challenger Bill Clinton, the Clinton campaign hung a sign at campaign headquarters that was to become very famous. It simply said: "The Economy, Stupid." The message it [was] sending with this simple phrase was basically the economy was something that affects every American and needed to be at the forefront of the campaign."[1]

If jobs, growth and trade mattered so much in rich America, then it would matter thousand times more in poor Ethiopia. The bulk of Ethiopians who live close to or below the poverty line is simply daunting. If decisive economic policy action has not taken place to improve the lives and livelihoods of ordinary citizens, then I fear that the delay would inevitably endanger popular support for PM Abiy's Administration. There is no justification to take such an excessive risk.

Excuses such as "the government does not have money so it would take time to improve lives and livelihoods" should not have any place. There are plenty of options available to the authorities, as illustrated towards the end of this piece.

The Double-Digit Growth Illusion

I wonder if the myth built around Ethiopia's miraculous double-digit growth has been so powerful that even our pioneering reformers have subscribed to it. Can the silence about economic reform be explained by such logic that: "well, it was just our politics that went so bad and needed radical revamping, otherwise miracles have already been happening in the economic sphere"?

If that is the case, then I strongly urge PM Abiy to rethink and accept the fact that it was just an illusion; such a miracle has never happened in the Ethiopian economy. If he needs evidence, I urge him to get clues from ordinary citizens, not from official publications (the Central Statistical Authority, the World Bank or IMF).

I vividly recall a speech made by an elderly man at a public gathering in Bale. The meeting was called by Aba Duula Gamada in the middle of the Oromo Protest. This is what the wise elderly man said (in Afaan Oromo): "*itto qulla deemnuu uuffattan jedhamna, itto beelofnuu quuftan jedhamna*", roughly translated, *our body is naked and our stomach empty, but the authorities keep telling us as that we are well dressed, we are well fed!*"

This speaks the truth more emphatically than thousands of pages of those rosy economic reports that the Ethiopian government, the World Bank and the IMF have regularly been churning out on the Ethiopian economy during the last two decades.

The Paradox

Delaying the economic reform agenda is counter-intuitive, actually paradoxical. I cannot comprehend why brave reformers who dared to confront political reforms would delay economic reform. Political reforms, although must be done, would inevitably generate enemies.

On the contrary, in the Ethiopian context, economic reform would certainly generate millions of friends for the reformers. It would enhance their already strong popular support. Above all, it is much easier and straightforward to undertake economic reform. It is not as if there are not burning issues regarding economic governance. The Ethiopian economy has been riddled with policy blunders. These have been accumulated over many years, sprinkled in all sectors. All are waiting to be resolved.

To mention just a few, fertilizer supply and distribution has been a monopoly of a handful of interest groups. This has been adversely affecting the lives and livelihoods of millions of farmers in all parts of Ethiopia. There are a handful of exporters, monopolizing all sectors, paying farmers and small producers unreasonably low prices. Ethiopia's natural resources have been depleting at alarming rates, and they urgently require regeneration.

Ethiopia's rural extension staff are literally unemployed labor force, actually doing nothing. Not that they did not want to help the farmers but there is no policy framework to activate their engagements. Farmers have acres of land (marginal and productive) but they do not have credit facilities to invest and undertake essential land improvements, without which increase in agricultural productivity is unthinkable.

Farmers cannot use their land as collateral to borrow from the banks. However, if a city slicker, who calls himself an "investor", arrived in the village and evicted that same farmer, he would be entitled to borrow using that same plot of land as collateral.

Costly Loyalty Cards

Now about more subtle issues related to commitment to a successful economic reform. Successful economic policy design and implementation require highly technical skills. This is not to say that economic matters are more important than other aspects in which a society functions but just that it requires a very specific and abstract set of skills.

In this regard, I am not sure the extent to which our pioneering reformers have recognized this fact and surrounded themselves with capable advisors and technocrats. In my view, Economy and Finance should not be subjected to party loyalty or quota based allocations of ministerial portfolios.

For instance, when he was choosing Ethiopia's Army Chief of Staff, PM Abiy had to think very seriously. IIis choice was not largely subjected to party loyalty criteria, although there could be some element of that in that decision. He did not pick a middle or low ranking army officer. PM Abiy knew very well he had to pick from among the most senior generals, knowledgeable in military affairs.

Similarly, Ethiopia's team of technocrats running the economy and finance portifolio should be based on merit, coming from among the most senior and highly experienced Ethiopian economists and bankers. There is no scarcity for that kind of expertise; Ethiopia is blessed with lots of highly skilled professionals working all over the world.

There is a trade-off between sticking to party loyalty and merit based assignments. The former is inevitable, but it is necessary to go for merit-based assignments in some cases. This can be a tough choice but it is good to be aware that the choices being made in allocations of human resources to ministerial portfolios are not cost free and some choices are more costly than others!

Still White Elephants?

It is unclear what economic development strategy PM Abiy has in mind for Ethiopia. There is no clue whether the old style developmental state will be retained or it would be reshaped to become the kind of citizen friendly developmental state that I have briefly discussed earlier. In this regard, I have to confess I have some worries that perhaps the old style may be allowed to persist, perhaps inadvertently.

I can adduce a few evidences as sources of my concerns. There were very few times that PM Abiy has had time to engage in economic matters, and all of them without exception were either visits to or opening up of Industrial Parks (IPs), EPRDF's latest brand of white elephants. IPs have been favorite destinations of dignitaries of high profile visitors, including heads of states. In a few occasions, there were times I have observed other engagements but still about big projects.

This indicates that the EPRDF may have steadfastly committed to mega infrastructures, destined to serve big businesses of both domestic and foreign origin. The trouble with mega infrastructure projects and big business-based development models is that they are not only extremely expensive to set up and run, but more worryingly, their rationales hinge on some hope that benefits would begin to be generated from them at some distant future, and then hopefully the benefits would trickle down to the poor.

This is a matter of faith though; no guarantee that benefits would be materialized, and, if they ever do, they may not necessarily trickle down to reach the poor. If the benefit would not accrue then the huge investment incurred to build them would become a sunk cost to society.

The fact is that the people of Ethiopia do not have the luxury of sitting and waiting for such benefits to reach them in some distant future. What is required is to undertake innovative interventions that would yield quick returns, small returns that add up to a large sum in terms of wealth creation.

There is a disease inherited from the old EPRDF style that economic policies are pursued only if they have propaganda value. This inevitably necessitated a focus on large and visible projects. PM Abiy need to make a clear departure from that sentiment. There is a desperate need to shift to low cost investment activities whose returns are certain to happen.

For instance, improvements of agricultural lands and natural resource regenerations (such as afforestation) would certainly yield returns in not so distant future. Promotions of small businesses in cities and towns through facilitation of credits and training would immediately create hundreds of thousands of more jobs, dwarfing jobs that might be created at the mushrooming IPs.

Job Creation Schemes

On a few occasions, I have heard PM Abiy mentioning scarcity of funds as constraints to getting things done. If this is really the case, then it is highly likely that he was not presented with the full options available to him, particularly untapped domestic investment resources. Here again we observe a paradox in that persisting with extremely costly and adventurous mega projects such as commitments to IPs is not consistent with prudent ways of managing scarce investment resources.

PM Abiy and his team have plenty of investment options to energize and vitalizing the Ethiopian economy. The importance of job creation for the unemployed urban labor forces and the excessively underemployed rural labor force can by no means be overemphasized. The urban labor force can be supported through credit facilitation and training to start small businesses.

Similarly, the disguisedly unemployed rural labor force can be employed in large public schemes, engagement in nationwide natural resource regenerations, terracing and afforestation. As stated earlier, smallholder rural agricultural producers should be linked to the banking sector, so that they engage in extensive investments to improve their agricultural lands.

Inflation, the Bogeyman

All of the above require mobilization of domestic credit facilities. If banks have to provide so much credit, then it would inevitably follow that money supply has to be increased and perhaps increased substantially. Some would begin to worry about catastrophic inflation. The excessive concerns regarding inflation as a bogeyman of economic ills emanates only from figments of imaginations by experts of the multilateral agencies – the World Bank and the IMF, whose primary preoccupation is to safeguard the interest of lenders in rich countries, not job creation particularly in poor economies like ours.

The misconceptions about inflation have been told so much that even serious economists would not think twice to pass judgments on the "dangers" of inflation, without even thinking about the economic contexts. I would illustrate this point by referring to three cases, one theoretical and the other two empirical.

Economic Theory

In principle, one should begin to worry about expansion in money supply leading to inflation only if that economy has reached full employment, that is to say, unemployment is down to near its natural rate (somewhere between 3% to 5%) and also other man-made and natural capital operating at their full capacity.

In an economy like Ethiopia where national unemployment rate is somewhere around 30% and large chunks of marginal and productive agricultural lands still lying idle, there should not be excessive concerns about inflation. That was why development economists have always found it prudent to use "inflationary financing" as a legitimate means of fostering economic development.

Ethiopia Recent Experience

For the last two and a half decades, the Ethiopian government was pouring billions of birr into the economy. The mega projects were not producing "teff", but only using cements and producing concrete slabs, none of which entered supermarkets for consumers to buy.

Most importantly, Ethiopia's banks were encouraged (rather arm-twisted) to lend hundreds of billions to METEC and perhaps more hundreds of billions to adventurous cowboy investors. None of them used those investment resources to produce a single blade of grass. That is why they all got their debts written off.

These reckless credit expansions did not cause horrors. Of course, inflation happened in Ethiopia but for completely different reasons – supply side constraints. For instance, farmers were not supported to produce food and supply to the market. One can imagine if all those several hundreds of billions were lent to Ethiopia's smallholder farmers and small-scale industry producers. There would be no chance for inflation to enter double digits at any time.

"Quantitative Easing"

The multilateral agencies, IMF and the World Bank, have been quiet regarding the so-called "quantitative easing" in Europe and USA. Quantitative easing was coined to hide the obvious fact that governments in the developed world were desperate to save their banks.

They have done so by encouraging the banks to lending at massive scales so that their economies would emerge economies from recessions. Governments in developed countries had to print trillions of euros or dollars and poured onto their economies. In other words, they had to create trillions of more money, that is to say increase the quantity of money in circulation (hence quantitative easing). Money was pumped into their economies but we have not heard about catastrophic inflation happening over there either.

In other words, it is perfectly reasonable, legitimate, and logical for PM Abiy to make extensive use of domestic credit facilities and mobilize domestic investment resources. This is the only way the economy can be vitalized by using domestic money, with no or little need for hard currency. For instance, natural resource regeneration through seedling propagation and tree plantation requires labor and birr, zero dollars.

If the IMF raised questions about Ethiopia's money supply, then PM Abiy, in his typical polite manner, would respond: "I am just doing quantitative easing".

References

[1] Paul Dillon. It's 'The Economy, Stupid', The Guardian, Feb 26, 2018. https://www.theguardian.pe.ca/opinion/letter-to-the-editor/opinion-its-the-economy-stupid-188979/

ABOUT THE AUTHOR

Ayele Gelan is an economist with over two decades of research experience with many national and international institutions. His research experience encompasses developing as well as developed economy contexts. He has published a good number of articles in peer reviewed journals.